D1440846

· HEGEL   AND   SKEPTICISM ·

HEGEL

AND

SKEPTICISM

Michael N. Forster

HARVARD UNIVERSITY PRESS

CAMBRIDGE, MASSACHUSETTS

LONDON, ENGLAND

1989

Library of Congress Cataloging-in-Publication Data

Forster, Michael N.
Hegel and skepticism / Michael N. Forster
p.   cm.
Bibliography: p.
Includes index.
ISBN 0-674-38707-4 (alk. paper)
1. Hegel, Georg Wilhelm Friedrich, 1770–1831
—Views on skepticism.
2. Skepticism—History—19th century. I. Title.
B2949.S54F67 1989
149'.73'09—dc19   88-24294
                                    CIP

FOR MY PARENTS,

MICHAEL AND KATHLEEN FORSTER

Acknowledgments

This work was completed during periods as a student at Princeton University and Heidelberg University and as a teacher at the University of Chicago. I enjoyed the benefit of fellowship support from the William Alexander Fleet Foundation, the King Edward VII British-German Foundation, and the Mrs. Giles Whiting Foundation.

Among the many people who have assisted me in this work, several deserve special mention: Ralph Walker of Magdalen College, Oxford University, Tim Scanlon of Harvard University, and John Cooper of Princeton University, who provided intellectual stimulation and help bearing indirectly on this project; Allen Wood of Cornell University, who made helpful suggestions on ways in which to improve the book; Lindsay Waters of Harvard University Press, who enabled me to bring the study to publication; Michael Frede of Princeton University, who gave generously of his time to teach me much of whatever I may know about skepticism and gave me the benefit of his reactions to a draft of this work; Hans Fulda of Heidelberg University, whose published work on Hegel stimulated some of my own reflections and who devoted much time to reading and discussing with me an early draft; and above all Raymond Geuss of Columbia University, who, as my adviser at Princeton, read and made very helpful criticisms of several drafts of this work, devoted many hours of conversation to the topics with which it deals, and in general gave me far more encouragement and support than any advisee could reasonably expect or hope for.

Finally, I would like to acknowledge a special debt to my parents, Michael and Kathleen Forster, and to my wife, Noha Aboulmagd.

Contents

· HEGEL AND SKEPTICISM ·

Introduction

PHILOSOPHICAL books of the "X and Y" variety ("Wittgenstein and Buddhism") often share with comic partnerships of that variety ("Laurel and Hardy") a capacity for eliciting amusement by their juxtaposition of incommensurable quantities. This is a virtue in a comic partnership, but not in a piece of philosophical literature. A work bearing the title *Hegel and Skepticism* may seem to be guilty of just such a juxtaposition of incommensurables. And indeed, there is comparatively little in the existing literature on Hegel to suggest otherwise. However, I wish to make two claims in explanation and stout defense of the subject of this book. First, Hegel's interpretation of the skeptical tradition in philosophy and his reaction to this tradition are absolutely fundamental to his philosophical outlook, so that large regions of his thought must remain obscure until this interpretation and reaction are properly understood. And second, Hegel's reflections on the nature of the skeptical tradition have considerable intrinsic merit, containing original insights from which contemporary historians of philosophy and philosophers concerned with skepticism can profit.

In this study I shall distinguish three aspects of Hegel's relation to the skeptical tradition: his critical interpretation of views within the tradition, his pursuit within his own philosophy of history of themes arising from this critical interpretation of skepticism, and his effort to construct a philosophical position capable of withstanding the assaults of the skeptics. The book is divided into three parts dealing with each of these topics in turn.

Part One is devoted to Hegel's critical interpretation of the skeptical tradition, found primarily in his unduly neglected 1802 essay *The Relation of Skepticism to Philosophy: A Presentation of Its Various Modifications and a Comparison of the Newest Skepticism with Ancient Skepticism* and in the chapters of his *Lectures on the History of Philosophy* (hereafter *History of Philosophy*) which deal with the New Academy and Pyrrhonism. Hegel has distinctive and closely thought-out views on the skeptical tradition. In particular, he draws a sharp distinction between the characters of ancient and modern skepticism, and holds that while ancient skepticism is of great philosophical importance, modern skepticism has little or no philosophical merit. Hegel's account of the difference between ancient and modern skepticism and his argument for the superiority of the former over the latter emerge as both original and, by and large, convincing. Judged for accuracy of interpretation and depth of critical insight, Hegel's treatment of the skeptical tradition is far superior to his comparably detailed and more widely discussed treatment of Platonic philosophy, for example. It is probably this aspect of Hegel's relation to skepticism from which today's historians of philosophy and philosophers concerned with skepticism have most to learn.

The modern reader of Hegel is likely to have a conception of skepticism based on acquaintance with its modern rather than its ancient forms. For this reason, it is essential to understand the Hegelian views on the nature and comparative value of ancient and modern skepticism just alluded to in order to perceive the role that skepticism plays within the broader framework of his own philosophy. For naturally, not everything which has historically gone by the name of skepticism comes to have this larger impact on his work—only those forms of skepticism which he considers to be philosophically important, its ancient forms. This is one reason for dealing with Hegel's critical interpretation of the skeptical tradition before examining the broader impact of skepticism on his thought.

Part Two attempts to show that the skeptical problems which Hegel finds to be of philosophical importance in the skeptical tradition play a considerable and interesting role within his own philosophical understanding of history. In particular, the *Phenomenology of Spirit* of 1807 (hereafter *Phenomenology*) and the *Lectures on the Philosophy of History* (hereafter *Philosophy of History*) indicate that Hegel understands the emergence of these skeptical problems to have had a decisive impact at a certain historical point on the development of human culture, an impact extending far beyond their impact on the development of philosophical thought in the narrow sense.[1] That historical point was the transition from the unified and harmonious culture of the Greek polis, which Hegel refers to as Ethical Life (*Sittlichkeit*), to the cultural conditions of Roman and subsequent Judeo-Christian history, in which men are intellectually alienated both from God and from their natural and social environment. The case which Hegel argues is in many respects a deep and thought-provoking one.

Part Three is devoted to Hegel's highly original, elaborate, and ingenious attempt to render his own philosophical system invulnerable to those skeptical problems which he considers philosophically important, as the central component of a somewhat broader project of achieving epistemological security for this system. There is a long tradition in the literature on Hegel which either overlooks his profound interest in epistemology or explicitly holds that he was dismissive or careless about it. This is in large measure attributable to a failure to pay sufficient attention to Hegel's critical interpretation of the skeptical tradition—the subject of Part One. Once one does so, it becomes clear that there are several features of his philosophy which are conceived by him to constitute a network of defenses of his own philosophical system against the only skeptical problems which he considers it necessary to defend *any* view against, namely those characteristic of ancient skepticism. And when this is recognized, it becomes possible to make out the contours of an even larger epistemological enterprise in Hegel's work of which this network of defenses against skepticism is a fundamental part. Thus it turns out that, far from being cavalier about epistemological issues, Hegel spent much time, particularly during his early years in Jena (1801–1807), in an almost obsessive pursuit of epistemological security for his system. His developing struggle to achieve that security can be traced above all in his sketches and expositions of the Jena Logic (a different discipline from the Logic of Hegel's mature system), in several of his essays published in the *Critical Journal of Philosophy* during the Jena period, and in the *Phenomenology* of 1807, which in certain respects marks the culmination of his efforts in the field of epistemology. So predominant is the epistemological component in these works that their character and development must remain largely unintelligible until Hegel's epistemological designs are understood. Hegel's epistemological, and in particular antiskeptical, strategy disproves the quite erroneous and damaging impression of him—and to some extent of German Idealism generally—as an epistemological delinquent building metaphysical castles on sands which the first flood of skepticism would be bound to wash away.

One interesting twist in Hegel's epistemological enterprise is that his attempts to defend his own system against skeptical assault and in general to make it epistemologically secure involve essential and extensive use of a procedure which he characterizes as itself skeptical. It is in this sense, for example, that he refers to the procedure of the *Phenomenology* as one of "self-completing skepticism."[2] In Hegel's texts it is in fact far easier to identify the role of skepticism as an influence on his conception of this procedure than to see that skepticism also provided some of the problems which the use of this procedure was designed to solve.[3] This use of a "skeptical" procedure to help solve skeptical or other epistemological problems may have a superficial air of paradox about it, but his strategy can be partly clarified by means of the following imperfect analogy: just as fideists have sought to provide an epistemological defense of the claims of faith by using skepticism to discredit the competing claims of reason, so Hegel attempts to provide an epistemological defense of his system by using a "skeptical" procedure to discredit all claims which compete with those of his system.

Hegel's critical interpretation of the skeptical tradition in philosophy proves, then, to be the key with which to unlock both an important part of his philosophy of history and the whole of his epistemological enterprise. By unlocking his epistemological enterprise, it also offers glimpses behind several further closed doors in the Hegelian philosophical edifice. For example, three major aspects of Hegel's philosophy remain to a large extent obscure in motivation until their role within his epistemological enterprise is explained. The first aspect is the enigmatic doctrine of the overcoming of the distinction between concept and object, or thought and being, in the true philosophical view of things. This doctrine is salient in the *Science of Logic* and in Hegel's later works, but it began its career in the early Jena period. And at this early date Hegel explicitly formulated it as (among other things) part of the network of defenses designed to protect his own philosophical system against what he saw as the threat posed by the skeptical tradition. The second aspect is Hegel's dialectical method, which from an early period was intended to play a variety of essential roles within his epistemological enterprise in general and his antiskeptical enterprise in particular (the dialectical method is the "skeptical" procedure mentioned earlier). Its early introduction and development were largely, though not exclusively, motivated by this epistemological function.[4] The third aspect is Hegel's difficult Jena texts themselves, particularly the Jena Logic and the *Phenomenology,* many features of which are only properly intelligible as attempts to realize his epistemological project. In particular, much in the development of these texts over time first becomes intelligible as an expression of Hegel's progressive striving to meet a certain epistemological standard which he holds dear.

Part Three, I would note, is written in a rather different spirit from the earlier parts. Whereas they are largely written in a spirit of qualified approval of the Hegelian views they expound, Part Three is intended to be no more than sympathetic exegesis. This different approach is mainly for reasons of economy of space: merely giving a sympathetic description of Hegel's complicated and mostly unexplored epistemological project is a lengthy business, and formulating a verdict concerning this project's viability would have prolonged the account intolerably. But since the question of my own verdict is bound to cross the reader's mind, I should perhaps acknowledge here a case of what might be called "the Descartes commentator's syndrome," or the condition of finding Hegel's conception of the skeptical difficulties confronting beliefs ultimately more persuasive than his attempts to solve those difficulties—the originality and ingenuity of his attempts notwithstanding.

PART I

HEGEL ON THE HISTORY OF SKEPTICISM

ONE

The Superiority of Ancient to Modern Skepticism

T HE TENDENCY in much discussion of the skeptical tradition in the modern period has been to regard comparatively restrained varieties of modern skepticism, of the kind advocated by Hume, for example, as more philosophically defensible and important than the radical skepticism of the ancient Pyrrhonists.[1] Among Hegel's predecessors, Hume himself famously held this view.[2] So too did Fichte, who in the *Science of Knowledge* wrote of an extreme skepticism like ancient Pyrrhonism "which doubts whether it doubts":

> Never yet, in good earnest, has there been a skeptic of this kind. A critical skepticism, such as that of Hume, Maimon or Aenesidemus [i.e., Schulze, not the ancient Pyrrhonist], is another matter; for it points out the inadequacy of the grounds so far accepted, and shows in doing so, where better are to be found. And if knowledge gains nothing as to content from this, it certainly does as to form—and the interests of knowledge are but poorly recognized in denying to the sharp-sighted skeptic the respect which is his due.[3]

Against this orthodox view Hegel argues that radical ancient skepticism, and particularly Pyrrhonism as preserved in the writings of Sextus Empiricus, is philosophically far superior to the more restrained modern forms of skepticism. This is what he means when he writes in *The Relation of Skepticism to Philosophy* that "the ideas about skepticism in common circulation are extremely formal and the noble nature which skepticism possesses when in its true form is habitually perverted into a general hidingplace and excuse for nonphilosophy in the most recent times."[4]

What, then, is the crucial difference which Hegel sees between ancient and modern skepticism and which in his view explains ancient skepticism's philosophical preeminence and modern skepticism's philosophical worthlessness? In order to answer this question, one must first see that in Hegel's view—and, I think, also in fact—the great merit of ancient skepticism lies in its possession of a general method: the method of setting into opposition equally strong propositions or arguments on both sides of any issue which arises and thereby producing an equal balance of justification on both sides of the issue. This is the method of "equipollence" (*isostheneia,* or "equal force on both sides"). It is used by the ancient skeptics as their means of inducing a suspension of belief (*epochē*) about any issue which arises.[5] That the method of equipollence is quite fundamental to the self-conscious practice of the Pyrrhonists can be seen from the remark of Sextus Empiricus: "The main basic principle of the skeptic system is that of opposing to every proposition/argument (*logos*) an equal proposition/argument (*logos*); for we believe that as a consequence of this we end by ceasing to dogmatize."[6] In the *History of Philosophy* Hegel draws attention to this method of ancient skepticism when discussing the ancient skeptical tropes, or patterns of argument, which provide the method's detailed articulation:

> We must now consider . . . the method in which the skeptics proceed, and it consists in this, that they have brought the universal principle that each definite assertion has to be set over against its "other," into certain forms, not propositions. Thus, in view of the nature of skepticism, we cannot ask for any system of propositions . . . Sextus hence says that skepticism is no selection . . . of dogmas, it is not a preference for certain propositions, but only that which leads, or rather which directs us . . . to live rightly and think correctly; thus it is in this way rather a method or manner by which only universal modes of that opposition are shown.[7]

As this passage indicates, Hegel considers the equipollence method a *method* in three specific senses. First, it is a method in the sense of being a quite general procedure for attacking claims or beliefs regardless of their content, rather than being restricted in its attack to claims or beliefs having a specific kind of content. Hegel thus says that *each* definite assertion is to be set over against its "other." Second, equipollence is a method in the sense of being a means for achieving a goal positively valued by the skeptics, the suspension of belief, rather than merely constituting a difficulty which demands a solution. For the ancient skeptics valued suspension of belief as the key to mental quietude (*ataraxia*) and hence happiness (*eudaimonia*)—the common goal of the various Hellenistic schools of philosophy—regarding the striving for and possession of beliefs (especially evaluative ones) as the source of all avoidable mental disquietude (*tarachē*) and mental disquietude as the source of all unhappiness.[8] Thus Hegel notes that the method is supposed by the skeptics to lead us to "live rightly and think correctly."[9] Third, equipollence is a method in the sense of being a procedure for inducing a suspension of beliefs which does not require the retention of *other* beliefs, the holding firm of *other* claims, as the basis for its attack on the beliefs being undermined. Hegel emphasizes this point in the passage just quoted when he insists that the skeptic's tropes are not supposed to be propositions and that skepticism is not supposed to involve a preference for certain propositions. That equipollence is a method in this third sense is what enables it to have the generality of application required for it to be a method in the first sense.

Modern skepticism is in general not founded on a method in any of these three senses, as Hegel is well aware. It is rather founded on a cluster of *specific problems*—in the correlative threefold sense of problems which arise for some kinds of claims or beliefs but not for others, which are raised not in the service of any positive goal but simply because they seem to demand solutions, and which essentially rely on the presupposition of the correctness of certain *other* claims or beliefs. Typically the modern skeptic's specific problems concern the legitimacy of proceeding from claims about a certain kind of subject matter, the knowledge of which is assumed to be absolutely or relatively unproblematic, to claims about a second kind of subject matter, the knowledge of which is not felt to be unproblematic in the same way. At one time the unproblematic subject matter might be one's own (current) mental states, and the problematic subject matter the external world. At another time the unproblematic subject matter might be the external physical world, and the problematic subject matter the objects of religious belief. Schulze, the modern skeptic with whom Hegel is directly concerned in *The Relation of Skepticism to Philosophy*, is understood by Hegel to emphasize the latter kind of skeptical problem, while Hume's writings contain examples of both kinds of problems.[10].

The third sense just distinguished in which ancient skepticism is based on a method, whereas modern skepticism is based on specific problems—namely, by virtue of ancient skepticism's use of the equipollence method as a means of calling any given claim into question without essentially presupposing other claims in order to do so, in contrast with modern skepticism's essential reliance upon such presuppositions—is absolutely fundamental to Hegel's case for the superiority of ancient over modern skepticism. He holds (I think, rightly) that modern skepticism has in general lost sight of the method of equipollence and, as a consequence, has had recourse to procedures for calling one belief or set of beliefs into question which essentially rely on the presupposition of some other belief or set of beliefs. This makes modern varieties of skepticism essentially *dogmatic* in the sense of being founded on beliefs themselves vulnerable to skeptical attack, and hence restricted in scope, in a way that ancient forms of skepticism were enabled not to be by virtue of their possession of the equipollence method. Hence the sorry tale which Hegel tells in *The Relation of Skepticism to Philosophy* of the gradual degeneration into dogmatism of the skeptical tradition through history. The tradition began with "the old and genuine skepticism" of the ten tropes of Aenesidemus but already in the five tropes of Agrippa entered a decline into dogmatism, which proceeded "until [skepticism] finally in the most recent times sinks so far with dogmatism that now for both the facts of consciousness possess undeniable certainty and for both truth lies in the temporal sphere, so that because the extremes touch each other in these happy times the great goal is . . . attained by them that dogmatism and skepticism fall together in their decline and each reaches out to the other most warmly the hand of friendship." [11]

The ancient skeptics used the method of equipollence to motivate a quite general suspension of belief rather than merely a suspension of some beliefs the motivation of which essentially depended on the retention of other beliefs. For the ancient skeptics' strategy of setting up opposing propositions or arguments of equal weight on each issue in order to induce a suspension of belief did not require that they believe any of the propositions or arguments thus deployed. When, for example, they set up some argument hostile to a piece of dogmatic theory, such as the Stoic theory that the "cataleptic impression" provided a criterion of truth, or the theory that there were gods having such and such a nature, this was never because they believed their destructive argument, regarding it as decisive against the dogmatic theory or more convincing than arguments available in favor of the dogmatic theory. On the contrary, they no more identified with this destructive argument than with the constructive arguments which the dogmatists had provided in support of their theory. For the whole point of the ancient skeptics' procedure of adducing arguments on both sides of an issue was that they should find the arguments on neither side more convincing than those on the other. If the ancient skeptics' *practice* emphasized the development of destructive arguments, this was purely a function of the fact that the constructive cases had already been argued sufficiently well by the dogmatists themselves, so that the skeptics could concentrate their efforts on arguing the destructive cases required for the establishment of an equal balance of arguments on both sides of each issue. Thus Sextus Empiricus, as too often goes unnoticed, will conclude a thoroughly destructive argument against the existence of a criterion of truth which has extended over some twenty pages of text with the following brief but crucial reminder:

> But one should notice that we do not propose to assert that the criterion of truth is unreal (for that would be dogmatism); but since the dogmatists

appear to have established plausibly that there really is a criterion of truth, we have set up counter-arguments which appear to be plausible; and although we do not positively affirm either that they are true or that they are more plausible than their opposites, yet because of the apparently equal plausibility of these arguments and of those propounded by the dogmatists we deduce suspension of judgment.[12]

The objection might be raised that even if the ancient skeptics do not have to believe any of the propositions or arguments they adduce on both sides of a question in order to bring about a suspension of belief, still they must believe that the propositions or arguments on both sides are equally strong. But as the preceding passage shows, Sextus Empiricus does not claim that this *is* the case, only that it *appears* to him to be the case. And we shall see later that claims about appearances made by the skeptics should not be understood as expressions of belief.

In contrast to ancient skepticism with its equipollence method, modern skepticism with its various specific problems is supposed by Hegel to contain an essentially dogmatic component. Perhaps the general basis for this claim is already clear from the examples of two kinds of such problems which I gave. But in order to pursue Hegel's case in detail, let us focus on one of those problems, the problem of our knowledge of the external world, or what Berkeley called the problem of a "veil of perception." This problem looms so large in modern formulations of skepticism (whether by antiskeptics like Descartes, Berkeley, and Moore or by skeptics like Hume) that it at times seems to risk being equated with skepticism itself. The problem might be formulated as follows: How, given the fact that we have immediate knowledge only of the contents of our own minds, are we ever to know that these contents represent things outside our minds as they really are, or indeed even that there is anything outside our own minds at all—since everything of which we have immediate knowledge and which we might therefore use to decide this question could be just as it is regardless of how, or even whether, things are outside our minds? Hegel states this favorite theme of modern skepticism in *The Relation of Skepticism to Philosophy*: "According to this newest skepticism the human faculty of knowledge is a thing which has concepts, and because it has nothing more than concepts it cannot go out to the things which are outside it. It cannot find out about them or explore them—for the two things are . . . different in kind. No rational person in possession of the representation of something will imagine himself at the same time to possess this something itself."[13] Now in Hegel's view, to the extent that one's skepticism either includes or is exhausted by the veil of perception problem, it is based on dogmatic assumptions which the ancient skeptic, far from sharing, would subject to skeptical destruction by means of the method of equipollence. Hegel draws attention to three such dogmatic assumptions, and we should now consider these, indicating how Hegel would envisage the ancient skeptic's attitude in each case.

The first dogmatic assumption made in veil of perception skepticism is that we have certain knowledge of at least one kind of fact, namely facts concerning our own (current) mental contents. This was the point of Hegel's remark that modern skepticism has sunk so far with dogmatism that for both "the facts of consciousness possess undeniable certainty." [14] Modern skeptics suppose that no skeptical difficulties can arise about their own (current) mental contents, and so feel themselves justified in retaining beliefs about them as part of the basis of their skeptical attack on beliefs about the external world.

Now to designate this assumption "dogmatic" and contrast it with the absence of dogmatism in ancient skepticism may appear to do the veil of perception skeptic an injustice. First, it might be objected that there really is no way of generating a coherent skeptical doubt about one's own current mental states. Second, it might be objected that the ancient skeptic is in exactly the same position as the modern veil of perception skeptic on this issue. For Sextus Empiricus remarks in a chapter of the *Outlines of Pyrrhonism* devoted to the topic of whether the skeptics abolish appearances: "When we question whether the underlying object is such as it appears, we grant . . . that it appears, and our doubt does not concern the appearance itself." [15] And furthermore, the ancient skeptic's whole position will collapse if he is not able to retain this modest residue of beliefs about how things appear to him. For it is only by identifying with them as appearances that he is able to retain that minimal identification with propositions no longer dogmatically held by him to be true which is necessary to sustain his philosophical position and the coherence of his life. Thus, the only way the ancient skeptic can consistently hold the kind of view which he must hold in order to have a philosophical position at all—such as the view that the suspension of belief is the means to the achievement of mental quietude or that such and such an argument for a claim is counterbalanced by such and such an argument against it—is by understanding these claims not as positive assertions that things are that way but as claims about how things appear to the skeptic himself to be. [16] And he can only consistently hold the kind of view which he must hold in order to sustain coherent daily activity by likewise having this view constituted not by assertions that things are thus and so but only by his own appearances to that effect. Hence Sextus Empiricus's description in the *Outlines of Pyrrhonism* of the skeptics' regulation of their lives by appearances drawn from four sources: "Adhering, then, to appearances we live in accordance with the normal rules of life, undogmatically, seeing that we cannot remain wholly inactive. And it would seem that this regulation of life is fourfold . . ." [17] This then is a second objection to Hegel's idea that modern skepticism's presupposition of facts about one's own current mental states makes it dogmatic in a way that ancient skepticism is not. It would seem that the beliefs about his own current mental contents which the modern skeptic allows himself are after all ones that the ancient skeptic allows himself too, and that these beliefs are no less important to the ancient skeptic as a basis for his skepticism than they are to the modern skeptic as a basis for his.

We shall see the kind of answer Hegel would give to the first of these two objections in the course of considering his answer to the second. His general response to the second objection is to *deny* that the ancient and the modern skeptic really take the same position on their own current mental states. But Hegel seems to vacillate between two mildly incompatible ways of arguing this case. According to one argument he gives, the ancient skeptic would reasonably disapprove of the modern skeptic's belief in his own current mental states and would distinguish his own position from that of the modern skeptic, on the ground that the modern skeptic, unlike himself, envisages these states as a kind of certain *reality*. According to Hegel's other argument, the ground for disapproval and disagreement would rather be that the modern skeptic, unlike his ancient counterpart, envisages these states as a kind of *certain* reality. Since both arguments are of considerable interest, I shall discuss each in turn.

The first argument holds that the ancient skeptic, unlike the modern skeptic, did not accept that expressions of one's current mental experience were expressions of reality or truth. Thus in the *History of Philosophy* Hegel states: "To assert [what is in our immediate consciousness] to be the truth did not occur to [the older skeptics]."[18] On this reading, the exceptionless refusal of the ancient skeptics to assert that anything really was a certain way which Hegel emphasizes in *The Relation of Skepticism to Philosophy* was sustained in the face of their liberal avowals of their own current mental contents by their never having considered these mental contents to be parts of reality.[19] And on this reading the same circumstance justifies the claim that a modern, Cartesian-inspired critic of the ancient skeptics who points out that "when they doubt everything, still this 'I doubt,' 'it seems to me,' etc., is certain"—who in this way points out in reply to the ancient skeptics "the reality and objectivity of the activity of thought"—is in fact only pointing to the "formal illusion of an assertion" and therefore making an erroneous criticism.[20] For on this reading the ancient skeptics did not consider their mental activity to be real or objective. And they therefore did not consider their pronouncements about their mental activity to be assertions or expressions of beliefs, since to assert or believe that *p* is essentially to assert or believe that *p* represents reality or expresses truth.

This surprising claim by Hegel of a radical difference in character between, on the one hand, the modern skeptic's conceptions of his mental states (as real) and his acquaintance with them (as belief or assertion, descriptive of reality and true) and, on the other hand, the ancient skeptic's corresponding conceptions has recently received support from Burnyeat:

> When the skeptic doubts that anything is true . . . he has exclusively in view claims as to real existence. Statements which merely record how things appear are not in question—they are not called true or false—only statements which say that things are thus and so in reality . . . If the modern reader finds this an arbitrary terminological narrowing, on the grounds that if I say how things appear to me my statement ought to count as true if, and only if, things really do appear as I say they do . . . the answer is that this objection, though natural, is anachronistic. The idea that truth can be attained without going outside subjective experience was not always the philosophical commonplace it has come to be. It was Descartes who made it so, who (in the second Meditation) laid the basis for our broader use of the predicates "true" and "false" whereby they can apply to statements of appearance without reference to real existence. . . . If *epochē* is suspending belief about real existence as contrasted with appearance, that will amount to suspending all belief, since belief is the acceptance of something as true. There can be no question of belief about appearance, as opposed to real existence, if statements recording how things appear cannot be described as true or false, only statements making claims as to how they really are.[21]

A rather direct piece of evidence in support of the Hegel-Burnyeat contention that the ancient skeptics did not consider correct expressions of appearances to be expressions of truths is found in Sextus Empiricus's discussion of the Cyrenaic philosophy in *Against the Logicians*.[22] For there he condemns the Cyrenaic position that our mental affections and nothing beyond them furnish us with a criterion of truth as no less dogmatic and open to skeptical attack than any other position which offers a criterion of truth. He presumably could not have taken this view if he had regarded his own expressions of his mental affections or appearances as not only undogmatic and immune to skeptical attack (as he certainly did) but also expressive of truth.

Someone bent on pressing the similarity between the modern veil of perception skeptic and the ancient skeptic in the face of this argument might respond that even if the ancient skeptic *overlooked* the fact that his expressions of how things appeared to him were expressions of reality or truth and hence *overlooked* the circumstance that they articulated beliefs and were assertions, still these things *were* the case. But it would, I think, be a mistake to suggest that the ancient skeptic was guilty of simply overlooking the true character of his activity in this way (as someone might overlook the fact that he was dribbling food down his shirt, for example). First, it does not seem plausible in the light of the ancient skeptic's acquaintance with the Cyrenaic position to suggest that he simply overlooked the circumstance that his expressions of appearances were expressions of reality or truth. Rather, one seems bound to conclude that he either did not have quite the same concepts of reality and truth as the Cyrenaic (and the modern skeptic) but instead analogues of them having, and recognized by him to have, no application to his own appearances, or else had the same concepts of reality and truth but conscientiously (if perhaps wrongly) disagreed with the Cyrenaic (and the modern skeptic) in denying their application to appearances. And in neither of these possible cases could it be said that the ancient skeptic was, in any ordinary sense, expressing reality or truth when he reported his own appearances. Second, in either of these two possible cases the suggestion that the ancient skeptic was expressing beliefs or assertions about his own appearances without realizing the fact would run into grave difficulties. For to assert or believe that p is essentially to assert or believe that p represents reality or expresses truth, and in neither of the two possible cases are these essential conditions met by the ancient skeptic. In the first case they are not met because the ancient skeptic (a) does not use the concepts of reality or truth but only analogous concepts and (b) denies that even these analogous concepts apply to his own appearances. In the second case it is not met because although he uses the concepts of reality or truth, he denies that these apply to appearances.[23]

This, then, is one of the two lines of argument which Hegel uses to distinguish the positions of the ancient and the modern skeptic on the issue of their own current mental states: the ancient skeptic reasonably refuses to consider these mental states a source of certain *reality*. Hegel summarizes the thought by saying that, where these current mental items are concerned, "certainty alone is in question, and not truth."[24]

According to Hegel's second, mildly incompatible argument, what distinguishes the ancient from the modern skeptic is rather that the ancient skeptic, unlike the modern, does not allow that his mental items constitute a kind of *certain* reality. Thus in *The Relation of Skepticism to Philosophy* Hegel says of ancient skepticism: "Through its turning against knowledge in general it finds itself, because it here opposes one thinking to another and combats the 'is' of philosophical thinking, driven likewise to overcome the 'is' of its own thinking."[25] And he maintains that through the ten tropes of Aenesidemus "everything which appearance . . . gives is made unstable."[26]

These claims encounter two prima facie problems. First, the claim that the ancient skeptic is driven to apply the equipollence method to the "is" of his own thinking presupposes that he initially conceives of his thoughts as belonging to reality, and this conflicts with the claim Hegel made in his previous argument that the ancient skeptic never thought of his own appearances as part of reality (this is the mild inconsistency between Hegel's two arguments). Second, Sextus Empiricus explicitly rejects the inclusion of appearances among the objects of skeptical attack, so that Hegel's contrary claim involves a misinterpretation.[27] In view of these prima facie problems, I would suggest that Hegel's second argument should be understood not as an argument about what Sextus Empiricus *in fact* had to say concerning appearances (Hegel writes that way, but we may put that down to carelessness) but rather as an argument about how the logic of Sextus Empiricus's position *would have* required him to treat the issue of appearances *if* he had possessed or developed a conception of them as part of reality. This eliminates both Hegel's internal inconsistency and his direct conflict with Sextus Empiricus's texts. So understood, Hegel's argument is that, insofar as the skeptic conceived of appearances as real in nature and conceived of correct expressions of them as true, the logic of his position would "drive" or require him to apply the equipollence method to claims about his own appearances as to claims about any other subject matter.

Nor would such a hypothetical extension of the logic of the ancient skeptic's position be by any means a superfluous exercise. For first, Sextus Empiricus's general assumption that appearances are by nature not part of reality and that their correct expressions are innocent of truth seems disturbingly arbitrary. There is surely force in the objection to it that, as in the case of other declarative statements, the declarative statement that things appear thus and so to me should be accounted true if and only if things do appear thus and so to me. (Burnyeat calls this objection "anachronistic" but his ground for doing so—namely, that it was quite generally assumed in the age of the ancient skeptics that truth could not be attained without going outside subjective experience—is mistaken, as the example of the Cyrenaic position shows.) And whatever initial appeal there may be in the idea that an individual's correct statements of his own appearances do not express truth or reality, this appeal evaporates when one reflects on other people's correct statements of that individual's appearances. For denying that *these* express truth or reality has no appeal at all, initial or otherwise. And yet it is hard to resist the intuitive suggestion that they *say the same thing* as the statements which the individual makes about himself, only from a different point of view, so that if the former express truth or reality, then the latter must do so as well. Second, at many points in Sextus Empiricus's texts he certainly *seems* to conceive of appearances as part of reality. For example, in the *Outlines of Pyrrhonism* he says that the name "appearance" is given by the skeptics "to what is virtually the sense-presentation (*dynamei tēn phantasian*)," where the Stoic tradition from which the term *phantasia* was borrowed considered these items sufficiently real to be physical in nature.[28] Again, the very fact that it makes sense for Sextus Empiricus to raise the question of whether the skeptics abolish appearances suggests that he has some conception of them as real.[29] Thus Hegel would be performing an important task if he could show that in the hypothetical circumstance that the ancient skeptic came to conceive of his appearances as real in nature the logic of his position would require that he not accept these appearances as a sphere of certain reality in the manner of the modern skeptic but rather subject claims about them to skeptical attack like all other claims about reality.

The burden of Hegel's second argument is that the ancient skeptic is *driven* by his use of the equipollence method in combating claims about reality in general to apply this same method to his claims about his own appearances (so far as he conceives appearances to be real in nature). If, as might reasonably be maintained, the equipollence method in some sense defines the character of ancient skepticism, then the fact—if it is a fact—that the method lends itself to an application to appearances (conceived as real in nature) no less than to other subject matters provides a clear sense in which the logic of the skeptic's position compels him to combat appearances (so far as he conceives them to be real in nature) by this method. It is because of the intrinsic tendency of the equipollence method to territorial expansionism that Sextus Empiricus eschews belief in the skeptic's own formulae ("No more one thing than another," "I determine nothing," etc.), saying that they are "virtually cancelled by themselves" and that the skeptic "in his enunciation of these formulae ... states what appears to himself and announces his impression in an undogmatic way."[30] That is to say, it is because Sextus realizes that his destructive strategy of setting up an equal balance of arguments on both sides of each issue is as applicable to his own formulae as to anything else, that he must indeed apply the strategy to those formulae, see them succumb to a suspension of belief, and be content to identify with them only as appearances. The rhetorical question of Hegel's second argument is, then, why the skeptic, having been forced by the internal dynamic of the equipollence method to undermine every claim with which he identifies and to turn it into a claim merely about how things appear to him, is not equally forced by the internal dynamic of the equipollence method to undermine these claims about appearances themselves.

Hegel's remarks about the skeptic's conception of appearances as by nature not real or truth-sustaining provide one answer to this question. But hypothesizing, as we have been, that the skeptic were to give up this conception and instead think of appearances as by nature real and truth-sustaining, would he have an alternative answer? Sextus Empiricus does have certain arguments which might do service, but they are not very persuasive. One such argument is that statements about appearances are invulnerable to skeptical attack because they are agreed on by everybody: "We declare that the view about the same thing having opposite appearances is not a dogma of the skeptics but a fact which is experienced not by the skeptics alone but also by the rest of philosophers and by all mankind; for certainly no one would venture to say that honey does not taste sweet to people in sound health or that it does not taste bitter to those suffering from jaundice."[31] The grounds for this commitment to the common views of all mankind are somewhat unclear, but whatever they may be, it seems unlikely that any good case against extending the method of equipollence to claims about appearances could be based upon it. First, Sextus Empiricus's commitment to the common views of men, although it surfaces at several points in his texts, has the appearance of being more a random accretion from external sources than an essential component of his skeptical position like the equipollence method.[32] Consequently, it can by itself constitute for the skeptic only a weak objection to extending the equipollence method to appearances. Second, the fact that all people have actually agreed on an issue constitutes no obstacle to skepticism via any inhibiting effect on the construction of equipollence arguments, since, as the practice of Sextus Empiricus illustrates, the skeptic can always himself construct a *new* argument against a proposition never in fact argued against before.[33] Third, if appearances were being considered as a potential part of reality, it would in any case by no means be clear that all philosophers known to Sextus Empiricus *had* agreed even on the question of their existence. For example, Gorgias had argued that *nothing* exists, an argument which Sextus Empiricus himself does not scruple to make use of elsewhere.[34]

If there is no effective barrier within the ancient skeptic's position against the application of the equipollence method to one's own current appearances when these are understood to be a potential part of reality, the question arises how exactly the method lends itself to such an application in the way that Hegel implies it does. Unfortunately, Hegel does not himself explain how the equipollence method can be used to generate a skeptical doubt about one's current appearances. However, it is easy to envisage that an equipollence skeptic might nowadays adduce arguments against the existence of appearances or mental states in general, and therefore against the existence of his own current appearances or mental states in particular, in order to produce a balance between these negative arguments and the positive arguments which he has for thinking that they *do* exist, thereby motivating a suspension of belief on the issue. For there are a number of carefully argued cases in favor of one or another variety of eliminative materialism on the philosophical market which constitute arguments against the existence of mental states in general (on the ground, for example, that they are essentially just postulates of a false theory about human behavior embodied in everyday language, in much the way that phlogiston was just a postulate of a false theory about combustion).[35] The fact that these cases against mental states are *already* on the market means that a modern Sextus Empiricus reluctant to extend his skeptical attack to appearances would not even be able to use the fig leaf argument from the agreement of the "philosophers and . . . all mankind" in order to justify his timidity.[36]

Of course, philosophers wedded to Cartesian notions about the transparency of the mind are likely to balk at the suggestion that the skeptic could come to doubt his own current mental states. A first response to this resistance would be to point out that eliminative materialists appear to *deny* quite seriously that they are ever in a mental state, and that it is hard to see how, if such serious denial is possible, doubt should not be. But perhaps the Cartesians' case merits closer inspection before we dismiss it as an attempt to frustrate the onward march of equipollence skepticism against the bastion of beliefs about the mental. The alleged transparency of the mind appears to consist in two principles: first, the principle that if one is in some mental state S having a character C, then one necessarily believes and knows this (the principle of *evidence*), and second, the principle that if one believes oneself to be in a mental state S having a character C, then one necessarily is in such a state and one's belief necessarily constitutes knowledge (the principle of *incorrigibility*). Each of these principles might be thought to cause problems for a skeptic intending to raise skeptical difficulties concerning his own mental states. The skeptic might, of course, seek to dispel such problems at their source, using his ingenuity to produce an equal balance of arguments for and against, and hence a suspension of belief in, the principles of evidence and incorrigibility upon which the problems rest. However, it seems to me very doubtful whether, even if the truth of these principles were admitted, they would really give rise to problems for the skeptic with whom we are concerned, and this is the point on which I would like to focus.

One problem to which the principle of evidence might be thought to give rise is the following. Suppose that the skeptic were in fact in certain mental states and yet expressed skepticism about being in them; in that case he would be guilty of a factual error because his expression of skepticism would involve a denial that he believed or knew himself to be in those mental states although it is a necessary consequence of his being in them together with the truth of the principle of evidence that he does believe and know himself to be in them. This apparent problem rests on a misunderstanding of the equipollence skeptic's position, however, for he does not typically *deny* that he believes or knows anything, but rather suspends belief on this as on other questions. This is implied in a passage in which Sextus Empiricus distinguishes Pyrrhonism from the position of the New Academy: "The adherents of the New Academy, although they affirm that all things are non-apprehensible, yet differ from the skeptics even, as seems probable, in respect of this very statement that all things are nonapprehensible (for they affirm this positively, whereas *the skeptic regards it as possible that some things may be believed and apprehended*)."[37] A second problem which appears to arise due to the principle of evidence is as follows. If the skeptic were in fact in certain mental states, this would entail by the principle of evidence that he believed and knew that he was, but then how could he as a skeptic simultaneously suspend belief on that question? In response to this apparent problem, one might first point out that people quite often find themselves in a psychological condition which would naturally and properly be described as one of simultaneously believing that p and suspending belief on the question whether p or even denying that p. Consider, for instance, the fairly normal case of a scientist or philosopher who simultaneously believes in an unreflective way that the car parked outside his office is really yellow (that it does not merely look that way because of an unusually glaring reflection of the sun, for example) and due to scientific considerations in a more reflective way suspends belief on the question whether, or even denies that, secondary qualities like yellowness are real qualities of objects like cars. Not only is such a psychological condition possible and common, but it is also a condition which typically involves no absurdity, since, for example, the attitude of belief or the sense of "reality" involved on its two apparently conflicting sides is not the same. It could then quite well be the case that the skeptic, rather like the scientist or philosopher in our example, simultaneously and without absurdity believed in an unreflective way that he was in certain mental states while in his role as skeptic in a more reflective way suspending belief on that question.

Turning to the principle of incorrigibility, a Cartesian might raise the following objection to a skeptic who was attempting to induce him to call his own current mental states into question: "Since I believe that I am currently in mental states X, Y, and Z and since the principle of incorrigibility is true, I must really currently be in mental states X, Y, and Z." But this objection is even less troublesome for the skeptic than the previous ones, for its argument is flagrantly question-begging—assuming as a premise that the objector *believes* that he is in such and such mental states, whereas belief is itself a mental state and hence precisely the kind of thing whose existence in the world the radical skeptic is calling into question.

Two pieces of historical evidence lend support to Hegel's view that it belongs to the logic of the ancient skeptic's position that he should react to a conception of his appearances as by nature real or truth-sustaining by extending the equipollence method to them and thereby inducing a suspension of belief about them. First, when Sextus Empiricus in *Against the Logicians* considers the real or truth-sustaining conception of their own mental affections espoused by the Cyrenaics, he attacks their belief that they possess such affections in exactly the same way as he attacks any other proffered criterion of truth, namely by adducing counterarguments against it with a view to establishing an equal weight of arguments for and against and hence motivating a suspension of judgment. This would seem to commit him to proceeding in the same fashion in response to any real or truth-sustaining conception of his own appearances which he might *himself* develop. Second, Galen reports on the existence of a group of radical Pyrrhonists who indeed did, unlike Sextus Empiricus himself, seek to generate a suspension of belief on the subject of their own appearances.[38] And in one place at least Galen characterizes the Pyrrhonist position in general as one which goes so far as to call into question whether we are thinking.[39]

Supposing the ancient skeptic were to extend his skeptical attack to appearances in the manner described, would it still be possible for him to retain the kind of identification with a view of things which would sustain his philosophical position and the coherence of his life? Hegel hints at one way in which he might be able to do this—namely by continuing to direct himself philosophically and practically by thoughts about appearances, but understanding these thoughts as implying an infinite regress of "it appears to me" qualifications. For example, instead of directing himself by means of the thought "It appears to me right to sacrifice to Zeus" simpliciter, he would now direct himself by this thought reinterpreted in such a way as to imply the further qualification "It appears to me that it appears to me right to sacrifice to Zeus" and so on ad infinitum. Hegel seems to have such a regress of qualifications in mind as the only consistent option left to skeptics who conceive of their own mental states as a potential part of reality when he writes of a modern skepticism which conceives of its mental states in such terms, namely as the "possession of a representation" where the representation is a "something":

> We do not read anywhere that this skepticism is consistent enough to show that . . . no rational person will imagine himself to be *in possession of a representation* of something. Since of course the representation too is a something, the rational person can only imagine himself to possess the representation of the representation, not the representation itself, and again not the representation of the representation either . . . but only the representation of the representation of the representation and so forth to infinity.[40]

We have now considered both of Hegel's arguments designed to show that the ancient skeptic's position on his own mental states is after all not the same as that of the modern skeptic, so that the modern skeptic may reasonably be charged with being dogmatic on this subject in a way that the ancient skeptic is not. Hegel summarizes the difference between the ancient skeptic and his modern counterpart by saying that ancient skepticism reached an "extreme of the highest consistency, namely one of negativity or subjectivity which did not limit itself to the subjectivity of character which is at the same time objectivity, but became a subjectivity of knowing which directed itself against knowing." [41] A skepticism that limited itself to a "subjectivity of character which is at the same time objectivity" would be one which, like that of Descartes or Hume even in their most extreme skeptical moments, adhered to the view that the realm of our own current mental states furnishes us with reality which we can know with certainty. The skepticism of the ancients, which was not limited in this way and instead became "a subjectivity of knowing which directed itself against knowing," was more radical and an "extreme of the highest consistency" in its rejection of *all* claims about reality. Hegel has two explanations of how this was so—explanations which seem inconsistent at first reading but which prove to be complementary when it is understood that one of them concerns the historical position of the skeptics and the other concerns the position to which the inner logic of skepticism would have driven the skeptics if, as did not happen, they had understood appearances to be a potential part of reality. These explanations are respectively that the ancient skeptics simply did not conceive of the appearances to which they restricted themselves as real in nature and that the ancient skeptics, if they *had* thought of appearances as a potential part of reality, would have subjected them to equipollence attack, suspended belief about them, and retained identification with them, if at all, by deflating claims about them in advance with an infinite number of "it appears to me" qualifications (thereby depriving those claims of the "full stop," the existence of some order at which such qualifications cease, which would be necessary for them to constitute genuine assertions or expressions of belief).[42]

In the course of backing up Hegel's charge that modern skepticism unlike ancient skepticism is dogmatic on the subject of one's own current mental states against the objection that the modern and ancient skeptics take the same view of this subject we have also answered the other objection which was raised against Hegel's charge: the objection that there is no way of raising a genuine skeptical doubt about one's own current mental states. For, as we saw, the skeptic might very well generate such a doubt by arguing with equal weight on both sides of the issue of whether our mentalistic vocabulary has application to reality at all.[43]

The second dogmatic assumption which Hegel detects in modern veil of perception skepticism is the assumption that the mental facts which this skepticism holds us to have immediate knowledge of concern a kind of mental *thing* with which we are acquainted by means of a kind of inner *perception*. It is, I think, true and important that the way of formulating skepticism in the modern period has been strongly influenced by a more or less literal understanding of mental states as *things,* which goes beyond but requires and reinforces the modern understanding of them as belonging to reality. Under the influence of Descartes above all, many skeptics and antiskeptics in the modern period tend to reject the vague and natural conception of mental states as states or properties of persons and the vague and natural conception of our relation to our own mental states as one in which we are simply the conscious bearers of those states or properties. Instead they think of mental states and our relation to our own mental states in terms of a specific set of concepts originally drawn from discourse concerning things in the physical world and our perception of them. Mental states thus become a kind of *object* existing in a sort of inner *space* and apprehended by a sort of immediate *perception*. In Descartes, for example, statements like this one from the *Principles* appear frequently: "By the term conscious experience I mean everything that takes place *within ourselves* so that we are *aware* of it, in so far as it is an *object* of our awareness."[44] The same kind of language used to describe the mental and our relation to it is as familiar from many other modern philosophers concerned with skepticism, such as Berkeley and Hume. However literally or metaphorically such language is understood by modern skeptics and antiskeptics, it exercises a powerful influence on their conception of the nature of skeptical problems. This is particularly true of the skeptical veil of perception problem itself. Berkeley's "veil" metaphor is much more than an ornament in that it makes vivid the assumption underlying the problem that mental states constitute a kind of object which immediately confront our faculty of perception. Thence arises the disturbing picture of these mental objects obstructing our line of (visual) perception to any other objects which may lie beyond them.[45] Hegel's view is that since ancient skepticism did not conceive of appearances as part of reality a fortiori it did not in the manner of modern skepticism conceive of them as a kind of thing, existing in an inner space or apprehended by a sort of immediate perception: "What the newest skepticism always brings with it is . . . the concept of a thing, which lies behind and underneath the appearance-things . . . [Ancient skepticism] for its part stops at the subjectivity of appearance. But this appearance is not a sensuous *thing* for it, behind which dogmatism and philosophy would claim there to be yet other things, namely the supersensuous ones. Since it refrains altogether from expressing a certainty and reality, it certainly has for itself no thing . . . about which it could have knowledge." [46]

The third and final dogmatic assumption made by the modern veil of perception skeptic is that there is a general and sharp distinction between concepts and their instances in the world, of a kind making it conceivable that any concept might exist without having or ever having had instances in the world. For it is assumed by the veil of perception skeptic that those of our mental items which are *essentially* conceptually articulated (such as our beliefs, thoughts, and intentions) could exist just as they are without there being or ever having been anything in reality instantiating the concepts which articulate them—or even without there being or ever having been anything in reality at all beyond the mental items themselves. Hegel emphasizes this assumption of modern skepticism and vigorously attacks it in *The Relation of Skepticism to Philosophy* where he notes that, "According to this newest skepticism the human faculty of knowledge is a thing which has concepts, and because it has nothing more than concepts it cannot go out to the things which are outside it. It cannot find out about them or explore them—for the two things are . . . different in kind." [47]

Now Hegel holds—rightly, I think—that this third assumption is one which the modern veil of perception skeptic *shares* with the ancient skeptic. The ancient skeptic, too, assumes the existence of a general and sharp distinction between concepts and their instances in the world, of a kind making it conceivable that any concept might exist without having or ever having had instances. In the *History of Philosophy* Hegel particularly associates this assumption with the Academic skeptic Arcesilaus. And that he is in general right to associate it with the ancient skeptics may be illustrated by the example of Sextus Empiricus, who not infrequently makes it a background assumption when advancing equipollence arguments. Thus Sextus in *Against the Physicists* prefaces an inquiry into the question of whether or not gods exist—an inquiry during which, in wonted equipollence fashion, he sets arguments for and against their existence in opposition with one another—with this comment: "Since not everything which is conceived partakes also in existence, but it is possible for a thing to be conceived and not exist—like a Hippocentaur and Scylla—after our inquiry about the conception of the gods we shall have to examine also the question of their existence." [48] The assumption articulated here that we might always be in possession of a concept corresponding to nothing in reality is clearly intended to be more than merely a part of one side of an equipollence argument, advanced without any identification on the part of the skeptic. For it is stated by Sextus Empiricus in propria persona *before* he proceeds to set forth equally balanced arguments. Rather, Sextus seems to understand the assumption to be one with which the skeptic himself identifies—presumably in something like the way in which he identifies with his own formulae (such as "No more one thing than another" and "I determine nothing").

This assumption made by the ancient skeptics of a general and sharp distinction between concepts and their instances, making conceivable the existence of the former without the latter, is important because it forms the basis of a special type of equipollence difficulty which the ancient skeptics raise: a type in which, having made the assumption in question, the skeptics ask whether particular concepts in fact have any instances and then adduce arguments of equal weight on both sides of this issue in order to motivate a suspension of judgment on it. Sextus Empiricus's difficulty concerning the existence of the gods was of this type. I shall henceforth distinguish equipollence difficulties of this special type from equipollence difficulties in general as "concept-instantiation" difficulties. Together with equipollence difficulties in general, they constitute the aspect of ancient skepticism which has the deepest impact on Hegel's own philosophy, as we shall see in Parts Two and Three of this work.

But if modern and ancient skepticism *share* this assumption, how can it be pointed to as another case in which modern veil of perception skepticism is dogmatic whereas ancient skepticism is not? Although Hegel does not directly address this question, a plausible answer is easy to find, for there is bound to be a crucial difference between the ways in which the modern and the ancient skeptic make the assumption. The modern veil of perception skeptic simply holds it to be true and is therefore guilty of dogmatism. The ancient skeptic, in contrast, is bound to "assume" it only in the qualified sense in which he "assumes" any of the formulae essential to his position: he will recognize that, when positively asserted, it is as susceptible to skeptical attack by means of the equipollence method as any other positive assertion, will in consequence suspend judgment on the question of whether or not it is true, and will then identify with it only qua appearance.

This, then, is Hegel's case for thinking that modern veil of perception skepticism is essentially based on dogmatic assumptions in a way that ancient skepticism is not. To summarize his main charges, modern veil of perception skepticism dogmatically assumes that we have certain knowledge of at least one kind of fact, namely facts concerning our own current mental states. Moreover, it dogmatically conceives of these mental states as a kind of thing, existing in an inner mental space and grasped by a sort of immediate perception. Finally, in radicalizing the problem of "seeing beyond" these mental states to the extent of raising the possibility that there might be nothing in the world corresponding to any of the concepts which articulate them, or even no external world at all, it dogmatically assumes a general and sharp distinction between concepts and their instances, of a kind making it conceivable that the former might always exist without the latter.

Now it might with justification be pointed out at this stage that there is a good deal more to modern skepticism than its veil of perception variety, and that Hegel's case for saying that modern skepticism as a whole has, in losing sight of the equipollence method, become essentially dogmatic therefore remains to be made out. In partial response to this reservation I include in an endnote remarks on another domain in which Hegel sees modern skepticism as typically falling into a timid dogmatism due to its lack of the equipollence method in contrast with ancient skepticism which again has a cogent equipollence attack to launch: the laws of logic.[49] But here I propose to respond to the reservation by briefly testing Hegel's charge that modern skepticism as a whole is guilty of dogmatism against the general skeptical practice of two of modern skepticism's foremost spokesmen, Hume and the Descartes of the *First Meditation*.

Hume, like most other modern representatives of skepticism, makes no significant use of the ancient skeptic's equipollence method. In Hume, skepticism is in the main reduced to a practice of producing arguments against various sorts of claims—where the arguments' premises and the validity of their inferences together with their conclusions as to the falsehood of the claims attacked are believed by Hume and are supposed to be believed by his readers. This is quite different from the practice of the ancient skeptics. The latter did not use arguments in order to come to or induce a belief in their conclusions (even if these conclusions were negative in character) but rather in order to bring about a suspension of belief regarding the questions at issue in those conclusions. And they did not believe their negative arguments' premises and the validity of these arguments' inferences or intend them to be believed, but instead found them and intended them to be found just equally plausible with the premises and inferences of the positive counterarguments which it was in their eyes equally important to adduce in order to bring about suspension of judgment. Measured by the standards of the ancient skeptics, Humean skepticism is merely a kind of negative dogmatism, shot through with beliefs which should be subjected to equipollence attack.

For example, in Section Seven of *An Enquiry Concerning Human Understanding* Hume believes and intends his readers to believe the negative conclusion that it is a mistake to think of the fact of a causal relation between some particular events A and B as a fact constituted by a necessary connection between events A and B themselves (and indeed, more positively, that this causal relation is essentially comprised of facts concerning the regular conjunction of A-like and B-like events in the same temporal sequence in the past and facts about the propensity of the mind to anticipate that A-like and B-like events will continue to be conjoined in this way in cases as yet unobserved). And he believes and intends his readers to believe the premises and the validity of the inferences belonging to the argument which he gives in support of this negative conclusion. He would be quite unready to conclude this argument in the manner of Sextus Empiricus with an acknowledgment that there are equally strong counterarguments in favor of the view he has been attacking.

Naturally, Hume's belief in his negative arguments consists first of all in a belief in their premises. These premises generally concern alleged features of our mental experience. Such, for example, is the general principle that every idea originates from an antecedent impression—the principle which is the basis of Hume's skeptical arguments concerning causation, external existence, the self, and so forth. That Hume feels comfortable assuming premises of this kind is in large part due to an underlying dogmatic assumption of his which we encountered earlier in connection with the veil of perception problem—the assumption that we can have certain knowledge of the existence and character of our own current mental states or, in Hume's terminology, impressions and ideas. Thus even during one of his most skeptical moods in *A Treatise of Human Nature* Hume still treats "those perceptions, which are immediately present to our consciousness" as a point beyond which skeptical doubts can be pushed no further.[50] In the *Encyclopedia* Hegel explicitly points out this dogmatic foundation of Humean skepticism and notes its vulnerability to ancient skepticism.[51] A consideration of Hume's general skeptical practice would tend, then, to support Hegel's contention that modern skepticism is essentially dogmatic in character.

The Cartesian skeptic of the *First Meditation* is equally neglectful of the ancient skeptic's equipollence method. Descartes' methodical doubt consists of a suspension of belief on everything which is "not entirely certain and indubitable," and this includes everything for which he can find "some reason for doubt."[52] This Cartesian route to suspension of belief is quite different from and much less demanding than that of the ancient skeptic. Whereas the ancient skeptic sought arguments against each proposition of *equal strength* with those existing for it in order to induce a suspension of belief, the Cartesian skeptic demands of himself no more than "*some* reason for doubt." And as Descartes' practice in the *First Meditation* shows, this need amount to no more than finding a hypothesis under which the proposition to be called into question is false and which is not itself conclusively disprovable. This hypothesis may quite well, as in the case of the Evil Genius Hypothesis, lack intrinsic plausibility and plausible grounds and be less plausible than the proposition which it is supposed to call into question.[53]

Despite its difference from the ancient skeptic's equipollence method, the Cartesian procedure of setting aside all beliefs for which one can find "some reason for doubt" in the modest sense just described is arguably free of any essential reliance on dogmatic assumptions. And so it might seem that this Cartesian procedure constitutes a counterexample to Hegel's judgment that modern skepticism is essentially dogmatic. In response to this I would suggest that the Cartesian method of doubt—despite its use of traditional skeptical materials, Descartes' talk of using it to achieve suspension of judgment, and his occasional description of it as skeptical—is not, and was not really understood by Descartes to be, a form of skepticism at all. There are several reasons why not.

First, the Cartesian procedure, if I have characterized it correctly, would clearly, unlike the ancient skeptic's equipollence method, be unsuited to the task of motivating a genuine suspension of belief or calling into question claims to knowledge. Were these really the goals of the Cartesian method, this unsuitedness would be the dear price paid for the ease of only having to provide "*some* reason for doubt" rather than *equally strong* reasons on both sides. For suppose it does turn out that given beliefs or all beliefs succumb to the method of doubt in the sense of its being shown that there is some hypothesis under which they are false and which is not itself conclusively disprovable. Why should this circumstance incline anyone to give up those beliefs if he still has stronger reasons for believing than for disbelieving them (unless he is afflicted with some bizarre inclination to withhold assent from any proposition for which he can find some hypothesis of error which is not conclusively refutable)? And why should it incline anyone to think that those beliefs cannot constitute knowledge (unless again he begins from the very odd assumption that the absence of any conceivable, not conclusively refutable hypothesis of error is a necessary condition of knowledge)?

But second, Descartes does not even seem particularly serious about using his method of doubt to achieve a genuine suspension of belief. Even if his voluntarist theory of judgment may sometimes incline him to think he could achieve this with the aid of the method, his talk about doing so often has the appearance of mere theater. He is at any rate quite happy to concede in the Synopsis of the *Meditations* that the very kinds of propositions to which the method gets applied during the course of the work—such as that there is a world and that men have bodies—"never have been doubted by anyone of sense." [54]

Third, the above-mentioned divergence of Descartes' method of doubt from the spirit of skepticism is explained by the fact that the method is intended by Descartes to constitute not a form of genuine skepticism but rather a close relative of genuine skepticism designed by him to play a role within a particular antiskeptical strategy which he has devised. [55] The method is designed so as to be able to set aside *at least* all those beliefs which it would be possible for the genuine skeptic to call into question, in the hope and expectation that when the method is applied, there will prove to be a residue of beliefs recalcitrant to it which the skeptic could therefore not possibly call into question (the setting aside of beliefs by the method is theatrically represented by Descartes as a suspension of belief or even a rejection of the beliefs as false). The method is supposed to accomplish this as follows. First, it focuses on a single necessary condition of raising any genuine skeptical difficulty for a claim: that there be some conceivable state of affairs in which that claim is false and which one cannot be certain does not obtain.[56] Second, the method does its utmost to show that this necessary condition is met by as many beliefs as possible, and it sets aside all such beliefs (here Descartes uses traditional skeptical materials liberally). Third, the method eventually confronts some beliefs by which, try as it might, it cannot find the necessary condition to be met. This residue of beliefs is thus seen to be invulnerable to skeptical attack.

Since the Cartesian method of doubt is not, and was not really understood by Descartes to be, a form of skepticism, it cannot constitute a counterexample to Hegel's general judgment that modern skepticism is essentially dogmatic. Furthermore, the whole bearing of the Cartesian method on genuine skepticism lies in the anticipated outcome of its application that some beliefs will prove not to satisfy the necessary condition of raising skeptical difficulties described above and will therefore be shown to be immune to skepticism (if the application of the method failed to have this outcome, it would have no consequences for skepticism at all—not antiskeptical ones, for obvious reasons, but not skeptical ones either, for reasons given earlier). And the essential foundation of the residue of beliefs which Descartes anticipates surviving the rigors of his method is beliefs about one's own mental states (*cogitationes*). Hence in a sense the whole bearing of Descartes' method of doubt on skepticism rests on his view that these beliefs about one's own mental states cannot be subjected to any hypothesis of their falsehood which is not conclusively refutable, so that they cannot possibly succumb to skeptical problems. But as our earlier discussion of veil of perception skepticism showed, this view is very dubious. Beliefs about one's own mental states seem on the contrary to be quite as vulnerable to such hypotheses (for example, the hypothesis of eliminative materialism) as are other beliefs, and there seem to be good prospects of raising skeptical equipollence problems against them.

I defer to the endnotes a response to two further reservations which might be raised concerning Hegel's thesis that the history of skepticism exhibits a displacement of the cogently radical equipollence skepticism of the ancients by a modern skepticism which, in its lack of the equipollence method, has fallen into dogmatism and is itself vulnerable to equipollence problems. These reservations concern the ancient end of Hegel's thesis. The first and less serious of them is the suggestion that this thesis is guilty of oversimplifying, of seeing ancient skepticism as more homogeneous in character than it really is, and in particular of failing to take into account the moderate character of the form of ancient skepticism propagated by the Academic skeptics.[57] The second and more serious reservation is the suggestion that Hegel's thesis rests on a fundamental misinterpretation of Pyrrhonism itself, attributing to it a kind of radicalism which it does not possess.[58]

This concludes my exposition of Hegel's most important and philosophically interesting insight into the history of skepticism. It is also the insight whose recognition is most essential if one is to understand the role which skepticism plays within the broader framework of Hegel's philosophy. According to this insight, the philosophical importance of the skeptical tradition lies in its development of the method of equipollence, of bringing equally plausible arguments on both sides of each issue into opposition with one another. This method was central to the self-conscious practice of the ancient skeptics, enabling them to generate an unrestricted skepticism free of any dogmatism, but it has been lost sight of by the skeptics of the modern period, who have developed in its place problems which are essentially founded on dogmatic assumptions—assumptions that are themselves susceptible to skeptical attack by means of the method of equipollence.

This argument for the superiority of ancient over modern skepticism is persuasive without the benefit of an acquaintance with any specifically Hegelian theories. The same cannot be said of a second argument for the superiority of ancient over modern skepticism to which Hegel attaches equal importance. Whereas the first argument in effect charges modern skepticism with not being radical enough in certain directions, with failing to extend its skeptical questioning to various dogmatic assumptions which it makes, the second argument holds that it is *too* radical in another direction, namely in its pretensions to undermine the claims made by Hegel's own philosophy or Philosophical Science, the discipline which he understands to articulate the true nature of the Absolute.[59] It attempts to do this on the basis of assumptions which Hegel regards as both dogmatic and false. This side of Hegel's criticism of modern skepticism can by fully understood only against the background of his account of how the content of Philosophical Science is immune to even the strongest form of skeptical assault, and we shall first come to examine this account in detail in Part Three. My brief description of Hegel's position here should be read with this in mind.

The Relation of Skepticism to Philosophy distinguishes three phases of the skeptical tradition in relation to the question of an illegitimate skeptical attack upon the claims of Philosophical Science. The first phase was "the old genuine skepticism" of the ten tropes of Aenesidemus (mistakenly attributed by Hegel to Pyrrho himself).[60] This skepticism was, according to Hegel, properly directed solely against the common Understanding, the faculty which articulates views less exalted than Philosophical Science, and not at all against Philosophical Science.[61] The next phase was the skepticism of the five tropes of Agrippa which already represented, in Hegel's view, a corruption of the skeptical tradition to the extent that these tropes were not only properly directed against the more theoretical dogmas of the Understanding but were also improperly directed against genuine Philosophical Science.[62] The final phase, on this account, was the complete corruption of skepticism in the modern period when a "skeptic" like Schulze could refrain from attacking the dogmas of the common or theoretical Understanding and instead direct all his skeptical energies against the claims of genuine Philosophical Science.[63]

Hegel has at least two fundamental criticisms of a skepticism which attacks Philosophical Science in the manner of Schulze. The first criticism is that Schulze, having made the dogmatic assumption of a certainly knowable world of mental and physical things answering to the concepts of the mere Understanding, compounds his sins by making the further dogmatic assumption that we can understand the claims which Philosophical Science makes about the Absolute in terms of the same common concepts of the Understanding (something which Hegel vigorously denies). In this way Schulze arrives at the idea that the Absolute is supposed to be a *thing* which *exists* and somehow lies *behind* that world of mental and physical things which he takes us to know with certainty. Hegel expresses this criticism with a lavish confusion of metaphors:

> It is not possible to understand the Rational [i.e. the Absolute] and Speculation [i.e. Philosophical Science] in cruder terms. Speculative Philosophy is constantly presented as though, before it, common experience lay there insurmountably as its iron horizon, spread out in the immovable form of its common reality, and as though Speculative Philosophy suspected and wished to spy out behind this horizon the *things-in-themselves* pertaining to the horizon as mountains of an equally common reality which that other reality carried on its shoulders. Herr Schulze cannot conceive of the Rational, the in-itself, otherwise than as a rock beneath snow. For the Catholic the host changes into a divine, living thing; what happens here is not what the devil demanded of Christ, that he change stone to bread, but rather the living bread of Reason transforms itself eternally into stone.[64]

Such an attempt to grasp the Absolute by using the concepts of the mere Understanding constitutes in Hegel's view not only a hopeless distortion of the Absolute's true character but also an attempt to grasp it in concepts which ultimately turn out to be self-contradictory.

Hegel's second major criticism concerns the character of a series of skeptical objections raised by Schulze against the claims of Philosophical Science. These objections are conceived in the spirit of Kant's refutation of the ontological proof of God's existence, which refutation Schulze wholeheartedly embraces. Hegel accuses Schulze of making in this series of objections the same dogmatic and false presupposition which Kant had made in his attempted refutation of the ontological proof: the presupposition that quite generally "that which is thought, because it is something thought, does not at the same time include a being within itself."[65]

Kant had argued that the ontological proof rested on the false assumption that existence was a concept, whereas in truth it was the satisfaction of a concept by something, and that consequently, contrary to the ontological proof, nothing could follow from any concept we might have of God and his perfections as to his existence since, "Whatever ... and however much our concept of an object may contain, we must go outside it if we are to ascribe existence to the object."[66] Hegel objects that Kant's case rests on the assumption that every kind of concept is distinguishable from the instances which satisfy it in such a way that it could be present without this instantiation, and that this assumption is not only thoroughly dogmatic but also false precisely where the subject matter in question is God, or the Absolute with which Philosophical Science deals. Hence Hegel comments on Schulze's use of the same dogmatic assumption as Kant in his skeptical attacks on the claims of Philosophical Science: "This division of the Rational, in which thinking and being are one, into the opposites thinking and being, and the absolute holding fast of this opposition ... constitutes the basis, repeated ad infinitum and applied in every case, of this dogmatic skepticism."[67] The Kant-Schulze dogmatic assumption of a sharp distinction between the concept of God or the Absolute and its instantiation in reality is a special case of the third dogmatic assumption which we detected behind modern veil of perception skepticism—the assumption that all concepts are distinct from their instances in the world in such a way that they could exist without this instantiation. Hegel is particularly critical of the Kant-Schulze special application of this more general assumption because, in his view, it is precisely in relation to God or the Absolute that the more general assumption breaks down.[68]

In Hegel's view ancient skepticism in its purest form is vulnerable to neither of the preceding criticisms which he levels against Schulze. Since, according to Hegel, the ten tropes of Aenesidemus do not attack the claims made by Philosophical Science about the Absolute (and the five tropes of Agrippa do not do so when properly employed, that is, exclusively against the Understanding), a fortiori they do not attack these claims either on the basis of a misconception of the nature of the Absolute arising from an inappropriate application to it of the concepts of the mere Understanding or on the basis of a falsely assumed distinction between the concept of the Absolute and its instantiation in reality.

This concludes my account of the two major lines of thought which lead Hegel to claim that modern skepticism is inferior to ancient skepticism. It should be clear from the aspects of Hegel's interpretation of ancient skepticism which we have examined so far that he takes a rather sensitive and sympathetic view of it. However, in order to complete our account of Hegel's critical interpretation of the skeptical tradition we should now do something to test the limits of this sensitivity and sympathy.

TWO

The Limitations of Ancient Skepticism

THE HIGH level of sensitivity and sympathy in Hegel's account of
ancient skepticism emphasized so far does have limits. In this
chapter we shall explore some of those limits.

We should begin by considering a series of puzzling features of Hegel's
interpretation of ancient skepticism not yet mentioned. At first sight
these appear to constitute merely a series of unconnected insensitivities
or misconceptions in his interpretation, and no doubt the undue neglect
of his interpretation has been largely due to this appearance. However,
these puzzling features prove, on closer inspection, to be neither unconnected nor mere insensitivities. Rather, they have a single complex
source—a certain complex ideal for a "skeptical" discipline of Hegel's
own devising. And they constitute less a series of insensitivities in interpretation than a unified and typically Hegelian critique of ancient skepticism—a measuring of it against, and charitable interpretation of it in
the light of, the complex ideal of his own "skeptical" discipline.

One of the puzzling features of Hegel's interpretation is his startling
claim that "the older skepticism does not doubt, being certain of untruth
. . . it does not flit to and fro with thoughts that leave the possibility that
something may still be true, but it proves with certainty the untruth of
all." [1] This seems to involve a complete misinterpretation, since the ancient skeptics did not aim to prove anything and did not attempt to show
in any way that claims were untrue. Instead, they merely sought to show
that the arguments for and against claims appeared to be equally strong
so that we should suspend judgment. A second puzzling feature is Hegel's
suggestion that ancient skepticism points out self-contradictions in
views. He writes, for example, that the skeptics "show in the same thing
the contradiction that exists, so that of everything that is presented the
opposite also holds good." [2] This, too, looks like a misinterpretation,
since the ancient skeptics did not understand themselves when they set

up arguments on opposing sides of issues to be demonstrating the self-contradictoriness of the views involved.[3] A third puzzle concerns some surprising statements Hegel makes about the five tropes of Agrippa in the *History of Philosophy*, where he gives a much more positive evaluation of them than in *The Relation of Skepticism to Philosophy*. Thus he says that they are "exhaustive as regards the determinate," that they exhibit a "profound knowledge of the categories," and that they are "necessary contradictions into which the Understanding falls."[4] Perhaps the claim about their exhaustiveness is not too puzzling, since in economy and in generality of application they may represent an improvement on the ten tropes of Aenesidemus. However, the basis for Hegel's other two claims is quite obscure. A fourth puzzle lies in Hegel's claim in *The Relation of Skepticism to Philosophy* that Plato's *Parmenides* is the most perfect example of skepticism: "What more perfect and self-contained document and system of genuine skepticism could we find than in the Platonic philosophy the *Parmenides,* which encompasses the whole field of [finite] knowing through concepts of the Understanding and destroys it? This Platonic skepticism does not aim at a *doubting* of these truths of the Understanding, which knows things as diverse, as wholes which consist of parts, as a coming to be and passing away, a multiplicity, similarity, etc., and makes objective claims of that kind, but at a complete negation of all truth of such a knowledge."[5]

The single, complex source of these puzzling features of Hegel's account of ancient skepticism lies in the fact that Hegel, as part of his epistemological enterprise to be considered in Part Three, develops a negative discipline of his own for the purpose of discrediting all the claims of the mere Understanding and thinks of this discipline as a kind of skepticism. This negative discipline, unlike historical skepticism, is designed to realize the following ambitious ideal: it must effect a discrediting of the claims of the Understanding which is *exhaustive* by demonstrating the *self-contradictoriness* of each member of a *system* of *categories* or fundamental concepts belonging to the Understanding. We shall consider the nature and role of this "skeptical" discipline in detail in Part Three. What is important for now is that the ideal which Hegel tries to realize in it at certain points acquires a strong influence on his interpretation of historical skepticism. Sometimes this influence takes the form of a presupposition of some aspect of the ideal as a standard by which to criticize ancient skepticism. At other times it has the more disconcerting appearance of a projection of some aspect of the ideal onto the texts of the ancient skeptics. Here are two examples of the former kind of influence. At one point Hegel criticizes historical skepticism by presupposing his own ideal that self-contradiction should be exhibited *systematically*, saying that "if the philosophic Idea is . . . implicitly dialectic, it is so not in a contingent manner," whereas historical skepticism "on the contrary, exercises its dialectic contingently, for just as the material comes up before it it shows . . . that implicitly it is negative."[6] At another point he criticizes historical skepticism by presupposing his own ideal that self-contradiction should be exhibited of *categories* or fundamental concepts, saying that the ten tropes of Aenesidemus exhibit a lack of development since in them "the content . . . shows its change only, without showing its contradiction in itself, i.e. in its concept."[7] Here are two examples, encountered above, of Hegel's more disconcerting practice of apparently projecting an aspect of his own ideal onto historical skepticism. At one point he appears to project the ideal of *exhaustiveness*, saying that skepticism's tropes are "exhaustive as regards the determinate."[8] At another point he projects onto historical skepticism the ideal of exhibiting *self-contradictoriness*, saying that the skeptics "show . . . the contradiction that exists."[9]

The puzzling features of Hegel's interpretation of ancient skepticism mentioned earlier are all readily explicable in this light. Thus Hegel's puzzling suggestion that the older skepticism proves the untruth of all the Understanding's claims results from a projection onto ancient skepticism of his ideal that the *self-contradictoriness* of the Understanding's claims should be demonstrated (by demonstrating this of the Understanding's fundamental concepts) and that this should be effected *exhaustively*. His puzzling suggestion that ancient skepticism was involved in the exhibition of the self-contradictoriness of views is intelligible once again as a projection onto it of his ideal that *self-contradictoriness* be demonstrated. His suggestion that the five tropes of Agrippa are "exhaustive as regards the determinate" involves the not altogether implausible projection onto them of the *exhaustiveness* which his own ideal demands; while his more puzzling claims that they exhibit a "profound knowledge of the categories" and are "necessary contradictions into which the Understanding falls" involve the projection onto them of his ideal of demonstrating a *system* of *self-contradictory categories*. Finally, Hegel's puzzling praise of Plato's *Parmenides* as the most perfect example of genuine skepticism rests on his conviction that it manifests all the aspects of his ideal, being a "system of genuine skepticism" (*systematicity*) which "encompasses the whole field of [finite] knowing through concepts of the Understanding" (*exhaustiveness* and *categories*) and "destroys it" (*self-contradictoriness*).

Now even in the cases where Hegel apparently *projects* his own ideal upon ancient skepticism it would, I think, be a mistake and an injustice to accuse him of simply misinterpreting his historical sources. Rather, he is working with a model in mind of a form of "skeptical" discrediting of dogmatic claims which he believes to reflect the metaphysical realities of the case, and he is inclined to interpret the historical skeptics charitably as striving more or less adequately to express what is present in that model (something he does more convincingly at some points and less so at others). This is merely a particular example of Hegel's general method in the history of philosophy (or of art or religion, for that matter) of presupposing the metaphysical truth of his own philosophy and then proceeding to interpret the philosophies of the past charitably in its light. Unlike Aristotle, who in practice writes the history of philosophy in a similar way, Hegel self-consciously embraces this approach and is prepared to defend it with arguments.[10]

Measuring or interpreting ancient skepticism by means of the ideal of his own "skeptical" discipline constitutes one of Hegel's forms of criticism of it. However, there are several others in addition. For example, Hegel sometimes suggests that ancient skepticism is guilty of some form of self-contradiction. Indeed he has at least three versions of this criticism. The first version appears in the *Phenomenology*, where it forms the basis of the dialectical development from the "shape of consciousness" Skepticism to the next shape, Unhappy Consciousness. Hegel holds that the skeptic, in his effort to maintain the identification with a view of things which he needs in order to live and to criticize dogmatism, unavoidably becomes susceptible to his own criticism, so that he inevitably oscillates between identification with a view and rejection of it.[11] Strangely, this somewhat naive criticism of the ancient skeptic was one which Hegel himself had already seen beyond five years earlier in *The Relation of Skepticism to Philosophy*.[12] There he had raised the similar argument that the skeptic faces the dilemma that he must either give up identifying with a position altogether because of his general proscription of objective claims, in which case his skepticism destroys itself, or he must identify with a position, in which case he commits himself to some objective claim or other and falls into inconsistency with his general proscription of this.[13] But instead of *accepting* this argument against the skeptic in *The Relation of Skepticism to Philosophy*, Hegel had rightly pointed out that while Sextus Empiricus is quite ready to comply with his general proscription of objective claims, applying the equipollence method to his own formulae when these are construed as such, this does not destroy his position because he can still identify with his own formulae as expressions of *appearances* rather than as objective claims. In this way Sextus avoids both the fate of the self-destruction of his position and the fate of inconsistency.[14] Why then, did Hegel resurrect an objection to skepticism in the *Phenomenology* which he had already successfully answered on skepticism's behalf in *The Relation of Skepticism to Philosophy*? It is hard to avoid the conclusion that he did so mainly because the form of the objection, namely an allegation of self-contradictoriness, fitted in conveniently with the dialectical method used in the *Phenomenology*, a method which involves making the transition from one shape of consciousness to the next through the development of a self-contradiction.

A second version of the self-contradiction criticism depends on some substantial Hegelian claims about the significance of skepticism as a stage in the history of philosophy. Hegel thinks that the retreat into subjectivity characteristic of skepticism signifies a result which, "positively expressed, is that self-consciousness itself is reality," so that skepticism "marks the standpoint at which self-consciousness knew itself in its thought to be the Absolute." [15] Its role in the history of thought is thus to prepare the way for and express implicitly the idealist insight that the subject himself is or constitutes all reality. Skepticism itself is not in a position to recognize this, however; it is only in the idealism of Neoplatonism that self-consciousness "receives a consciousness respecting that which it has thus become, or its essential nature becomes its object." [16] Now Hegel perceives a contradiction between, on the one hand, the idealist significance of the skeptic's retreat into subjectivity, the significance that the subject himself is or constitutes all reality, and, on the other hand, the contingency and disorder with which appearances seem to confront the skeptic, their lack of any subjection to his ordering will. [17] This is the point of a passage in the *History of Philosophy*:

> Skeptical self-consciousness . . . is this divided consciousness to which, on the one hand, motion is a confusion of its content; it is this movement . . . in which what is offered to it is quite contingent and indifferent . . . On another side its simple thought is the immovability of self-identity, but its reality, its unity with itself, is something that is perfectly empty . . . As this simplicity and at the same time pure confusion, skepticism is in fact the wholly self-abrogating contradiction. [18]

The sense in which "contradiction" is at issue here is clearly a rather extended one, and the criticism of skepticism involved could only begin to appear convincing to someone who had already accepted some substantial and questionable Hegelian views about the role of skepticism in the history of philosophical thought.

The third and perhaps most persuasive version of the self-contradiction criticism of ancient skepticism is contained in Hegel's remark in the *Phenomenology* that skepticism's "deeds and its words always belie one another." [19] This seems to echo the view championed by Hume in the modern period that the Pyrrhonist ideal of a life without belief proves vain in the face of action, which of necessity involves beliefs, so that "the great subverter of *Pyrrhonism* or the excessive principles of skepticism is action, and employment, and the occupations of common life." [20]

Another, more original criticism of ancient skepticism which Hegel offers is that while it succeeds in making itself immune to refutation by its retreat into the subjectivity of only saying how things appear to the skeptic, this victory is a completely hollow one: "The invincibility of skepticism must undoubtedly be granted, only, however, in a subjective sense as regards the individual . . . To keep oneself in individuality depends on the will of the individual; no one can prevent a man from doing this, because no one can possibly drive another out of nothing." [21] The skeptic's success in avoiding refutation is hollow in much the same way as the success in avoiding refutation of a man who restricted himself to using ejaculations like "Oh joy!" or "My goodness!" would be a hollow success. A skeptic who restricts himself to utterances about how things appear to him is simply not engaging in the *kind* of activity with which someone can take issue or in the *kind* of activity which can be a taking issue with someone and is therefore not engaging in the *kind* of activity in which someone can be refuted: "This purely negative attitude, which wishes to remain mere subjectivity and appearance, ceases precisely in this way to be something for knowing. Whoever remains attached to the vanity that it appears so to *him,* that *he* thinks so, and wishes his utterances not to be taken for objective thought and judgment at all, must be left to himself—his subjectivity concerns nobody else, still less does it concern philosophy or does philosophy concern it." [22] This would not be so clear if what were in question were the modern skeptic's truth-sustaining or factual appearance statements, for it might then seem that the skeptic's activity of making claims about his own appearances *was* an activity of the kind in which one could take issue with people and be taken issue with and therefore *was* an activity of the kind in which one could be refuted, and that any immunity to refutation was simply a noteworthy and laudable feature of this special case of that general kind of activity—just what the skeptic required. But in question here are rather the nonfactual appearance statements which Hegel ascribes to the ancient skeptics—statements which the skeptic either simply does not intend to express truths or which he uses in such a way that they imply an infinite series of deflating "it appears to me" prefaces. And Hegel's idea that in expressing one's own appearances in either of these ways, one is simply not engaging in the *kind* of activity in which one can take issue with people or be taken issue with, in which one can refute someone or be refuted, has considerable force. This surely does cast a somewhat dubious light on the skeptic's immunity to refutation in this area.

Hegel has one final line of critical thought about ancient skepticism which should be described here, though only in a preliminary way since it will be explained in some detail in Part Three. In *The Relation of Skepticism to Philosophy* he emphasizes that there are bounds to the sphere of legitimate application of the difficulties raised by ancient skepticism. Since he believes that "the old, genuine skepticism" of the ten tropes of Aenesidemus does not overstep these bounds, his point does not exactly amount to criticism of ancient skepticism, but it would be criticism of any attempt to give *unrestricted* application to ancient skepticism's difficulties. The alleged bounds are a function of certain conditions of the applicability of equipollence difficulties in general or of concept-instantiation difficulties in particular, conditions which the ancient skeptic implicitly (if undogmatically) assumes to hold in cases where he raises these difficulties, but which in Hegel's view do not hold universally because they do not hold for the subject matter of his own philosophy. In short, equipollence and concept-instantiation difficulties can find no application in this special case.

As Hegel's previous criticism of ancient skepticism implied, when the ancient skeptic's claims that equipollence or concept-instantiation difficulties arise for some subject matter are understood merely as claims about how things appear to him, they are incontestable and irrefutable. This might seem to render futile Hegel's attempts to set bounds to the application of these difficulties. The other side of the coin of Hegel's previous criticism, though, is that when the skeptic's claims merely concern appearances, they do not challenge anything that anyone else believes. In order for them to do so, they must be reconstrued as claims about how things really *are*, such as that the arguments for and against such-and-such a proposition really *are* of equal plausibility, or that there really *is* a difficulty about establishing that such-and-such a concept corresponds to anything in reality. It is therefore such dogmatic forms of the skeptic's claims that Hegel will be concerned to challenge and in these forms they are indeed contestable and perhaps refutable. At the same time, although the claims in the different forms in which the skeptic makes them, namely as claims about appearances, are immune to any possibility of refutation, this does not mean that the answer to them which Hegel provides by pointing out the conditions of applying the skeptical difficulties and their nonfulfillment for the special case of his own philosophy must have no force against the skeptic. For the conditions of raising equipollence and concept-instantiation difficulties which Hegel lays bare and challenges for the special case of his own philosophy have probably never actually been reflected on as assumptions of his skepticism by the skeptic. And this gives Hegel some ground for hope that by making them explicit and arguing that in this special case they do not hold, so that the skeptical difficulties cannot arise here, he might shake the skeptic's confidence in or dissuade him from an unrestricted skepticism even though he cannot strictly contest or refute what the skeptic says.

The condition of the applicability of the equipollence method in general which the skeptic implicitly assumes to hold when he applies it is that the proposition to which it is applied has a negation. For in order to find equally plausible arguments *for and against* a proposition *p*, as the method requires, one must obviously find an argument against *p*, but finding an argument against *p* just is finding an argument for *not-p* (the negation of *p*). The condition of the applicability of the concept-instantiation difficulty in particular which the skeptic assumes to hold when he applies it is that the concept to which the difficulty is applied could exist without there being anything in the world instantiating it. Both these assumptions may appear universally true and uncontroversial but, as we shall see, Hegel believes that neither holds for the content of his own philosophy.

PART II

SKEPTICAL CULTURE IN HEGEL'S PHILOSOPHY OF HISTORY

THREE

The Theory of a Historical Ur-teilung

HEGEL'S understanding of the nature of ancient skepticism plays an important and generally neglected role within his philosophy of history, manifesting itself there in his conception of what he at one point refers to as "skeptical culture" (*skeptische Bildung*).[1] Hegel sees the historical emergence of this skeptical culture as a key to understanding the collapse of the general form of cognition and the religious and ethical attitudes that characterized the pagan Greek city-states and their replacement by the general form of cognition and the religious and ethical attitudes characteristic of the ascendant Judeo-Christian tradition. It is my hope that an examination of this view will achieve two things. First, it should draw out one of the more interesting and persuasive threads in the complex weave of Hegel's philosophy of history and thereby enhance our understanding and appreciation of the latter. Second, it should reveal a body of Hegelian reflections on the broader cultural preconditions and impact of skepticism which deserve attention for their own sake.

Hegel nowhere gives a really definitive or unequivocal statement of the theory of skeptical culture's role in history in which I am interested. The form it takes varies considerably from one text to another, and it always retains something of an experimental character. It is nevertheless possible to distill a consistent and plausible version of the theory from the materials provided in a number of texts and this will be my main goal.

Lest this qualification give the impression that Hegel was half-hearted in assigning to skeptical culture a role within his philosophy of history, I should emphasize immediately that, on the contrary, as time went on, he assigned to its impulse an increasingly central and exclusive role in explaining the historical transition from pagan Greek to Judeo-Christian culture. This process can be traced through three works: *The Positivity of the Christian Religion*, the *Phenomenology*, and the *Philosophy of History*.

In the *Philosophy of History* it is above all the Sophists who are the representatives of what I am calling skeptical culture. This may prompt the question in what sense the cultural phenomenon to which I am referring deserves to be called a *skeptical* culture. The answer is that it is for Hegel characterized by a lively awareness of the two kinds of epistemological difficulties which we have seen him to identify as distinctive of ancient skepticism: first, the general equipollence difficulty of how to decide questions of fact when the claims or arguments on both sides appear equally strong; and second, the more specific concept-instantiation difficulty of how to decide whether concepts correspond to anything in the world, given that it appears possible for any concept to exist without instantiation in the world and that the arguments for and against instantiation in the case of particular concepts appear equally strong. A skeptical culture, then, is one in which difficulties of the kind raised by the ancient skeptics are taken seriously and (an obvious but, as we shall see, important corollary) in which the intellectual *preconditions* of raising these difficulties are established.

It is important to consider the origin and nature of Hegel's idea of the general structure of the historical change from pagan Greek to Judeo-Christian culture which the emergence of a skeptical culture is supposed to explain. For doing so will provide us with a broad framework within which to place and understand the details of his account of that change and in particular the role of the emergence of a skeptical culture in the account. Hegel's idea of the general structure of the historical change in question had a peculiarly a priori origin. It would hardly be an exaggeration to say that he started out with a certain structure in mind and only then looked for the historical phenomena to instantiate it.[2] What is really surprising, though, is the degree to which he was successful in this search.

The ultimate author of the structural idea which Hegel applied to the transition from pagan Greek to Judeo-Christian culture was Hoelderlin. Hoelderlin had a metaphysical theory owing much to the historical Parmenides according to which a primordial, undivided Being was subjected to an *Ur-teilung* ("judgment," but also "original division") which first established the division between subject and object that is present for human consciousness. This theory finds its most concise and explicit statement in the fragment *Judgment and Being*.[3] However, a different expression of it in a preface to *Hyperion* will help to illustrate an important ambiguity in Hoelderlin's view:

> The blessed unity, Being, in the only sense of the word, is lost to us and we had to lose it if we were to strive for it and win it . . . We have fallen apart from Nature and what formerly, as one may surmise, was one, now struggles in opposition, and rule and slavery alternate between the two sides. Often it seems to us as though the world were everything and we

nothing, but often too as though we were everything and the world nothing
. . . To put an end to that eternal struggle between our self and the world,
to restore the peace of all peace which is higher than all Reason, to unite
ourselves with Nature to an infinite whole, that is the goal of all our striving, whether we understand ourselves in this or not.[4]

The ambiguity in this passage concerns the question of whether Hoelderlin supposes the state of "blessed unity, Being" and the event of our
becoming conscious of a separation from Nature to fall *within* human
history or whether he supposes them rather to fall within a time prior to
human history or even to be supratemporal. That they at least fall within
time is suggested by the phrase "what formerly . . . was one." That they
in addition fall within human history is suggested by the statement that
Being "is lost to us" (since we can only lose what we once had).[5] However, Hoelderlin's theory encounters a major internal problem if it says
that they fall within human history, and this is why his position is ambiguous. The problem is that Hoelderlin himself plausibly suggests that it
would make no sense to suppose that there existed conscious subjects
prior to any recognition of a subject-object distinction, since "a consciousness without an object is . . . unthinkable" and consciousness of
an object is necessarily consciousness of it as distinct from the subject,
while equally consciousness without the self-consciousness of the subject
is unthinkable—"How can I say 'I' without self-consciousness?"—and
consciousness of a subject is necessarily consciousness of it as distinct
from an object.[6] If this is so, then the idea that the original unified Being
and its division into the subject-object distinction might occur *within*
human history is absurd.

Despite the apparent incoherence in this idea, Hoelderlin's friend
Schelling explicitly adopted the view that the original state of unity and
the event of Ur-teilung do occur within human history. This is shown by
the fact that he identified mythical thought (meaning primarily the mythical thought of the Greeks) as belonging to a period *before* Ur-teilung.[7]
We may represent Hoelderlin's and Schelling's versions of the theory of
Ur-teilung schematically (figure 1).

This theory of Hoelderlin's and Schelling's about the Ur-teilung or
original division of a state of perfect unity looks singularly unpromising
as the basis of an interpretation of concrete events within human history.

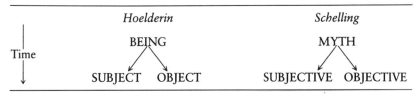

Figure 1

It is not even clear that Hoelderlin, who invented the account, really intended it to have this kind of historical application at all. As pointed out, there is at least one apparent absurdity in giving it such an application as it stands. Furthermore, neither Hoelderlin nor Schelling gives more than the vaguest indication of which historical period might be involved, and neither makes an attempt to find hard historical evidence to support the theory.[8] Finally, neither Hoelderlin nor Schelling gives any explanation of why such an event as Ur-teilung should have occurred at the time when it allegedly did.[9]

Nevertheless, Hegel took over the basic structure of this theory, applied it unequivocally to events within human history, and succeeded in generating an interesting account. In order to do so, he had to remedy the shortcomings of the theory just mentioned, and this inevitably involved a radical alteration of the theory itself, leaving in the end little more than an abstract structure in common between his own version and the earlier versions of Hoelderlin and Schelling.

Hegel does not actually use the word *Ur-teilung* to refer to a historical division of an original unity, reserving this term for his ahistorical Logic instead.[10] However, in the *Phenomenology* he describes a historical division of an original unity which is far too similar in structure to the theories of Hoelderlin and Schelling to have been conceived independently. For the Hegel of the *Phenomenology* the original state of unity and harmony, corresponding to Hoelderlin's Being or Schelling's Myth, is the historical period in which the Greeks possessed a unified, harmonious Ethical Life. Thus Hegel refers to Spirit at this stage of its development as a "simple substance" and speaks of its "beautiful harmony and tranquil equilibrium."[11]

The character of the Ur-teilung which disrupts and brings a division into this harmonious unity is different from that envisaged by Hoelderlin in being unequivocally held to take place in a community of men who are already conscious subjects, possessing a consciousness of themselves as distinct from the objective world standing over against them.[12] And it is correspondingly different from that envisaged by either Hoelderlin or Schelling in not being conceived as the source of consciousness of a subject-object distinction. Hence the incoherence which threatened the Hoelderlin-Schelling version of the historical theory does not afflict Hegel's version.

According to Hegel, the original division instead takes the form of a division of the objects of human consciousness into, on the one hand, a social and natural world having a harsh, objective character and, on the other hand, a remote, inscrutable, and despotic divinity. This is described most clearly in the "Spirit" chapter of the *Phenomenology,* where Hegel depicts the downfall of the Ethical Life of Spirit and the emergence of a

Spirit dirempted into Culture (*Bildung*), on the one hand, and Faith (*Glaube*), on the other. He says of this diremption that "Spirit, which henceforth is divided within itself, traces one of its worlds, the *realm of Culture*, in the harsh reality of its objective element; over against this realm, it traces in the element of thought the *world of Faith*, the *realm of essential being*."[13] Spirit is thereby "divided and expanded into *this world* and the *beyond*."[14] We can represent this theory from the "Spirit" chapter schematically (figure 2).

So far so good. It is crucial though for our purposes to recognize that this treatment of a historical Ur-teilung in the "Spirit" chapter is not the only depiction of that event in the *Phenomenology*. As Lukács has pointed out, the *Phenomenology* contains not just one treatment of the whole course of history but three such treatments, each considering it under a different aspect.[15] First, there is a treatment of the whole of history under the aspect of the individual consciousness in the chapters "Consciousness," "Self-consciousness," and "Reason." Then there is a second treatment of the whole of history under the aspect of the developing social order in the "Spirit" chapter. Finally, there is a third treatment of the whole of history under the aspect of the developing artistic, religious, and philosophical views of men which express the Absolute in the chapters "Religion" and "Absolute Knowing." Thus the historical event described in the "Spirit" chapter as the division of the harmonious unity of Ethical Life into the realms of Faith and Culture is treated at other points in the *Phenomenology* as well. Of particular importance here is the fact that the Spirit divided into the realms of Culture and Faith which we meet in the "Spirit" chapter corresponds to the dirempted Unhappy Consciousness described in the earlier "Self-consciousness" chapter. Hence, Hegel remarks in the course of his discussion of Faith in the "Spirit" chapter: "Religion . . . in the form in which it appears here as the Faith belonging to the world of Culture, does not yet appear as it is in and for itself. We have already seen it in other characteristic forms, viz. as the Unhappy Consciousness, as a shape of the insubstantial process of consciousness itself."[16] Of less importance for our purposes is the correspondence between the Unhappy Consciousness, and hence the Spirit divided into Faith and Culture also, and the stage of the "Religion" chapter which Hegel calls Revealed Religion.[17]

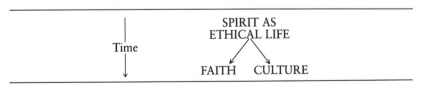

Figure 2

Why is the correspondence between the Spirit divided into Faith and Culture in the "Spirit" chapter and the dirempted Unhappy Consciousness of the "Self-consciousness" chapter so important? The reason is that the explanation given in the "Spirit" chapter of why the harmonious unity of Ethical Life was disrupted, giving way to a Spirit divided between the realms of Faith and Culture, is rather meager. If this divided Spirit corresponds to the Unhappy Consciousness of the "Self-consciousness" chapter, though, that meager explanation can be filled out by Hegel's account of the emergence of the Unhappy Consciousness in this earlier chapter of his text. Thus, to hear Hegel's full explanation of why the harmonious, unified Ethical Life of the Greek polis gave way to an ascendant Judeo-Christian culture in which man's world was characterized by a division between, on the one hand, a harsh, objective natural and social environment and, on the other hand, a remote, inscrutable, despotic God requires consideration of not only the account of this event in the "Spirit" chapter but also the stages of the "Self-consciousness" chapter which deal with Lordship and Bondage, Stoicism, and Skepticism and which are supposed to explain the emergence of the Unhappy Consciousness.

If the Spirit divided between the realms of Faith and Culture corresponds to the Unhappy Consciousness, one may ask how the *other* stages of the "Spirit" chapter involved in the Ur-teilung of Ethical Life correspond to counterparts in the text's earlier treatment of history under the aspect of the individual consciousness. First, the harmonious unity of Ethical Life in the "Spirit" chapter corresponds to the "Consciousness" chapter as a whole (comprising the stages Sense Certainty, Perception, and Understanding). Thus Hegel writes of Spirit in the simple form of Ethical Life: "Spirit is, in its simple truth, Consciousness and forces its moments apart . . . In this separation of the moments of Consciousness, the simple substance has, on the one hand, preserved the antithesis to Self-consciousness [i.e. the content of the chapter following the "Consciousness" chapter] and, on the other, it equally exhibits in its own self the nature of Consciousness."[18] Second, as this passage already suggests, stages of the "Spirit" chapter *subsequent* to the harmonious unity of Ethical Life are correlated with the "Self-consciousness" chapter. Thus, Hegel says of the germ of opposition already present in Ethical Life: "The way in which the antithesis is constituted in this ethical realm is such that Self-consciousness has not yet received its due as a particular individuality."[19] To be more specific in this respect, Hegel explicitly correlates the stage of the "Spirit" chapter called "Legal Status," in which the Roman Empire with its abstract laws is depicted as a period of transition from Greek Ethical Life to the divided Spirit of Faith and Culture, with the Stoicism and Skepticism stages of the "Self-consciousness" chapter. Thus he remarks of Legal Status: "Personality . . . has stepped out of the life of the ethical substance. It is the independence of Consciousness which has *actual* validity. The nonactual thought of it which came from renouncing the *actual* world appeared earlier as the *Stoical Self-consciousness*."[20] And he similarly brings skepticism into relation with this Roman phase of Spirit: "Like Skepticism, the formalism of legal right is . . . by its very nature without a peculiar content of its own; it finds before it a manifold existence in the form of 'possession' and, as Skepticism did, stamps it with the same abstract universality, whereby it is called 'property.'"[21]

Diagrams of the two treatments of a historical Ur-teilung in the *Phenomenology* which are of particular interest to us, the treatment in the "Spirit" chapter and the treatment in the "Consciousness" and "Self-consciousness" chapters, show the correspondences just considered and point up once again the debt which the structure of Hegel's account owes to the inferior historical account developed by Hoelderlin and Schelling (figure 3).

This model of a historical Ur-teilung in the *Phenomenology* already looks more promising than the Hoelderlin-Schelling model. The Ur-teilung is unambiguously supposed to be a historical event. It does not fall victim to the absurdity of positing something as an event within human history (the emergence of a subject-object distinction for consciousness) which is a precondition of there being any conscious subjects to have a history. It is based on a consideration of concrete historical facts from a relatively well-defined period of history. These facts concern the decline of the confident culture of early Greek history, in which men felt an organic proximity to their natural and social environment and worshiped understandable, accessible, and relatively human gods, and the

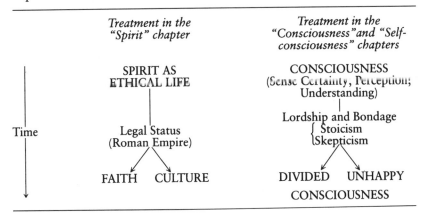

Figure 3

supersession of this culture through the rise of Rome by a culture in which the natural and social environment had a harsher, more alien character and in which revealed religion posited an inscrutable, remote, omnipotent and despotic deity in place of the gods of polytheism. Finally, it attempts to offer an explanation, and indeed a relatively naturalistic as opposed to a merely metaphysical explanation, of the historical Urteilung which these historical events constitute.[22]

In what remains of this part of the book we shall explore in more detail Hegel's account of the historical process whose general structure we have just considered, with a view particularly to understanding his explanation of why it took place and the role within this explanation of a skeptical culture and of the skeptical difficulties which characterize such a culture.

FOUR

The Collapse of Greek Ethical Life

EGEL sometimes depicts the collapse of the unified, harmonious Ethical Life of early Greece in the language and images of
the biblical Fall of Man. Like the biblical Fall, the collapse of
Greek Ethical Life represents the destruction of a state of harmony and
innocence through the acquisition of a certain kind of insight, and like
the biblical Fall, it represents a loss of innocence which leads man to hide
from God.[1] An example of such a use of the biblical story which illustrates the *skeptical* character of the insight Hegel considers responsible
for the collapse of Ethical Life is found in the account from the *History
of Philosophy* of the Academic skeptic Carneades's visit to Rome. Hegel
reports how Carneades caused a stir by arguing in public on successive
occasions the cases for and against justice, and how this skeptical practice of balancing equally convincing arguments on both sides of a question found a receptive audience among the Roman youth but created
alarm among older Romans concerned to uphold the prevailing ethical
order, "because the youths were thereby turned away from the strictness
of ideas and virtues which prevailed in Rome."[2] Hegel says of the mea-
sures which were taken to avert this consequence:

> But this taint can no more be avoided than could in Paradise the desire
> for knowledge. The knowledge which is a necessary moment in the culture
> of a people thus makes its appearance as the fall from innocence, and as
> corruption. An epoch such as this, in which thought appears to veer about,
> is then regarded as an evil so far as the security of the ancient constitution
> is concerned. But this evil of thought cannot be prevented by laws etc.; it
> can and must be the healer of itself through itself alone.[3]

Hegel is here concerned only with the destruction of a Roman analogue
of Greek Ethical Life through the introduction of skeptical difficulties.

But his mature explanation of the historically more important destruction of Greek Ethical Life itself takes a similar form.

Hegel's interest in the causes of the collapse of a unified, harmonious early Greek culture spans texts as remote in time as the Bern essay *The Positivity of the Christian Religion* and the Berlin *Philosophy of History*. However, it is an important question, and one not answerable by a casual survey of the texts, just what this unified, harmonious Greek culture whose collapse Hegel wishes to explain is supposed to consist in.

In *The Positivity of the Christian Religion* the question why the harmonious and unified culture of early Greece (and Rome) collapsed is primarily the question why Greek (and Roman) polytheism, with its deep roots in all aspects of daily life, was supplanted by Christianity:

> How could a religion have been supplanted after it had been established in states for centuries and intimately connected with their constitutions? What can have caused the cessation of a belief in gods to whom cities and empires ascribed their origin, to whom the people made daily offerings, whose blessings were invoked on every enterprise, under whose banners alone the armies had conquered, who had been thanked for victories, who received joyful songs and earnest prayers, whose temples and altars, wealth and statues, were the pride of the people and the glory of the arts, and whose worship and festivals were but occasions of universal joy? . . . How strong must the counterweight have been to overcome the power of a psychical habit which was not isolated as our religion frequently is today, but was intertwined in every direction with all men's capacities and most intimately interwoven even with the most spontaneously active of them?[4]

In those parts of the *Phenomenology* and the *Philosophy of History* which are most concerned with the destruction of Greek culture, Hegel's interest may at first sight seem to be directed toward the collapse of the ethical views and practices of the early Greeks rather than toward the collapse of their polytheistic religion. His very use there of the term Ethical Life to characterize the original state of Greek harmony and unity which is destroyed may suggest such a reading. However, this reading is correct only insofar as the Ethical Life of Spirit certainly is characterized by distinctive views and activities belonging to the sphere of ethics in the usual sense, ethical views and activities which are distinctive as to both form and content. Their content is described in general terms in the *Phenomenology* as the "human" and "divine" laws which competitively regulate activity within Ethical Life.[5] Their form is a harmonious and markedly communal ethical practice in which the community enforces ethical norms and the ethical verdict of the community automatically has prior authority, both in principle and in fact, over the ethical verdict of the individual. This contrasts sharply with the individualistic Morality (*Moralität*) of a later age in which societal enforcement pertains to law but not to ethics per se and the locus of moral authority is the individual conscience rather than the community. Thus, when Hegel offers an explanation of the collapse of Greek Ethical Life, he certainly is offering an explanation of the collapse of this content and form of ethics in the usual sense. At the same time, this development in ethics in the usual sense is not all, or even the most important part, of what is involved in Ethical Life and its destruction.

For one thing, the question of why Ethical Life collapsed is not meant as an abandonment of the earlier question of why polytheism declined; Hegel is not substituting for his original question about the decline of this form of religion a question about a historically proximate decline in a particular type of ethical outlook and activity. Rather the question of why the Ethical Life of Spirit collapsed, as this question is posed in the *Phenomenology* and the *Philosophy of History,* encompasses *both* the question of why early Greek ethical views and activities declined *and* the question of why Greek polytheism lost its grip.[6] That Hegel is interested in considering the religious change along with the ethical when he explains the collapse of Greek Ethical Life is shown in the *Phenomenology* by such facts as that he identifies Greek religion as essentially belonging to the Ethical Life of Spirit and on occasion gives a simultaneous and identical explanation of the decline of both the religion and the ethics of the Greeks.[7] Again, this interest is shown in the *Philosophy of History* by such facts as that Hegel there understands the question of the corruption of Greek culture as a question about both the decline of Greek religion and the decline of Greek laws and emphasizes the raising of the question whether gods are and what they are as a symptom of the destruction of this culture.[8]

There is, however, a further reason why it would be wrong to see the ethical characteristics of Greek Ethical Life as the sole focus of Hegel's interest when he explains its destruction. This is the fact that Greek Ethical Life is distinguished not only by its ethics and religion but also by a set of features characteristic of its cognitive attitudes in general, be their subject matter religious, ethical, physical, or whatever. It represents a particular form of cognition in general.[9] Hegel emphasizes at least three distinctive characteristics of its particular form of cognition in general. First, in Greek Ethical Life there is an automatic harmony and agreement in the views of all members of the community on at least the fundamental principles governing any given subject matter.[10]

Second, this harmony is sustained by the disposition of the individual within the community to defer automatically and exclusively to the judgment of the community on all fundamental issues. His deference is automatic in the sense that once the community's verdict is clear, he does not hesitate to concur, and he concurs simply because the community's verdict is the way it is. His deference is exclusive in the sense that it involves the absence of any presumption on his part that he has a right to be convinced about fundamental issues (other than by being told the view of the community) and the absence of any inclination to seek to justify or ground fundamental judgments (other than by finding them to be agreed upon by his community). These possibilities do not even occur to him. Thus, when he defers to the community on some fundamental issue, he does so simply because the community takes the view it does—not, for example, because he finds it plausible that a view on which his fellows agree is likely to be right. For the subject matter of ethics in the usual sense this is one of the features which in Hegel's eyes distinguishes the ethical attitude of Greek Ethical Life from that of modern Morality. In Ethical Life the individual defers automatically and exclusively to the ethical norms of the community, whereas in Morality, even if deference occurs in practice, it rests on the authority of the individual's conscience and is based on ulterior reasons which he has. However, Hegel believes, I think, that this automatic and exclusive deference to the judgment of the community distinguishes the individuals within Ethical Life when they pass fundamental judgments on *any* subject, ethical or not. Hegel draws attention to the absence within Ethical Life of any claim on the part of the individual to a right to be convinced when he says of the laws within Ethical Life: "If they are supposed to be validated by *my* insight, then I have already denied their unshakable, intrinsic being and regard them as something which, for me, is perhaps true but also perhaps not true. Ethical disposition consists just in sticking steadfastly to what is right, and abstaining from all attempts to move or shake it, or derive it . . . By acknowledging the *absoluteness* of the right, I am within the ethical substance." [11] And in this passage he particularly emphasizes that when the individual within Ethical Life accepts fundamental principles on a topic solely with an eye to the verdict of the community any attempt to find justifications or grounds for them as the foundation of his acceptance is excluded: "These laws of the ethical substance are immediately acknowledged. We cannot ask for their origin and justification, nor can we look for any other warrant." [12]

The third characteristic of the form of cognition which distinguishes Greek Ethical Life is that individuals are in a sense unaware that their cognition of the world proceeds through the medium of thought. Hence this stage of Spirit is sometimes characterized by Hegel as "immediate." As the *Phenomenology* puts the point: "The *relationship* of self-consciousness to [the laws] is . . . simple and clear. They *are*, and nothing more; this is what constitutes the awareness of its relationship to them." [13] Or in the words of the *History of Philosophy:* "An undeveloped consciousness . . . usually knows nothing of what is present in addition to the content." [14] As in the case of the previous two characteristic features of cognitive activity within Greek Ethical Life, we are to assume here that the feature indicated belongs to the cognition of *any* subject matter, not only to the cognition of ethical matters in the usual sense. That individuals within Ethical Life are unaware that their cognition of reality proceeds through the medium of thought does not mean that they fail to recognize that they make assertions and possess beliefs which may on occasion be erroneous. [15] The immediacy which characterizes their conception of their cognitive relation to the world consists rather of two more subtle omissions. First, there is something which individuals within Ethical Life do not recognize about the *fundamental* principles upon which their judgments and those of the community as a whole rest—those principles by means of which the world is ultimately explained, which constitute the standard for evaluating and accounting for less fundamental judgments, and upon which in Greek Ethical Life the community is in complete and automatic agreement. They do not recognize that these fundamental principles belong to a medium of thought which is distinct from the world and through which the believer seeks to represent that world and possibly fails to do so. Thus in the *Phenomenology* Hegel writes of the human and divine laws which are the fundamental principles governing ethics in Greek Ethical Life: "In Self-consciousness they exist explicitly, whereas *in the ethical order they are only implicit.*" [16] And in the *History of Philosophy* he writes: "The natural man has no consciousness of the presence of opposites; he lives quite unconsciously in his own particular way, in conformity with the morality of his town, without ever having reflected on the fact that he practises this morality. If he then comes into a foreign land, he is much surprised, for through encountering the opposite *he for the first time experiences the fact that he has these customs.*" [17] It is a corollary of this point that within Greek Ethical Life a precondition of raising an unrestricted version of the skeptical equipollence difficulty is not yet met, for the most fundamental beliefs people have are not yet recognized by them *as such,* as belonging to the medium of thought in distinction from the world which that medium is supposed to represent, and a fortiori are not yet recognized by them as capable of misrepresenting the world. The second of the two omissions characteristic of individuals within Greek Ethical Life is their failure to recognize that all the concepts, both analyzable and basic, by which their beliefs and assertions are articulated belong to a medium which is quite distinct from the world which those beliefs and assertions strive to depict—a medium which might therefore turn out not to capture any of the features of that world. Thus, while individuals will recognize that a nonfundamental belief like "This is a pink rat" is merely a thought distinct from the reality which it strives to depict and that it might therefore be erroneous, they will not grasp the fact that the basic concept "rat" is quite distinct from the rats in the world, or that the basic concept "pink" is distinct from the pinkness in the world, and so will not grasp the possibility that these concepts might exist without corresponding to any kinds actually in the world. If this intellectual situation is hard to imagine, reflect on the difficulty that Socrates had in making clear to his interlocutors that his "What is X?" questions were questions about the definitions of single forms rather than about the various examples or species of X found in the world.[18] This is at least part of what Hegel has in mind when in the *History of Philosophy* he contrasts the relatively sophisticated individuals who belong to a skeptical culture with the kind of undeveloped consciousness which is found in Ethical Life. He says that the consciousness of the individual in a skeptical culture has "the power . . . to go back from itself, and to take as its object the whole that is present, itself and its operation included," whereas "an undeveloped consciousness, on the other hand, usually knows nothing of what is present in addition to the content."[19] It is a corollary of this point that within Ethical Life a precondition of raising an unrestricted skeptical concept-instantiation difficulty has not yet been met, since concepts have not yet been recognized as quite generally distinct from the features of the world which they are supposed to represent, and a fortiori have not yet been recognized as quite generally capable of failing to correspond to anything in the world.

Hegel's conception of the innocent and harmonious early Greek culture or Ethical Life whose decline he wishes to explain has, then, three essential components by the time of the *Phenomenology* and the *Philosophy of History:* early Greek polytheism, early Greek ethics, and the general form of cognition found in early Greece. When Hegel in these texts offers an account of the destruction of early Greek culture or Ethical Life, he is attempting to explain the demise of all three of these features. I shall argue that the mature version of the account presents the early Greeks' general form of cognition as the necessary foundation of their polytheism and ethics and ascribes the collapse of all three features to the collapse of their general form of cognition.

There are three texts in which Hegel seeks to formulate an explanation of why the harmonious and innocent culture of the early Greeks collapsed. The earliest of these is *The Positivity of the Christian Religion* whose framing of the problem in religious terms we considered earlier; the next is the *Phenomenology;* and the third and last is the *Philosophy of History.* There are considerable differences between the explanations given in each text, not to mention obscurities in the individual explanations. But the direction in which Hegel's thinking on the subject developed was toward regarding the establishment of the intellectual preconditions for raising the skeptical problems of equipollence in general and concept-instantiation in particular, and the actual raising of these problems, as the key to a naturalistic explanation of the collapse of early Greek culture or Ethical Life.

When Hegel in *The Positivity of the Christian Religion* raises the question of how Greek and Roman polytheism, with its deep roots in all aspects of private and communal life, could have lost its grip, the answer he gives makes no mention of skeptical problems at all and is instead socioeconomic in character. Simultaneously explaining the decline of Greek and Roman polytheism, Hegel argues that polytheism was of its essence the religion of a free people, of a people who freely participated in noncoercive social and political institutions. At a certain point in the history of both Athens and Rome wealth became concentrated in the hands of a military aristocracy who used it to acquire power and influence within the community, power and influence which were at first freely granted to them but soon came to rest on coercion. This emergence of coercion as the basis of social and political relations destroyed the freedom of the community's participation in social and political institutions which was essential to its polytheistic religion.[20] This explanation, at least for the Greek case in which we are mainly interested, has the unmistakable ring of falsehood, not only postulating an implausible connection between polytheistic belief and sociopolitical freedom but apparently also reversing the history of aristocratic and democratic institutions and correlating exclusively with democracy a form of religion which in fact had a considerably securer existence under aristocracy (the Greek Enlightenment with its occasional hostility to traditional religion was after all an achievement of democracy). However, this explanation is significant as an early attempt to answer the question why the harmonious, innocent culture of early Greece collapsed, and to do so in naturalistic terms, and it throws a certain amount of light on the more interesting explanation offered in the *Phenomenology,* to which we now turn.

As demonstrated in the previous chapter, the explanation in the *Phenomenology* of why Greek Ethical Life—as a unity of religious, ethical, and general cognitive characteristics—suffered decline appears at several points in the text. The most important of these points are the first three stages of the "Self-consciousness" chapter (dealing with Lordship and Bondage, Stoicism, and Skepticism) and the discussion of the disruption of Ethical Life in the "Spirit" chapter. Reading these various locations together one can see that Hegel's explanation has developed significantly beyond that in *The Positivity of the Christian Religion,* while at the same time retaining a certain amount in common with it. On the one hand, the Lordship and Bondage stage of the *Phenomenology* represents a degree of continuity with the earlier explanation. In both cases Hegel depicts the emergence of a set of relations between two social groups in which one group monopolizes wealth to the exclusion of the other group and wields coercive social or political power over the other group.[21] On the other hand, this common element represents only the first stage of the explanation in the *Phenomenology,* rather than the whole of it as in *The Positivity of the Christian Religion.* The subsequent stages of the explanation in the *Phenomenology* are found in the sections on Stoicism and Skepticism and in the "Spirit" chapter, and they concern the emergence of the intellectual preconditions for and the outbreak of the skeptical difficulties of equipollence and concept-instantiation.

The role of the Lordship and Bondage stage of the *Phenomenology* in the work's explanation of the collapse of Greek Ethical Life is not very satisfactory. Hegel does not explicitly say when or where the events described in this stage took place or who played the roles of lord and bondsman.[22] Partly because of this historical vagueness, the account of the transition from this social phenomenon to the intellectual phenomena Stoicism and Skepticism looks rather thin and unconvincing. The burden of the case is that the social deference which the bondsman must show to his lord and the accompanying intellectual deference which he must show to the objects on which he labors for the lord are (in contrast to the self-assertive "being-for-self" which is characteristic of the lord in his relation both to other men and to things) conducive, respectively, to introspection and the recognition of objectivity. And both of these outcomes are necessary for that awareness of a division between thought and objective reality which Hegel sees as the distinctive contribution of Stoicism. Thus concerning this awareness of a division between objective reality and thought, Hegel writes that "for the subservient consciousness as such, these two moments—itself as an independent object, and this object as a mode of consciousness, and hence its own essential nature—fall apart."[23]

This attempt to explain the intellectual causes of the disruption of a harmonious, unified Greek culture which the *Phenomenology* for the first time introduces in terms of prior social causes of the kind which had been central to the explanation of this disruption in *The Positivity of the Christian Religion* is not repeated in Hegel's subsequent accounts in the "Spirit" and "Religion" chapters of the *Phenomenology* or in the *Philosophy of History.* In these accounts intellectual causes are accorded explanatory priority. The role of Lordship and Bondage in the explanation found in the "Self-consciousness" chapter of the *Phenomenology* thus appears to be a symptom of a transition in Hegel's thought. From now on Hegel was concerned solely with intellectual rather than social causes of the disruption of a harmonious, unified Greek culture, namely with the establishment of the intellectual preconditions for raising the skeptical difficulties of equipollence and concept-instantiation and the emergence of these difficulties themselves.

Two themes in the explanation of the destruction of Greek Ethical Life found in the *Phenomenology* concern the establishment of the intellectual preconditions for the skeptical difficulties and the emergence of these difficulties themselves. Both themes point in the direction of Hegel's more considered explanation in the *History of Philosophy*. The first theme appears in the Stoicism and Skepticism stages of the "Self-consciousness" chapter. Hegel interprets Stoicism as a movement which establishes some of the intellectual preconditions for raising skeptical difficulties. It will be remembered that the form of cognition distinctive of Greek Ethical Life was characterized by the absence of an awareness of our concepts and principles as all belonging to a medium of thought distinct from the world which we use them to depict, and that this made it impossible to raise the skeptical equipollence and concept-instantiation difficulties in their full force and generality. In the *Phenomenology* Hegel holds that the distinctive achievement of Stoicism was to establish a consciousness of just such a general division between thought and the world, thereby making possible the full articulation of these skeptical difficulties. Explaining the Stoic development of a sharp distinction between the conceptually articulated medium of thought and the world that we aim to know through it, Hegel says that for the Stoic the concept is "straight-away *my* concept," so that "in thinking, I *am free*, because I am not in an *other*, but remain simply and solely in communion with myself . . . and my activity in conceptual thinking is a movement within myself," and that for the Stoic, "with the reflection of self-consciousness into the simple thought of itself, the independent existence of permanent determinateness that stood over against that reflection has . . . fallen outside of the infinitude of thought."[24]

Hegel is doubtless thinking here of, among other things, the Stoic theory about sense-presentations (*phantasiai*) and expressibles (*lekta*). For the Stoic the sense-presentations through which all knowledge is obtained are literally corporeal marks on the regent part of the soul caused by the impact of the world. This model brings with it a sharp distinction between the sense-presentations in the soul and the world causing them. Moreover, in the Stoic account the propositional articulation of sense-presentations proceeds through expressibles whose distinctness from the world which they are used to represent is still more striking in virtue of their status as incorporeal, abstract objects. In both these ways the Stoic theory of the relation between thought and reality is constructed in such a manner as to posit the kind of division between the two which suggests that in principle the elements on the "thought" side could be just as they are without in any way resembling or corresponding to anything on the

"reality" side. In this way Stoicism makes possible the unrestricted raising of skeptical equipollence and concept-instantiation difficulties.

Hegel explains the epistemological objections which the ancient skeptics urge against the Stoics and against dogmatists in general as ultimately arising because of this original Stoic invention of a sharp division
of thought from reality.[25] He represents the skeptics' success against the
Stoics and against dogmatists in general as resting essentially on a borrowing and thinking through of this sharp distinction. Hence in the *Phenomenology* the Skepticism section immediately follows the Stoicism section and depicts the skeptics as taking over the sharp Stoic division
between thought and reality but, instead of making the futile attempt to
validate claims about reality on the basis of an examination of thought
alone in the manner of the Stoics, renouncing claims about reality altogether.[26] In the *History of Philosophy* Hegel gives a clear statement of his
view that the Stoics first invented the sharp division between thought and
reality and then succumbed to it when the skeptics took it over as the
basis of their skepticism:

> Because to Stoic philosophy truth consists in the fact that thought de-
> clares some content of existence to be its own, and the conception as appre-
> hended gives its approbation to this content, the content of our conceptions,
> principles and thoughts undoubtedly appears to be different from thought,
> and the union of the two . . . only arises by means of some determinate
> content being taken up into the form of thought and thus being expressed
> as truth. But Arcesilaus saw this consequence, and his saying that appro-
> bation must be withheld is thus as much as saying that by thus taking up
> the content no truth comes to pass, but only phenomenon; and this is true,
> because, as Arcesilaus puts it, conception and thought likewise remain apart
> . . . Arcesilaus . . . makes the same celebrated distinction as in recent times
> has again been brought forward with so much force as the opposition be-
> tween thought and being, ideality and reality, subjective and objective.
> Things are something different from me. How can I attain to things? . . . It
> was of [the] unity of thought and reality that the Stoics ought to have given
> an account; and they did not do so . . . The logic of the Stoics hence re-
> mained formal merely, and the attainment of a content could not be dem-
> onstrated.[27]

Such is the skepticism-related theme offered in explanation of the collapse of Greek Ethical Life in the "Self-consciousness" chapter. The
second skepticism-related theme playing this explanatory role in the
Phenomenology appears in the "Spirit" and "Religion" chapters. The
"Spirit" chapter makes a general reference back to the movement of Self-
conciousness just considered but adds to and changes the characterization of this movement.[28] The addition concerns the emergence of two
related preconditions for raising the skeptical equipollence difficulty with

respect to fundamental principles, the subsequent emergence of that difficulty itself, and the discrediting of the principles for which it emerges. The change consists in the fact that now the context of the movement of Self-consciousness is no longer the philosophical schools of Rome but instead the living ethical practice of early Greek Ethical Life, governed competitively but harmoniously by two fundamental ethical principles, the human and divine laws.

It will be remembered that within Greek Ethical Life the individual had no awareness of the fundamental principles supporting his system of beliefs *as such*. A fortiori he had no awareness of conflicts between fundamental principles. Both of these factors, however, are preconditions for the emergence of an equipollence difficulty for the individual with respect to fundamental principles. In the "Spirit" chapter Hegel describes the simultaneous establishment of both these preconditions in connection with the fundamental human and divine laws: "These powers acquire the significance of excluding and opposing one another: in Self-consciousness they exist explicitly, whereas in the ethical order they are only implicit."[29] And he explains that the equal authority of these two conflicting laws for the ethical community then becomes apparent—in essence the equipollence problem of opposed principles having equal strength—and that this ensures their mutual elimination: "The movement of the ethical powers against each other and of the individualities calling them into life and action have attained their true end only in so far as both sides suffer the same destruction. For neither power has any advantage over the other that would make it a more essential moment of the substance."[30] The same account is repeated in the "Religion" chapter when Hegel discusses Greek religion.[31]

From these two themes of the *Phenomenology* it is clear that Hegel in this work assigns a central role to the establishment of the intellectual preconditions for raising the skeptical problems of equipollence and concept-instantiation and to the emergence of these problems themselves in his explanation of why Greek Ethical Life as a union of distinctive religious, ethical, and general cognitive characteristics suffered collapse. However, Hegel's explanation of that collapse receives its final form in the *Philosophy of History*, where it undergoes two important changes. First, the attempt to find a primary social cause which dominated *The Positivity of the Christian Religion* and found continued expression in Lordship and Bondage stage of the *Phenomenology* falls away entirely. The explanation in the *Philosophy of History* concerns more or less exclusively the rise of a certain intellectual movement which Hegel understands to represent equipollence and concept-instantiation difficulties and the intellectual preconditions for raising them. Second, whereas the *Phenomenology* saw the Roman schools of Stoicism and skepticism and the concrete ethical experience of the Greeks as the historically effective bearers of these skeptical difficulties and their preconditions, the *Philosophy of History* assigns the decisive role in the destruction of Greek Ethical Life to an early philosophical bearer of these same difficulties and preconditions: Sophism.

Thus, when Hegel in the *Philosophy of History* addresses the task of "understanding the *spoiling* of the Greek world in its deeper meaning," he refers in explanation to the Sophists (and Socrates, whom he associates with them), and particularly to their introduction of the two skeptical difficulties and their preconditions.[32] He writes regarding equipollence difficulties: "Thinking . . . appears here as the principle of corruption, and indeed of the corruption of substantial Ethical Life; for it sets up an opposition."[33] And regarding concept-instantiation difficulties and their intellectual precondition of a sharp division between conceptual thought and reality, he writes: "Through the ascendant inner world of subjectivity the breach with reality occurred . . . Now the question was raised, whether gods are and what they are."[34]

There was an obvious difficulty with the view presented in the *Phenomenology* that the philosophical schools of Stoicism and skepticism which as bearers of the two skeptical problems and their intellectual preconditions were decisive for the decline of Greek Ethical Life were the schools of Rome. The difficulty was that these schools had flourished as bearers of the skeptical problems and their preconditions in Greece well before they took root in Rome. The *Philosophy of History* avoids this difficulty, not by the obvious means of transferring the burden of the explanation to the corresponding Greek schools, but by shifting it to the even earlier philosophical movement of Sophism.

That Hegel is right to see the Sophists of the fifth century B.C. as early representatives of the two skeptical difficulties and their intellectual preconditions is evident from the views of the two leading Sophists, Protagoras and Gorgias (though of course their *reactions* to the skeptical difficulties were by and large different from the skeptical reaction of suspending judgment, a lonely exception being the stance taken by Protagoras to the question of the existence and nature of the gods). In the *Philosophy of History* Hegel alludes to the role of equipollence difficulties in Sophism by saying that this movement "sets up an opposition." He makes the point more explicitly in the *History of Philosophy* where he says of the Sophists' method of argumentation: "With such reasoning men can easily get so far as to know . . . that if arguments are relied upon, everything can be proved by argument, and arguments for and against can be found for everything."[35] That this was indeed the view of Protagoras can be surmised from his dictum, "On every topic there are two arguments contrary to each other," from the fact that in accordance with this dictum he wrote two books of "antilogic" or opposing arguments (which have not survived), and perhaps from his claim that he could make the weaker argument appear the stronger and his practice of teaching pupils to praise and blame the same things.[36] Protagoras formulated his relativist theory of truth partly in response to his conviction that equally convincing arguments could be provided for and against any conclusion and that this presented a difficulty for ordinary views about truth.[37] There is also a good deal of evidence to back up the claim that the Sophists were concerned with concept-instantiation difficulties and with the intellectual preconditions for raising such difficulties. In the *Philosophy of History* Hegel depicts the Sophists as responsible for the ascendance of the inner world of the subject and the breach between this inner world and reality, which he regards as the source of such questions as whether gods are and what they are. This question is a particularly radical example of a concept-instantiation difficulty because it concerns a basic, unanalyzable concept. And it is precisely the question which Protagoras first posed—answering it with agnosticism.[38] As for the intellectual precondition which Hegel mentions for raising such concept-instantiation difficulties, namely the recognition of the inner world of the subject's conceptual thought and its division from reality, in the *History of Philosophy* he rightly identifies the second and third parts of Gorgias's treatise *Concerning Nature or Concerning the Nonexistent* as articulating a conception of such a general division (indeed not only a general division between thought and reality but also a general division between language and reality).[39] In that treatise Gorgias argues for a sharp general distinction between thought or language, on the one hand, and the realm of existence (if there were one), on the other, in the course of supporting the last two of three alarming theses which he sets forth, namely the two skeptical theses that "even if anything exists it is inapprehensible to man" and "even if anything is apprehensible, yet of a surety it is inexpressible and incommunicable to one's neighbor."[40] Thus Gorgias is recognized in the *History of Philosophy* to have had a role in preparing the ground for skeptical difficulties analogous to that attributed to Stoicism in the *Phenomenology*.

Hegel's explanations in various texts of the collapse of Greek Ethical Life understood as early Greek polytheism, early Greek ethics in the usual sense, and a specific form of cognition in general possessed by the early Greeks make clear, then, the increasing importance he assigned as time went on to the establishment of the intellectual preconditions for raising the skeptical difficulties of equipollence and concept-instantiation and to the emergence of these difficulties themselves. Hegel's mature view is that these intellectual causes undermined Greek Ethical Life by in the first instance undermining its specific form of cognition in general. Since this form of cognition in general was the essential foundation of the polytheism and ethics of Greek Ethical Life, its destruction necessitated theirs.

In the course of our examination of the form of cognition in general characteristic of Greek Ethical Life and the explanations of the collapse of Ethical Life given in the *Phenomenology* and the *Philosophy of History* we have encountered several intellectual preconditions of raising the skeptical difficulties of equipollence and concept-instantiation in their full force and generality. There were two preconditions of raising equipollence difficulties in their full force and generality. First, there was the precondition that people be aware of the fundamental principles in their belief-system *as such,* as belonging to the medium of thought which attempts to depict the world in distinction from the world itself, and as therefore capable of misrepresenting the world. Second, there was the precondition that people come to recognize the existence of fundamental principles which stand in conflict with one another. An important point about these two preconditions is that Hegel thinks they are not sharply separable from one another. It is perhaps clear that the second requires the first, but Hegel also holds that the first requires the second, as we can see from a passage in the *History of Philosophy:* "The natural man has no consciousness of the presence of opposites; he lives quite unconsciously in his own particular way, in conformity with the morality of his town, without ever having reflected on the fact that he practises this morality. If he then comes into a foreign land, he is much surprised, for through encountering the opposite he for the first time experiences the fact that he has these customs." [41] The two preconditions are thus thought of as interdependent, and this is why Hegel appears to equate them in the *Phenomenology* when he says that the human and divine laws "acquire the significance of excluding and opposing one another: in self-consciousness they exist explicitly, whereas in the ethical order they are only implicit." [42] If appropriately qualified, this claim of interdependence has considerable plausibility.

The establishment of these preconditions with respect to fundamental principles is arguably not only a necessary condition of raising the equipollence difficulty in its full generality (that is, for fundamental as well as nonfundamental principles) but also a necessary condition of effectively raising it *at all.* Since it is not obvious why equipollence difficulties could not be raised about nonfundamental principles alone, for example about the myriad conflicting perceptual judgments emphasized in the ten tropes of Aenesidemus and other skeptical sources, it is important to consider why this might be so.

Sextus Empiricus certainly thought it was important that the skeptics should focus their equipollence attack on the fundamental principles of the dogmatists. At the beginning of *Against the Physicists* he makes the following declaration of strategy: "We shall attack the most important and comprehensive dogmas, as in the doubts cast on these we shall find the rest also included. For just as, in a siege, those who have undermined the foundation of a wall find that the towers tumble down along with it, so too in philosophical investigations those who have routed the primary assumptions on which the theories are based have potentially abolished the apprehension of every particular theory."[43] And he contrasts this Pyrrhonist approach of focusing skeptical attack on the fundamental principles of the dogmatists with what he regards as the inferior Academic approach of spending much time merely attacking their nonfundamental principles. His avowed reason for preferring the Pyrrhonist approach is simply that it is more economical. But perhaps there is also a hint of the view that arguing to equipollence merely on nonfundamental issues as the Academics often do is not only unnecessary but also ineffective. If so, then his insistence on the importance of focusing attack on fundamental principles perhaps shows some sensitivity to the following important point. If one does not establish equipollence for fundamental principles, one will not do so effectively for nonfundamental principles either, since an important part of the nature of fundamental principles is that they constitute grounds for deciding conflicts between less fundamental ones, or reasons for preferring one of two conflicting nonfundamental principles over the other. In other words, where a fundamental principle remains unchallenged, there will be a range of nonfundamental principles falling within the scope of its jurisdiction for which equipollence difficulties cannot be successfully raised, because the existence of this authoritative criterion prevents conflicts between those nonfundamental principles from becoming conflicts in which both sides appear to have equal justification. Consider, for example, the conflicts between perceptual judgments frequently encountered in the skeptical literature, such as the conflict between the yellow perceptions of the man with jaundice and the multicolored perceptions of the healthy percipient, or between the apparent roundness of a tower when viewed from a distance and its apparent squareness when viewed from close up.[44] Such conflicts are in themselves quite inadequate as grounds for suspending belief about the perceptible properties which are at issue, for as long as we have been shown nothing to the contrary we can confidently point out that we have more fundamental principles which enable us to decide such cases of disagreement, providing us with a stronger justification for preferring one of the conflicting judgments than we have for preferring the other. For example, we have a more fundamental principle to the effect that jaundice causes objects which are not in fact yellow to appear so. As a result, in the case where the man with jaundice perceives as yellow those objects which the rest of us perceive as multicolored, we who know this principle and know that the man has jaundice have a stronger justification for relying on our perceptions than we have for relying on his. And if the man himself shares this principle with us and the knowledge that he has jaundice, then he, too, has a stronger justification for the judgment that the objects are multicolored (although they appear to him yellow) than he has for the judgment that they are yellow. Similar remarks apply to the conflict between the appearance from a distance that a tower is round and the appearance from close up that it is square, for we have all sorts of more fundamental principles concerning the kinds of illusions which are produced by viewing objects at a distance and the explanation of why they take place and of how to correct them. A similar relation between fundamental and nonfundamental principles can be found for any subject matter with which the skeptic might deal. This explains why the generation of equipollence difficulties with respect to fundamental principles or the demonstration that one has no better justification for accepting any given fundamental principle than for denying it, is a necessary condition not only of the success of the equipollence method against these principles themselves and hence of its *unrestricted* success, but also of the success of the method against nonfundamental principles and hence of the success of the method *at all*.

The encountered precondition for raising concept-instantiation difficulties in their full force and generality was that one have recognized that the conceptually articulated medium of thought is in its entirety distinct from the world which we attempt to know through it, in such a way that the medium might exist as it is regardless of how, or even whether, the world is. In the *Phenomenology* Hegel attributes the establishment of this precondition to Roman Stoicism, whereas in the *Philosophy of History* he attributes it to the Sophists of the fifth century B.C. We have seen that his attribution to the Sophists of a conception of the medium of conceptual thought in general as distinct from reality has considerable plausibility. A further indication that he has here succeeded in dating a quiet but fundamental revolution in thought lies in Kahn's painstakingly researched thesis that the full existential use of the verb "be"—the use which we associate with such questions as "Does Zeus exist?" "Do gods exist?" and "Does color really exist?"—first emerges in the Greek language in the fifth century B.C.[45] For it seems likely that the full existential use of "be" and the conception of the medium of conceptual thought as in general distinct from and capable of misrepresenting reality are essentially interdependent.[46]

Hegel uses the establishment of these three intellectual preconditions for raising skeptical difficulties to explain the collapse of the most fundamental aspect of Greek Ethical Life, its special form of cognition in general defined by the three characteristics described earlier. Once these preconditions are present, one of the three defining characteristics has disappeared straightaway, namely the absence of any conception of fundamental principles as part of the medium of thought and therefore capable of misrepresenting reality, and the absence of any conception of a general division and possible failure of correspondence between the concepts which articulate thought and the features of the world which might instantiate them. How the establishment of the preconditions for raising skeptical difficulties also leads to the disappearance of the other defining characteristics of the form of cognition in general belonging to Greek Ethical Life, and hence to the complete removal of that form of cognition, is explained by Hegel's account in the *Philosophy of History* of what happens when the establishment of the preconditions for the skeptical difficulties ushers in the skeptical difficulties themselves in their full force.

Hegel argues that upon the full emergence for some subject matter, say ethics or religion, of the general equipollence difficulty of incompatible but apparently equally justified claims or the more specific concept-instantiation version of this difficulty concerned with the possibility that our concepts might not answer to features in the world at all, the immediate reaction to the problem in the culture where this happens is as follows. There arises a search for *reasons* by means of which the questions raised by these difficulties even concerning fundamentals might be settled, an attempt to establish an imbalance in the arguments for and against specific answers to these questions which will make rational a firm commitment to one answer rather than another. Hegel contrasts this situation with the one which obtains in Greek Ethical Life, saying that "the absolute is no longer regarded as valid in its own right, but only insofar as it has reasons to justify it." [47] This marks a further collapse of the form of cognition belonging to Greek Ethical Life. Only two of its three defining characteristics remained: first, the automatic agreement in judgment on all fundamental matters among all members of the community, and second, the deference shown by the individual to the verdict of the community on all fundamental matters, which was automatic and also exclusive in the sense that the individual made no claim to a personal right to be convinced and made no attempt to give reasons or grounds where such matters were concerned. But the search for reasons or grounds to secure even fundamental principles which arises in the wake of the skeptical difficulties destroys these remaining characteristics. It destroys the automatic and exclusive deference of the individual to the community on fundamentals because the availability of reasons or grounds replaces the community's verdict as the foundation of the fundamental judgments which members of the community are prepared to make, and this loss of authority by the community shifts the locus of decision on even fundamental issues to the judgment and conscience of the individual. When this happens, the collapse of the automatic agreement of judgments on fundamental matters in the community is also inevitable, for its underpinning was the automatic and exclusive deference of individuals to the community's verdict on these matters and when this underpinning disappears no stable patterns of reasons or grounds on which the whole community agrees can be found to replace it: "When no such reasons—i.e., no completely abstract universal principles—can be found as the basis of the laws . . . men's ideas of virtue begin to waver."[48] In this way the form of cognition in general characteristic of Greek Ethical Life disappears.

Hegel understands the establishment of the preconditions for raising the skeptical difficulties and the emergence of these difficulties themselves to destroy Greek Ethical Life with respect not only to its form of cognition in general but also to its polytheism and ethics. To begin with ethics, part of what distinguished this aspect of Greek Ethical Life was its unusual *form*, the circumstance that ethical judgment and activity had a harmonious communal character in which ethical norms were enforced by the community and the community's ethical verdict was automatically accepted in principle and in fact as more authoritative than the individual's. This is fundamentally a special case of the last two defining characteristics of Ethical Life's form of cognition in general discussed above: the automatic agreement of the community on fundamental matters, on the one hand, and the automatic and exclusive deference of the individual to the community's verdict on such matters, on the other hand. The explanation already considered of how these two defining characteristics disappeared due to the emergence of skeptical difficulties therefore also applies to the special case of the disappearance of the distinctive form of ethics belonging to Greek Ethical Life. Indeed Hegel's discussion of the general process in the *Philosophy of History* is written primarily with the special case of ethics in mind. In addition, the *content* of Greek ethics, made up of the human and divine laws which Hegel discusses in the *Phenomenology*, is of such a character that it allows no satisfactory defense against the challenge of the skeptical difficulties and so succumbs to them. When the step is taken in response to the recognition of an equal weight of justification for and against received ethical principles which the skeptical difficulties embody of ceasing to accept these received principles unquestioningly from the community and instead seeking ulterior reasons for them to restore the balance of justification in their favor, this search ultimately fails and so skepticism overcomes the received ethics. Thus in the *Philosophy of History* Hegel writes that, having become aware of the problem of the conflicts and equal weights of justification afflicting those ethical principles which it has inherited from tradition in the form of "belief, trust, and custom," consciousness "now has reasons for renouncing the latter and the laws which they impose. This is indeed the inevitable result of any search for reasons; and when no such reasons . . . can be found as the basis of the laws in question, men's ideas of virtue begin to waver."[49] Fundamentally the same point is made in the *Phenomenology* when Hegel explains that the absence of any greater strength of justification for either of the two conflicting fundamental ethical principles found within Greek Ethical Life, the human and the divine laws, was the reason for their simultaneous destruction.[50]

This situation of complete vulnerability to skeptical difficulties in which the content of pagan Greek ethics finds itself contrasts, in Hegel's view, with the more secure situation of the ethical content of the revealed religions. Hegel believes that whereas pagan Greek ethics was largely self-sustaining rather than wholly dependent on religion, the ethics of cultures committed to the revealed religions is wholly founded on the understanding that it has been commanded by God.[51] It is, to use Hegel's term, "positive" in the sense that it belongs to a "system of religious propositions, which is supposed to have truth for us because it is commanded to us by an authority to whom we cannot refuse to subjugate our belief."[52] Since, as we shall see, Hegel envisages the belief in God that distinguishes the revealed religions as in a certain way constructed to withstand skeptical difficulties, he regards the ethical views which in the revealed religions stand or fall with that belief in God as similarly forearmed against skeptical assaults, thus giving them an advantage over the ethical views of the pagan Greeks when they confront skeptical difficulties.

Turning from Greek ethics to Greek polytheism, Hegel sees a similar situation. He emphasizes in *The Positivity of the Christian Religion* that the rootedness of Greek polytheism in all aspects of communal life was one of the major sources of its strength.[53] Thus the general decline in the authority of the community which arose from the emergence of the skeptical difficulties and the consequent search for reasons and shifting of authority in cognitive matters to the individual's judgment of itself represented a blow at the foundations of this type of religion. But as with Greek ethics, Greek polytheism suffered from the further weakness that its content was as a matter of fact unable to withstand the challenge of the skeptical difficulties because it could afford no reasons in its favor which would upset the balance of opposed justifications which the skeptic pointed out, and hence no replacement for the lost authority of community tradition as its foundation. Hegel indicates this vulnerability of Greek polytheism in the *Phenomenology* when he refers to "the contingent character . . . which imagination lent to the divine beings" in Greek religion.[54] And he expresses it as follows in the *Philosophy of History*: "Zeus, who set limitations to the depredations of time [i.e., Chronos] and suspended its constant flux, had no sooner established something inherently enduring than he was himself devoured along with his whole empire. He was devoured by the principle of thought itself, the progenitor of knowledge, of reasoning, of insight based on rational grounds, and of the search for such grounds."[55] Again, Hegel holds that the religious belief of the revealed religions is in contrast to that of Greek polytheism somehow forearmed against the challenge of the skeptical difficulties and the ensuing demand for reasons, so that this challenge will not wreak the same havoc among believers in revealed religion as it did among the adherents of Greek polytheism.

This, then, is Hegel's account of the role played by the intellectual preconditions for the two skeptical difficulties and by these difficulties themselves in bringing about the destruction of Greek Ethical Life in its various aspects. However, the explanation of this destruction can be pursued one stage further back while still remaining within the bounds of both Hegel's comments on the subject and plausibility. When Hegel in the *Phenomenology* addressed the question of why the intellectual preconditions for the skeptical difficulties and these difficulties themselves emerged, his answers concerned events in the life of a *single* community. Thus in the "Self-consciousness" chapter the Lordship and Bondage stage, which was supposed to provide a social etiology of the intellectual developments depicted in the Stoicism and Skepticism stages, referred to lords and bondsmen who, to the extent that they belonged to a community at all, belonged to the same community. And the conflict depicted in the "Spirit" chapter as arising in ethical practice between the human and divine laws and leading to the conscious opposition of these laws and thence to their constitution of an equipollence difficulty also occurred within the confines of a single community. A more interesting and plausible explanation at which Hegel hints in other texts, however, sees the emergence of the preconditions for the skeptical difficulties and of these difficulties themselves as the result of events which essentially involve *more than* one community.

Perhaps the clearest statement of this explanation occurs in *The Relation of Skepticism to Philosophy*:

> [Skepticism] anticipates in the individual what the necessity which is drawn out in the finitude of time performs unconsciously on the unconscious species. What the species considers to be absolutely one and the same, permanent, eternal and everywhere similar, is torn from it by time, most generally by that acquaintance with alien peoples which extends itself by natural necessity—as for example the acquaintance of the Europeans with a new part of the world has had that skeptical effect for the dogmatism of their ordinary human understanding up to now and for the unimpeachable certainty of a mass of concepts about right and truth.[56]

The suggestion that it is above all an acquaintance with the ways of thinking (and behaving) of alien peoples which gives rise to skeptical culture—to a culture in which the intellectual preconditions for skepticism are established and skeptical difficulties emerge—is a plausible and important one.

Considering this thesis in crudely statistical terms to begin with, it does seem that skeptical ideas tend to gain ground in a society in proportion as it has a lively reflective acquaintance with the thoughts and ways of alien communities, and one can often establish this correlation at the level of individual thinkers too. Hegel refers in the preceding passage to a connection between the prevalence of skeptical ideas in the modern period and the discovery of the peoples of the New World. A good example of this connection at the level of the individual is Montaigne, a man who can take much of the credit for the salience of skepticism in modern thought.[57] Montaigne's essay *Of Cannibals* provides an excellent illustration of the sustenance which his skepticism found in reports of the unfamiliar thoughts and ways of recently discovered peoples in the New World.

An equally strong correlation between reflective acquaintance with the thoughts and ways of alien peoples and the popularity of skeptical ideas exists in the case of the ancient Greeks. The rise of skeptical ideas in the fifth century B.C. coincides with the appearance of Herodotus's anthropological *Histories*. At the level of individual thinkers, no reader of Sextus Empiricus can fail to have been struck by the enthusiasm with which he adduces descriptions (often drawn from Herodotus) of the views and practices of alien communities in support of skeptical conclusions, particularly on ethical subjects. Pyrrho, the figurehead of the Pyrrhonist movement, had firsthand acquaintance with the thought of foreign peoples, having "foregathered with the Indian Gymnosophists and with the Magi," if Diogenes Laertius is to be believed.[58] The Sophists, important early representatives of skeptical ideas, were notorious for their constant travel between different Greek city-states, and Protagoras in particular is alleged to have had a Persian education in his youth.[59] And important early representatives of skeptical themes outside the Sophistic movement, such as Democritus and Xenophanes, provide further examples of a correlation between these themes and a direct acquaintance with or reflection upon the thoughts and ways of alien peoples.[60]

So much for a significant statistical correlation between skeptical ideas and a lively reflective acquaintance with the thought and practice of alien communities. But Hegel's account of the various intellectual preconditions for a full-blooded skepticism and of the nature of Greek Ethical Life in which those preconditions are not yet established suggests more precisely *why* an acquaintance with the thought of alien communities was, at least initially, an indispensable stimulus to the formation of skeptical ideas. Thus the two interdependent preconditions for raising equipollence difficulties in their full force and generality—the explicit awareness of fundamental principles *as such* and the awareness of conflicts between fundamental principles—are described by Hegel himself in one passage as first coming about through an acquaintance with the views of alien peoples. This is because the communities where these preconditions are not yet established exemplify the general form of cognition characteristic of Greek Ethical Life, in which the community is in complete and automatic agreement on fundamental principles, so that it is only by going beyond the confines of their own communities and considering the views of alien communities that individuals can come to recognize the actuality or even the possibility of conflicts between fundamental principles. Hegel writes: "The natural man has no consciousness of the presence of opposites; he lives quite unconsciously in his own particular way, in conformity with the morality of his town, without ever having reflected on the fact that he practises this morality. If he then comes into a foreign land, he for the first time experiences the fact that he has these customs, and he immediately arrives at uncertainty as to whether his point of view or the opposite is wrong."[61] It was suggested earlier that an awareness of conflicts between fundamental principles and thence of equipollence difficulties for such principles is a necessary condition of equipollence difficulties having any force *at all*—that is, even for nonfundamental principles. It is plausible to assume therefore that the Greeks would not have developed their strong interest in equipollence difficulties if they had not become aware of conflicts between fundamental principles and of equipollence difficulties afflicting such principles in the way described, namely through the discovery of conflicts between the fundamental principles of different communities. This was the necessary background against which the myriad equipollence difficulties for nonfundamental principles could emerge and carry conviction. As Hegel's choice of examples to illustrate his case plausibly suggests, the establishment of this background will initially have taken the form of a discovery that the fundamental principles of one's own community conflicted with those of some other community in the fields of ethics and religion.[62]

FIVE

The Alienated Realms of
Culture and Faith

I N THE preceding chapter we investigated Hegel's account of the collapse of Greek Ethical Life, the unified and harmonious culture of
early Greece, and the role played by the emergence of a skeptical
culture in his naturalistic explanation of that collapse. This represents
Hegel's rewriting of the negative side of the Hoelderlin-Schelling theory
of a historical Ur-teilung. In the present chapter we turn to Hegel's account of the positive side of his version of a historical Ur-teilung: the
division of human experience between a harshly objective everyday
world of natural and social phenomena, on the one hand, and a divine
realm characterized by remoteness from the everyday sphere of natural
and social phenomena and habitation by an inscrutable, despotic God,
on the other. In Hegel's explanation of this positive development skeptical culture again plays a vital role.

Hegel discusses this positive outcome of Ur-teilung in both the *Phenomenology* and a number of earlier works. In the "Spirit" chapter of
the *Phenomenology* he reports that after the disruption of Ethical Life,
"Spirit, which henceforth is divided within itself, traces one of its worlds,
the *realm of Culture,* in the harsh reality of its objective element; over
against this realm, it traces in the element of thought the *world of Faith,*
the *realm of essential being.*"[1] Speaking of the corresponding stage of the
"Self-consciousness" chapter, Unhappy Consciousness, he refers to this
same opposition of two realms of reality: "One of them, viz. the simple
unchangeable, [the Unhappy Consciousness] takes to be the *essential*
being; but the other, the protean changeable, it takes to be the unessential. The two are, for the Unhappy Consciousness, alien to one another."[2]
And again he emphasizes the alien and objective character of the natural
side of this opposition, saying that the Unhappy Consciousness has an
"initially external relation" to "the incarnate unchangeable" (by which

he means Christ but also, in typical Hegelian fashion, Nature), which is thus experienced as "an alien reality."[3]

Hegel associates this positive outcome of Ur-teilung—the alienation of consciousness from, and opposition to one another of, a natural and social realm, on the one hand, and a divine realm, on the other—above all with Judaic and Christian culture. In the *Phenomenology* he identifies it mainly if not exclusively with Christianity. However, earlier texts see it in both Christianity and Judaism. Thus *The Positivity of the Christian Religion* describes the alienation from God which resulted when Rome adopted Christianity in place of polytheism: "The spirit of the age was revealed in its objective conception of God when he was no longer regarded as like ourselves, though infinitely greater, but was put into another world in whose confines we had no part."[4] *The Spirit of Christianity*, on the other hand, identifies the double alienation of man from God and Nature as characteristic of Judaism: "The fate of the Jewish people is the fate of Macbeth who stepped out of nature itself, clung to alien beings, and so in their service had to trample and slay everything holy in human nature."[5]

The works mentioned contain at least two lines of naturalistic explanation for the emergence of a consciousness alienated from a harshly objective natural and social world, on the one hand, and a remote, inscrutable, despotic deity, on the other. One line of explanation is connected with the theme of a skeptical culture. The other line, which is of equal importance to Hegel, but of less immediate importance to us, accounts for this positive outcome of the historical Ur-teilung by reference to the emergence of conditions of social and political subjugation.[6]

Concerning Hegel's explanation by reference to skeptical culture, one can see that he understands there to be an intimate relation between the divided consciousness of Christianity and the skeptical ideas which precede it historically from the immediate transition which he makes between Skepticism and the Unhappy Consciousness in the *Phenomenology*. We noted earlier that Hegel, in accordance with the general method used in the *Phenomenology* to dispose of each shape of consciousness, argues that Skepticism was implicitly self-contradictory, and we noted that one of the ways in which he understands this to be so consists in the idea that the deeper significance of the skeptic's dissolution of dogmatic truth was that "self-consciousness itself is reality" or "knew itself in its thought to be the Absolute," a significance which contradicted the confusion and lack of conformity to his will characteristic of the appearances with which the skeptical subject was confronted.[7] Now Hegel interprets the emergence of the alienated and divided Unhappy Consciousness of Christianity as an inevitable outcome or realization of this self-contradictory condition of Skepticism: the Unhappy Consciousness merely makes explicit, or "brings together" the two sides of, this self-contradiction implicit in Skepticism. It does so by projecting each side of the self-contradiction as a separate sphere of reality—the absolute self-conscious subject as a remote, infinite, omnipotent God, and the confused, uncontrolled appearances as a sphere of harsh, contingent everyday reality. This is the burden of the passage in which the transition from Skepticism to the Unhappy Consciousness is made:

> In Skepticism, consciousness truly experiences itself as internally contradictory. From this experience emerges a *new form* of consciousness [i.e. the Unhappy Consciousness] which brings together the two thoughts which Skepticism holds apart. Skepticism's lack of thought about itself must vanish, because it is in fact *one* consciousness which contains within itself these two modes. This new form is, therefore, one which *knows* that it is the dual consciousness of itself, as self-liberating, unchangeable, and self-identical, and as self-bewildering and self-perverting, and it is the awareness of this self-contradictory nature of itself.[8]

This account of how Skepticism gives rise to the alienated and divided Unhappy Consciousness of Christianity establishes the point that Hegel envisages an intimate etiological connection between the two phenomena. However, he gives more plausible hints elsewhere as to what exactly that connection might consist in and we shall focus on these hints in what follows. Our task, then, will be to clarify Hegel's account of the emergence of a consciousness, exemplified primarily in Christianity, for which reality is divided into an alienated natural and social "realm of Culture, in the harsh reality of [Spirit's] objective element," on the one hand, and an alienated divine "world of Faith, [a] realm of essential being," on the other.[9] And above all it will be to pursue Hegel's hints about how the development of a skeptical culture contributed to the emergence of such a consciousness. To this end we should now consider Culture and Faith in turn.

An explanation of how Hegel understands Culture to be distinguished by articulation in "the harsh reality of [Spirit's] objective element," or of how he understands Culture's conception of everyday reality to be characterized by harshness and objectivity, will make readily perceptible his account of why such a conception of everyday reality emerged and particularly the role of a skeptical culture in this account. Hegel's attempt to describe and explain the emergence of the harsh, objective conception of everyday reality distinctive of Culture is to be understood as an attempt to describe and explain the genesis of a conception of everyday reality which does not merely belong to some bygone age but has also endured and is constitutive of the modern (or at least, pre-Hegelian modern) mind.[10] That the various components of the conception of everyday reality characteristic of Culture and their etiology thus constitute something like an analysis and etiology of the modern world's conception of everyday reality in its distinctiveness and distinctness from that of other ages is part of what makes Hegel's account interesting.

Hegel's idea about the harshness and objectivity of this conception of everyday reality has at least four distinct components. The nature and the cause of the first three of these components are readily intelligible in the light of Hegel's already examined views about the collapse of Greek Ethical Life. The first component is the thought that the natural and social world which is left after the collapse of Greek polytheism is a world bereft of divine inhabitants. Once the gods were regular visitors to the natural and social world of men, intervened and participated in their activities, appeared to them, and were revealed in communal rites, but now the single God of Christianity has retired into remote aloofness from this human sphere.[11] As we saw, Hegel assigns a central role in the explanation of this disappearance of the gods of polytheism to the emergence of a skeptical culture.

The second component is the thought that when Greek Ethical Life disappears, the natural and social world loses an ethical meaningfulness with which the ethical aspect of Ethical Life had imbued it. Thus in the *Phenomenology* Hegel describes how in the transition from Greek Ethical Life to the conditions of Roman culture the ethical meaningfulness of the social community is lost, and value comes to reside only in the individual and his goals. The community becomes no more than "the soulless community which has ceased to be the substance . . . of individuals, and in which they now have the value of selves and substances, possessing a separate being-for-self."[12] Again, consider the ethical meaningfulness which Hegel supposes the natural process of human death to have had within Greek Ethical Life. In *The Positivity of the Christian Religion* he describes how the ethical outlook belonging to this Greek culture was one in which a man's country or state "was the invisible and higher reality for which he strove . . . it was the final end of *his* world or in his eyes the final end of *the* world."[13] In these circumstances the fact that the natural event of a man's death occurred in the service of his state and was recognized by his state to have done so transfigured it into something having absolute ethical meaningfulness. Thus Hegel says: "Confronted by this idea, his own individuality vanished . . . It could never or hardly ever have struck him to ask or beg for persistence or eternal life for his own individuality."[14] According to the *Phenomenology* it was the dead man's family that sustained the communal honor required for the ethical transfiguration of his natural death and therefore for the overcoming of its merely natural character.[15] Once this ethical outlook belonging to Greek culture disappears due to the destruction of the ethical meaning of the state and the emergence of the values of individualism, however, the ethical meaningfulness of the natural process of death falls away, and death becomes merely a terrifying natural destruction of a man's body and consciousness: "Death, the phenomenon which demolished the whole structure of his purposes and the activity of his entire life, must have become something terrifying ... since nothing survived him."[16] Since the emergence of a skeptical culture plays a central part in Hegel's account of the disappearance of the ethical aspect of Greek Ethical Life, it is central to his explanation of the disappearance of the ethical trans-figuration of natural and social phenomena which is part of the ethical aspect of Ethical Life.

The third component of Hegel's idea about the harshness and objectiv-ity of the conception of everyday reality within culture is the thought that, once Greek Ethical Life disappears, so too do certain aspects of its peculiar form of cognition in general which give it a less harsh and ob-jective, because more spiritualized, conception of reality. These aspects are, first, the absence of any sharp distinction between reality and the received views of the community and, second, the absence of any sharp distinction between reality and the medium of thought in general. Hegel touches on this question in *The Spirit of Christianity* in the course of a discussion of miracles.[17] He argues that the incongruity which modern religious sentiment may find between the infinite nature of Spirit and its alleged resort to miraculous activity within the finite arena of brute his-torical reality results in part from a difference in outlook between us moderns and the original believers in such miracles—namely the differ-ence that we conceive Spirit and brute reality to be opposed to one an-other in a way that they did not. Thus he writes: "Seen with the soul of the Apostles, the miracles lose the harshness which the opposition in them between Spirit and body has for us. The reason for this is that it is obvious that the Apostles lack the European intellectualism which ex-tracts all Spirit from the contents of consciousness and crystallizes the latter into absolute objectivities, into realities downright opposed to Spirit. Their cognition is more like a vague hovering between reality and Spirit."[18] This passage can be partly understood in light of the form of cognition in general which Hegel holds to distinguish Greek Ethical Life. Thus *one* thing he means is that we moderns, unlike the early believers in miracles, perceive a sharp distinction between the received views of the community (Spirit), on the one hand, and reality, on the other.[19] For within the form of cognition in general belonging to Greek Ethical Life the individual shows an automatic, unquestioning deference to the re-ceived view of the community on all fundamental principles. And in this sense he does not clearly distinguish between the received thought of the community, on the one hand, and reality, on the other. An early expression of this idea appears in Hegel's remark about the Greeks in *The Positivity of the Christian Religion:* "If anyone had been able to hit upon the question, 'How would you prove the divine origin of a command or prohibition?' he could not have called on any historical fact for his answer, but only on the feelings of his own heart and the agreement of all good men."[20] *Another* thing Hegel means is that we moderns, unlike the early believers in miracles, perceive a sharp distinction between the medium of thought in general (Spirit) and reality. For within the form of cognition in general belonging to Greek Ethical Life, the individual has no clear conception of fundamental principles or basic concepts as existents distinct from features of the world which they are supposed to depict and thus no clear conception of them as capable of misrepresenting the world. In this sense he fails to distinguish clearly between the medium of thought in general and reality. These two ideas account for Hegel's reference in the passage quoted to a "vague hovering between reality and Spirit" in the early individual's cognition, the early individual's possession of a spiritualized conception of reality. We have seen that Hegel understands the emergence of a skeptical culture to undermine the form of cognition in general peculiar to Greek Ethical Life, so that it turns the two mentioned points at which the spiritual and the real formerly fused with one another into points of sharp separation between the two, and hence turns a spiritualized into a harsher and more objective conception of reality.

The fourth component of Hegel's idea of a harsh, objective conception of reality is less easily explained in its nature and origin. Whereas the establishment of the first three components is a more or less straightforward implication of his account of the collapse of Greek Ethical Life in its religious, ethical and general cognitive aspects, the establishment of the fourth component is not. In the *Phenomenology* Hegel makes it clear that he understands the fourth component to be decisive in the formation of the harsh, objective conception of reality which belongs to Culture. It will be remembered that the "Spirit" chapter contains a description of a process in which Greek Ethical Life is disrupted by the development of an explicit awareness of its two fundamental ethical principles, the human and divine laws, and their conflict with one another: "These powers acquire the significance of excluding and opposing one another: in Self-consciousness they exist explicitly, whereas in the ethical order they are only implicit."[21] Hegel sees in the intellectual response to this discovery of conflicting fundamental laws the decisive source of the harsh and objective conception of reality which belongs to Culture. The emergence of this source, the fourth component, thus presupposes the establishment of the two preconditions for equipollence skepticism, namely the recognition of fundamental principles *as such* and as conflicting. As with the other components, therefore, the emergence of a skeptical culture has a vital role to play in explaining the emergence of the fourth component. The decisive source of Culture's harsh, objective conception of reality which emerges in response to the discovery of conflicting fundamental laws is the act of explicitly committing oneself in a certain way to one of the conflicting laws in rejection of the other. Thus Hegel writes in the *Phenomenology:*

> [Self-consciousness], just because it is a self to itself and advances to action, raises itself out of simple immediacy, and spontaneously splits into two. By this act it gives up the specific quality of the Ethical Life, of being the simple certainty of immediate truth, and initiates the division of itself into itself as the active principle, and into the reality over against it, a reality which, for it, is negative. By the deed, therefore, it becomes guilt. For the deed is its own doing, and "doing" is its inmost nature. And the guilt also acquires the meaning of crime; for as simple, ethical consciousness, it has turned towards one law, but turned its back on the other and violates the latter by its deed . . . The action is itself this splitting into two, this explicit self-affirmation and establishing over against itself of an alien external reality; that there is such a reality, this stems from the action itself and results from it.[22]

Hegel's general point is that it is in responding to the recognition of the existence of contrary fundamental principles by *consciously adopting a particular kind of commitment to certain fundamental principles in exclusion of other contrary ones* that a consciousness establishes the full harshly objective conception of reality which is distinctive of Culture. This seems to me a profound thought.

Hegel is here concerned with the emergence of a harsh, objective conception of reality, but closely bound up with the nature of one's conception of reality is the nature of one's activities of belief and assertion. For to believe or assert is essentially to believe or assert something to be real. Thus one would expect radical variations in the conceptions which people had of the nature of reality to be mirrored in variations in the nature of their activities of belief and assertion. In particular, it seems plausible to suppose that if the emergence of a radically new objective conception of reality took place in the way described by Hegel, then it was accompanied by the emergence of a corresponding objective kind of belief and assertion. That Hegel envisages such an extension of his account is clear from his denial in the *Phenomenology* that the attitude taken toward fundamental principles within Greek Ethical Life is literally one of belief and his claim that the attitude of belief pertains rather to a conception of reality as alien or objective, like that found in Culture. This is the burden of his statement that in Ethical Life consciousness "does not *believe* in [the laws], for although belief does perceive essential

being it perceives it as something alien to itself." [23] In light of this it is of
some interest that the classical scholar Snell argues, in a way which par-
allels and complements Hegel's account of the role of the fourth component in giving us a harsh, objective conception of reality absent from
Greek Ethical Life, that the early Greeks lacked our attitude of belief
because their corresponding cognitive attitude did not involve the commitment to fundamental principles over against explicitly recognized
contrary alternatives which is an essential component of our attitude of
belief:

> In fact, when we consider the religion of Homer and the creed of the
> Olympian gods which he created, we may well wonder whether this is a
> belief at all. Our notion of belief always allows for the possibility of disbe-
> lief . . . "Belief" . . . requires as its opposite a false belief, a heresy . . . All
> this was foreign to the Greeks; they looked upon their gods as so natural
> and self-evident that they could not even conceive of other nations acknowl-
> edging a different belief or other gods. [24]

The fourth component which Hegel supposes to be decisive for the
emergence of the harsh, objective conception of reality and attitude of
belief belonging to Culture is not, however, *exhausted* by the establishment of a conscious commitment to fundamental principles in exclusion
of contrary alternatives. *Had* it been so exhausted, this component
would have arisen with a high degree of inevitability once Greek Ethical
Life collapsed for the following reasons. The emergence of an awareness
of fundamental principles as belonging to the medium of thought and as
therefore capable of misrepresenting reality is an essential part of the
collapse of Greek Ethical Life as a form of cognition in general and depends on the awareness of contrary fundamental principles, so that if
only for this reason the collapse of Greek Ethical Life is inevitably accompanied by an awareness of contrary fundamental principles. And if
there is to be anything even remotely like a conception of the states of
affairs depicted in fundamental principles as real or anything even remotely like belief in these principles once such an awareness of contrary
alternatives is established, then it must involve a conscious commitment
to fundamental principles in exclusion of contrary alternatives. However,
due to the fact that there is more to the fourth component than just such
a conscious exclusive commitment to fundamental principles, it will
prove that the establishment of this component is not fully explained by
the collapse of Greek Ethical Life.

The crucial additional element of the modern objective conception of
reality and attitude of belief which Hegel specifies as part of the fourth
component concerns the *nature* of the conscious commitment to a fundamental principle in exclusion of contrary alternatives which they in-

volve. Where an awareness of contrary alternatives exists, any cognitive attitude to a principle which is to be even remotely like belief and any conception of the state of affairs represented by the principle which is to be even remotely like a conception of it as real must indeed involve some form of conscious exclusive commitment to the principle. But this is not to say that the cognitive attitude to the principle or the conception of the state of affairs which it represents must involve the very *kind* of conscious commitment to the principle in exclusion of contraries which is involved in the objective conception of reality and attitude of belief characteristic of us moderns. Thus, the collapse of Greek Ethical Life may make in some sense inevitable the replacement of an outlook in which there is no awareness of contrary fundamental principles and hence no conscious exclusive commitment to such principles but merely a passive acceptance of them from the community by an outlook in which there is a conscious exclusive commitment to these principles; and this may mean that the emergence of a conception of reality and an attitude of belief *more* like ours is in the same sense inevitable when Ethical Life collapses. But still, this does not imply that the emergence of *exactly* our modern conception of reality and attitude of belief is inevitable, since it does not necessitate that specific *kind* of conscious, exclusive commitment which is essential to them.

Thus Hegel describes the kind of conscious exclusive commitment which in fact arises when Ethical Life collapses and brings with it the harsh, objective conception of reality and attitude of belief belonging to Culture and hence to the modern world, in a striking way. In contrast to the passive acceptance of principles within Greek Ethical Life which Hegel refers to as "merely non-action, like the mere being of a stone, not even that of a child," the conscious exclusive commitment to principles found in Culture is said to have the character of a free deed or a self-affirmation.[25] Hegel writes of the conscious commitment of the subject to one ethical law in exclusion of another incompatible one as its "deed" (*Tun*) which brings with it guilt (since it is free), and as a "self-affirmation" (*sich fuer sich setzen*), not something which "could, or perhaps could not, be the action of itself, as if with the doing of it there could be linked something external and accidental that did not belong to it, from which aspect, therefore, the action would be innocent."[26]

This description of the kind of conscious exclusive commitment which is involved in Culture can perhaps be understood in light of the model of the freedom of the "finite will" presented in the *Philosophy of Right*. The finite will is restricted to the extent that its impulses and desires are given for it, just as the range of alternative contrary principles is given for the individual in Culture.[27] At the same time the finite will shares in freedom through not being the slave of the sum force of these impulses and desires but being able to transcend this force in choosing which impulses or desires to follow, just as, one may suppose, Hegel understands the individual in Culture to be free in his judgment in the sense that he is not determined in his commitment to any given principle in exclusion of contraries by the balance of forces of the alternatives but is somehow able to transcend this balance of forces in choosing which alternative to adopt.[28] The important point to draw from this analogy is that both in the case of the finite will and in the case of the individual judging within Culture, commitment to a course of action or a judgment is not simply an expression of the force of the reasons which the individual has for that commitment but is essentially an act going beyond any mere expression of the force of those reasons.

Hegel's characterization of the conscious commitment to fundamental principles in exclusion of contrary alternatives which arises after the collapse of Greek Ethical Life as a free deed or self-affirmation signifies, then, that this commitment is not merely an expression of a greater force in the objective reasons the individual has favoring the principles to which he is committed as compared to whatever force there may be in any objective reasons favoring the contrary alternatives which he excludes. One might have expected this in view of Hegel's insistence in the *Phenomenology* that the fundamental ethical laws whose conflict with one another gives rise to the free deed or self-affirmation of a commitment to the one in conscious exclusion of the other have *equally* strong objective justifications, and his remark in the *Philosophy of History* that the attempt at this stage to evade the equipollence difficulty by finding "completely abstract universal principles" as reasons fails. [29] There *are no* overriding objective reasons available for preferring certain fundamental principles to the exclusion of other contrary ones, so whatever form an exclusive commitment to particular principles may take at this stage, it cannot simply take the form of an expression of overriding objective reasons which one has. Hegel here captures an important feature of our conception of reality and attitude of belief. The commitment to a proposition which we express when we conscientiously claim that the world really is a certain way and which we attribute to someone when we say that he believes it to be that way essentially amounts to more than an expression of the preponderance of available objective reasons in that proposition's favor. Indeed it may occur when the person committed does not think there is such a preponderance of available objective reasons (as in the case of the religious belief of a fideist, for example).

But further, consider in the light of Hegel's model of a free deed or self-affirmation two very different kinds of conscious commitment to fundamental principles in exclusion of contrary alternatives which could equally well have resulted, for all that has been said so far, from the

collapse of Greek Ethical Life, including the failure to elude the equipollence difficulty by finding overriding objective reasons. The conceptions of reality and the attitudes of belief associated with these two possible forms of exclusive commitment would have been very different.

First, the resulting conscious commitment to a principle in exclusion
of contrary alternatives could have been in its essence no more than the
expression of a certain kind of subjective or egocentric reason for preferring it, that is, a reason recognized to fall short of the objective reasons
which were sought but not found and to be instead essentially relative to
the standpoint of the individual believer. For example, the conscious exclusive commitment to a principle might have been essentially just an
expression of the circumstance that the principle was the received view
of one's community, a principle which one was psychologically incapable
of giving up, a principle which fitted in well with one's other views, a
principle which had proved adequate in helping one to lead a satisfactory
life, or any combination of these or similar egocentric reasons. In saying
that the world "really was" the way a certain fundamental principle depicted it as being, someone in this situation would have meant no more
than that there were overriding reasons of the relevant subjective kind in
its favor, and his "belief" in the principle would have been of a kind
constituted by this sort of commitment. But this first model does not
correspond to the conception of reality and attitude of belief which we
moderns actually have. If *we* believe some principle on the basis of subjective reasons of the kind mentioned, we do so at most because we take
them to be *indicative* of its truth, not because they are what we are expressing by calling it true. And we may quite well believe it in the absence
of or even in opposition to such reasons. Hegel seems implicitly to acknowledge this point, for his suggestion that the kind of conscious exclusive commitment which arose when Ethical Life collapsed and which
persists in the modern world is a free deed or self-affirmation excludes a
situation in which the act of commitment is essentially nothing more
than the expression of the force of the subjective reasons one has, just as
much as it excluded the situation in which the act of commitment was
just an expression of the force of one's objective reasons. Hegel's suggestion requires that the act of commitment should transcend *any* mere
expression of the force of available reasons.

Second, the conscious exclusive commitment which arose could have
had the form in essence of some kind of simple, irreducible commitment
to a principle in exclusion of contrary alternatives going beyond any
expression of the force of available reasons. In this case the claim that
things "really were" as a given principle depicted them would have expressed a simple, irreducible commitment to that principle in exclusion
of contrary alternatives, and while a greater force of available reasons

might have been adduced to justify this simple commitment on occasion, it would not have been an essential part of what was expressed in that commitment. Correspondingly, the kind of belief established in this case would have been such as to involve essentially just the simple, irreducible commitment in question. This second model comes much closer to describing our modern conception of reality and attitude of belief. And Hegel seems to recognize this, for just this kind of model is required to do justice to his suggestion that the conscious exclusive commitment in Culture has the character of a free deed or self-affirmation—that is, a simple act which transcends any expression of the force of the reasons one has. The fourth component of the harsh, objective conception of reality (and attitude of belief) belonging to Culture is not, then, only the existence of a conscious commitment to fundamental principles in exclusion of contrary alternatives but also the existence of this kind of simple, irreducible commitment transcending the expression of the force of available reasons.

Hegel's mention in the *Phenomenology* of a free deed or self-affirmation seems, though, to describe not only the *practice* of conscious exclusive commitment distinctive of Culture itself but also the *origin* of this practice. Here the fact that the collapse of Greek Ethical Life through the emergence of a skeptical culture is not itself sufficient to establish the fourth component in all its aspects becomes important. That collapse leaves a real alternative to the kind of conscious exclusive commitment distinctive of the fourth component, namely a commitment in the form of an expression of the force of subjective or egocentric reasons. This situation contrasts with the high degree of inevitability with which the collapse of Greek Ethical Life caused by the emergence of a skeptical culture leads to the first three components of the harsh, objective conception of reality belonging to Culture and to the first part of the fourth component (the recognition of contrary fundamental principles and the emergence of *some* kind of conscious exclusive commitment). I suggest that Hegel envisages the historical adoption of the form of commitment which distinguishes Culture, rather than the alternative form of commitment consisting of an expression of the force of subjective or egocentric reasons, as itself the result of a free choice which was not inevitable and which is not fully explicable in the light of rational grounds possessed by the individuals who made the choice. That is, we are also to understand the deed which *originates* the practice of conscious exclusive commitment distinctive of Culture on the model of the finite will. In this respect Hegel's Ur-teilung retains an element of that ultimate inexplicability which the corresponding event in the accounts of Hoelderlin and Schelling possessed.[30]

Culture's harsh, objective conception of natural and social reality, whose origins in the emergence of skeptical culture we have considered, constitutes only the first half of the division and double alienation established on the positive side of Hegel's historical Ur-teilung. The other half is "the *world of Faith, the realm of essential being*."[31] Hegel sees the alienated religious outlook of Faith, which complements the harsh, objective conception of natural and social reality found in Culture, as likewise a consequence of skeptical culture. Hence the immediate transition from Skepticism to Unhappy Consciousness (corresponding to Faith) in the *Phenomenology*, which indicates that the emergence of skeptical culture is instrumental in bringing about this religious outlook. The account of the relation between skeptical culture and Faith on which I wish to focus is as follows. Hegel views the emergence and flourishing of the religious outlook of Faith, which is characteristic above all of Christianity, as partly explicable in terms of the suitability of this outlook as a defense of objective claims against the threat posed to them by skepticism. This religious outlook provides a kind of defensive rationalization of objective claims in the face of skepticism's threat.

For Hegel the positing of a remote, infinite God by the Christian Unhappy Consciousness is a mere projection of that consciousness itself into a distant realm as an alien entity, a projection which takes place because consciousness undergoes the experience of Skepticism. Thus Hegel writes, "The Unhappy Consciousness itself *is* the gazing of one Self-consciousness into another, and itself *is* both, and the unity of both is also its essential nature. But it is not as yet explicitly aware that this is its essential nature, or that it is the unity of both."[32] Hegel emphasizes that it is essential to the very purpose or function of this religious illusion that the God which it posits should be posited as alien and remote, in the sense of being quite distinct from men and undiscoverable by their cognitive strivings. Thus he writes of the "unattainable beyond" into which this God is projected that, "Where the 'other' is sought, it cannot be found, for it is supposed to be just a *beyond*, something that can *not* be found."[33] Part of Hegel's idea here is that these features of the religious conception belonging to the Unhappy Consciousness are essential to its constitution of that kind of defensive response to skepticism which it has the function of providing. Hegel distinguishes two sides of this defense against skepticism built upon God's imagined distinctness from men and his imagined unattainability by way of their cognitive efforts.

The first side of the defense may be understood as follows. When the Greeks originally became aware of the existence of contrary fundamental principles and of equally strong reasons on both sides, this constituted a threat to their belief because of their reliance on the discovery of superior reasons as the basis of beliefs exposed to competition from contraries. Such reliance caused no problems while the only beliefs recognized to face competition from contraries were nonfundamental ones which could be decisively justified or invalidated by appeal to more fundamental ones, but it caused problems in a situation where fundamental principles were recognized to face competition from contraries as well and were found to lack any decisive justification or invalidation by reasons. This same reliance on superior reasons as the basis of beliefs subject to competition from contraries continued to allow belief to be threatened when the Greeks reacted to their initial difficulty by seeking to develop *new* reasons which would establish an imbalance in the strength of the reasons for and against certain principles—the ambition of Greek rationalism—but discovered that "no such reasons—i.e., no completely abstract universal principles—can be found," or that the problem of an equal balance of opposed reasons was simply reiterated at the level of the new rationalist theories.[34] Now the religious outlook of the Unhappy Consciousness or Faith has the function of substituting for this reliance on the discovery of superior reasons as the basis of belief in principles exposed to competition from contraries a quite different basis of such belief, namely passive obedience to the commands of God. In this way the ubiquitous and inescapable occurrence of equipollence difficulties ceases to be a threat to belief.

Thus according to Hegel, whereas the reaction of the earlier Greeks when confronted by the skeptical difficulty of equipollence was to retain their reliance on superior reasons as the basis of beliefs exposed to competition from contraries and initiate a vain search for reasons which might withstand the skeptical difficulty in order to safeguard their beliefs, the reaction to skepticism of Neoplatonism—a philosophical movement which he closely associates with and often interprets in the light of Christianity—was quite different. This reaction consisted of altogether ceasing to rely in fundamental matters upon the reasons which the cognitive subject had or could find and instead passively accepting the beliefs commanded by God. Hegel says of this response to skepticism that, "with the rejection of the criterion for subjective knowledge, finite principles in general also disappear," so that in place of "the mere turning of the subject on himself," within Neoplatonism liberty, happiness, and steadfastness can now "only be brought about by turning to God, by giving heed to absolute truth" which is "the standpoint of reverencing and fearing God."[35]

Similarly in the revealed religions themselves the basis of beliefs is not the reasons which people possess or can discover for them but rather the supposed fact that a God who has revealed the fundamental truths (in the Torah, the Ten Commandments, the words of Jesus, or the Koran) has commanded belief in them, a command which must be passively obeyed. This foundation within the revealed religions of all belief on a passive obedience to God rather than on reasons was a theme whose importance struck Hegel early in his career. Hence the concept of "positivity" developed in *The Positivity of the Christian Religion* as a means by which to distinguish the nature of Christianity from that of Greek religion: "A positive belief is a system of religious propositions which is supposed to have truth for us because it is commanded to us by an authority to whom we cannot refuse to subjugate our belief."[36] Hence also Hegel's observation in *The Spirit of Christianity* that "the existence of God appears to the Jews not as a truth but as a command."[37] The same passive acceptance of beliefs from an external authority is emphasized in the *Phenomenology* as a feature of the religious outlook of the Unhappy Consciousness or Faith. Thus Hegel says that for the Unhappy Consciousness, when men work on the present world, they employ "faculties and powers, a gift from an alien source, which the unchangeable makes over to consciousness to make use of."[38] And he describes how this passive acceptance of belief from an alien authority undergoes an extension within Catholicism to become a passive acceptance of the demands of the priest, who is understood to communicate God's demands.[39]

The second side of the defense against skepticism which Hegel finds built into the religious outlook of Faith depends on this outlook's understanding of the God who commands belief in men as himself a believer or possessor of a cognitive perspective. Upon their discovery of conflicts between contrary fundamental principles and of ensuing equipollence difficulties, the Greeks' response was to seek to give new reasons in order to establish an imbalance in the reasons on the opposing sides of the conflicts. And their unhappy experience was that "no such reasons—i.e., no completely abstract universal principles—can be found," so that this strategy for answering the equipollence threat failed.[40] The revealed religions, we saw, do not attempt to evade the threat by in this way giving superior reasons, since they rather substitute for our reliance on discoverable reasons as the basis of our beliefs a passive obedience to God's commands. At the same time, however, they do not simply dismiss the requirement that our beliefs should have superior reasons but instead develop the idea of a cognitive perspective, namely God's, which possesses an absolute justification of certain principles over against others but which is quite distinct from the cognitive perspective of men, who can therefore have no share in this absolute justification. In this way the natural equation under which the Greeks labored of the idea that there *is* a superior justification for a principle with the idea that there is a superior justification of it which we can *give* is broken. As a result, the revealed religions can simultaneously hold that certain of our beliefs have a stronger justification than their contraries—indeed an absolute justification—and yet reject any expectation that we should be able to give that superior justification. This idea of an absolute justification, belonging to God, which is beyond the reach of any human capacity for justifying sustains belief in the face of the equipollence difficulty confronting those justifications which we can actually give. And it does so by making sense of the affirmation that a claim has a superior or absolute justification even though we are not able, and probably never will be able, to provide any justification for it which is not counterbalanced by an equally strong justification for a contrary claim.

Thus Hegel emphasizes that the God of Faith has a cognitive perspective on all facts. For example, he says of the natural and social world of Culture that "what is *present* has the significance only of an objective reality, the consciousness of which exists in a beyond." [41] And he hints at the nature of the absolute justification which this divine perspective possesses when he says that God not only thinks about the world but also thinks about it in such a way that his thinking of it is its *form:* "The *present* actual world has its antithesis directly in its *beyond,* which is both the thinking of it and its thought-form." [42] For the absolute justification of God's beliefs consists in the fact that God is the omnipotent creator of the world, for whom there is no distinction between his thought or wish that things are a certain way and their actually being that way (recall that Hegel saw a contradiction between the absoluteness of the self signified by skepticism and the contingency of the skeptic's appearances, their lack of complete subjection to his will). Hegel describes this situation as follows in the *History of Philosophy:*

> It is indispensable that God should be thought of in relation to the world and to man. This relation to the world is then a relation to an "other," which thereby at first appears to be outside of God; but because this relation is *His* activity, the fact of having this relation in Himself is a moment of Himself . . . God reveals Himself in Himself, and therefore establishes distinct determinations in Himself . . . In this manner, therefore, that which afterwards appears finite is yet produced by Him in Himself.[43]

Thus in the view of the revealed religions the immediate identity between God's thought or wish that things are a certain way and their actually being that way provides God with an absolute justification for all his beliefs, an absolute justification which he possesses but which it is beyond the capacity of human beings to give.

Hegel therefore understands the religious and ethical views which belong to the revealed religions to be forearmed against the assaults of skepticism in certain ways that the religious and ethical views belonging to Greek Ethical Life were not, and to be consequently better able to withstand those assaults. For of course it is above all religious and ethical beliefs which in the revealed religions receive both a "positive" foundation through revelation and an absolute justification in the cognitive perspective of an omnipotent, creative God going beyond any human capacity for justifying, and which are thereby protected against equipollence difficulties.

We have now seen the form taken by the theory of a historical Ur-teilung or original division in Hegel's work and the large role played by the emergence of a skeptical culture in his explanation of this historical Ur-teilung. There is one final question which we should briefly address: What happens to the division between a harsh, objective natural and social realm, on the one hand, and a remote, inscrutable, despotic divine realm, on the other, once it has been established for human consciousness in history?

In Hoelderlin's version of the theory, the original division, once established, remained a permanent feature of man's experience, however much its sharpness might be reduced in the course of time:

> To put an end to that eternal struggle between our self and the world, to restore the peace of all peace which is higher than all Reason, to unite ourselves with Nature to an infinite whole, that is the goal of all our striving, whether we understand ourselves in this or not. But neither our knowledge nor our action reaches in any period that point where all the struggle in opposition ceases, where all is one; the determinate line unites itself with the indeterminate only in an endless convergence.[44]

Hegel's version of the theory is by contrast a good deal more optimistic. For Hegel the division which afflicts man for a substantial part of his history is eventually overcome and gives way to a new condition of unity and harmony in some ways similar to, though higher than, that originally enjoyed in Greek Ethical Life. Thus the *Phenomenology* describes a gradual overcoming of the sharp division between the worlds of Faith and Culture through the stages of Pure Insight, Enlightenment, Morality, and Conscience, which constitute a route to the final restoration of unity and harmony in Hegel's own age:

> Both worlds . . . when grasped as Spirit . . . are confounded and revolutionized by the *Insight* [of the individual] and the diffusion of that Insight, known as the Enlightenment; and the realm which was expanded and divided into *this world* and the *beyond*, returns into self-consciousness which now, in the form of Morality, grasps itself as the essentiality and essence as the actual self; it no longer places its *world* and its *ground* outside of itself, but lets everything fade into itself, and, as *Conscience*, is Spirit that is certain of itself.[45]

And later the *Encyclopedia* gives more succinct expression to the same optimistic message: "Spiritual life in its immediacy appears first as innocence and unsophisticated trust. But it lies in the essence of Spirit that this immediate condition be overcome ... This standpoint of division (*Entzweiung*) is now likewise to be overcome and Spirit should return through itself to unity."[46]

PART III

THE EPISTEMOLOGICAL DEFENSE OF HEGEL'S SYSTEM

SIX

Hegel's Epistemology?

I N THIS chapter we approach the question of the epistemological security of Hegel's philosophical system, the system which receives its
final and most complete expression in Hegel's *Encyclopedia*. This
baroque system has been too well explored by others to require, and is
too complex to allow, anything but the briefest of summaries here. Its
governing principle, which is supposed by Hegel to encompass and explain everything, is Absolute Spirit or Hegel's version of the God of
Christianity. Each of the three parts of the *Encyclopedia* captures an essential aspect of the constitution or self-movement of Absolute Spirit.
The Logic expounds Absolute Spirit as the divine logos—an ascending,
self-moving conceptual hierarchy which permeates and explains all natural and spiritual phenomena. It expounds this divine logos in abstraction from such phenomena or, in Hegel's words, in the form of "God as
he is in his eternal essence before the creation of Nature and a finite
Spirit."[1] The Philosophy of Nature expounds the self-externalization of
the divine logos in Nature, which is accordingly ordered in an ascending,
self-developing hierarchy mirroring the earlier stages of the ascending,
self-moving conceptual hierarchy of the divine logos expounded in the
Logic. This natural hierarchy includes merely mechanical and physical
phenomena at the lower end and organic ones at the higher end. The
Philosophy of Spirit continues to expound the realization of the divine
logos, but at the higher level of mental or spiritual phenomena, which
are accordingly ordered in an ascending, self-developing hierarchy corresponding to the later stages of the ascending, self-moving conceptual
hierarchy of the divine logos. In doing so, it ascends from general mental
characteristics of men to the social and political institutions of the state
and their historical development and finally to art, religion, and philosophy, which express the truth about Absolute Spirit and hence constitute
Absolute Spirit's return to itself and its achievement of an essential

knowledge of its own nature. This philosophical system can be understood, on one level at least, as a defense or reworking of the Christian conception of God. In particular, its three parts represent an attempt to make sense of the Christian doctrine of a triune God: the Logic depicts God as he is in himself, the Philosophy of Nature depicts God the Son, and the Philosophy of Spirit depicts God the Holy Spirit.

Now it is not, I think, widely recognized that Hegel was seriously concerned about, or made significant efforts to ensure, the epistemological security of this extraordinary philosophical system. A first acquaintance with his works often produces the impression that it was erected in blissful disregard of epistemological problems, and that its metaphysical extravagance may be largely attributable to this fact. The feeling easily arises that Hegel might have spared himself much onerous and futile philosophical labor if only he had read his Hume a little more attentively. In something like this spirit Scruton recently wrote: "Much of Hegel's metaphysics develops independently of any epistemological basis. He avoids the first-person standpoint of Descartes not through any rival theory of knowledge, but by a process of abstraction which, because it abolishes the individual, leaves no evident room for the theory of knowledge at all. This makes Hegel's metaphysics so vulnerable to skeptical attack that it has now little to bequeath us but its poetry."[2]

The verdict of many Hegel specialists on the issue of Hegel's relation to epistemology has not been so very different. Thus many books on his philosophy simply ignore the question of his epistemology and even so sympathetic and generally reliable a critic as Baillie explicitly argues that Hegel is naively unconcerned about epistemological difficulties. According to Baillie, Hegel, "acting on the principle which he . . . described as learning to swim by entering the water . . . at once assumes that the knowledge which philosophy professes to furnish is possible, is not to be sought or justified by a preliminary inquiry, but has simply to be expounded and exhibited."[3] On Baillie's reading, "whether thought is able to know, or how far it can know being at all, is a problem which from the start [Hegel] never seems to have considered, at any rate never discussed at length."[4] Hegel's confidence in his philosophical principle was accordingly based on nothing more than the feeling that, as an explanation of reality, it "agreed with the needs of religion and the general conclusions of the philosophy of his time."[5] In sum, for Baillie's Hegel "there was . . . no initial problem regarding knowledge."[6]

In short, there is a widespread assumption that Hegel showed little or no interest in securing his system against epistemological challenges in general or skeptical attacks in particular. However, this common view is a misconception on a grand scale. An absolutely fundamental feature of Hegel's thought from as early as his first years in Jena was his development of a clear and exacting set of epistemological standards and his devotion of a large portion of his philosophical energies to meeting these standards on behalf of his own philosophical system. This epistemological struggle was first and foremost an attempt to meet the challenge of skepticism as Hegel conceived it, and his Jena years, specifically 1802–1807, constituted the period of its greatest intensity. Both of these facts are recorded in an unlikely but interesting source—a biographical poem composed in Hegel's honor in 1826 by the heavy Teutonic hand of his friend, Friedrich Foerster:

> And so our hero announced himself in early years,
> When the skeptics had sent him serpents of doubt.
> Faith! He crushes the monsters like Goettingen sausages,
> And only the empty husk of skepticism remained behind.[7]

The fact that Hegel's epistemological strivings are largely concentrated, and certainly most readily perceptible, in works of the Jena period, many of which have been relatively neglected until recently, goes some way toward explaining the common oversight of this quite fundamental aspect of his thought. Once one recognizes the form taken by his epistemology in these early works, though, his concern with the subject becomes readily perceptible in later writings as well.

Hegel's concern to confront epistemological difficulties in general and skeptical ones in particular in a sense puts him in the mainstream of German idealism. For contrary to another fairly widespread misapprehension, the German idealists as a group were by no means epistemologically irresponsible, dogmatic system-builders who carelessly left their systems open to skeptical attack. They were in fact distinguished by a shared recognition of the importance of skepticism and by a determined effort to answer it on behalf of their systems.[8] So much so that whether or not Fichte's comment is true of philosophy in general, a strong case can certainly be made for its truth of the development of German idealism from Kant to Hegel: "It cannot be denied that philosophical reason owes every noticeable advance it has ever made to the observations of skepticism on the precariousness of the position where it has for the moment come to rest."[9] Kant's debt to the skepticism of Hume, who by Kant's own confession "first interrupted my dogmatic slumber and gave my investigation in the field of speculative philosophy a quite new direction," is of course well known.[10] Less well known is the way in which Reinhold attempted to reform Kantian idealism by reconstructing it systematically on the foundation of a single, self-evident principle in response to his realization that Kant's own formulation of his idealism had left it resting on various presuppositions vulnerable to skeptical attack. Again, it was largely in response to criticisms of Reinhold's fundamental principle, the "proposition of consciousness," raised by the soi-disant skeptic Schulze that Fichte sought to derive that principle from an epistemologically firmer foundation, the deed or *Tathandlung* of the self's self-positing, and so generated his own idealist system.[11] And even Schelling paid lip service to this tradition of respect for skepticism, saying that skepticism was the necessary starting point of transcendental philosophy.[12] Hegel's concern to confront skepticism puts him in this tradition only "in a sense," though, because he has a distinctive and unusually well-thought-out conception of the skeptical difficulties which it is important to solve and, as we shall see, a quite original set of proposals for solving them having little in common with the solutions offered by his idealist predecessors.

Of course, Hegel's writings undeniably contain much which offers *prima facie* support for the common view that he was indifferent to skeptical or other epistemological difficulties. For example, there appears to be a shameless lack of self-criticism in his method of Critique as this is described and practiced in the *Critical Journal of Philosophy*, a method which consists essentially in presupposing the truth of his own system and then tracing hints of its standpoint in the works of other modern philosophers as a means to their evaluation.[13] Thus Haym interprets this method naturally enough as an expression of Hegel's dogmatic and uncritical conviction in the truth of his own philosophical principle.[14] Again, in *The Relation of Skepticism to Philosophy* Hegel says of his and Schelling's philosophy and its fundamental principle of identity: "There is . . . no truth in the claim that the new philosophy attempts to ground (*ergruenden*) the possibility of the identity presupposed in common life, for it does nothing but express and recognize that presupposed identity."[15] And in *The Difference between the Fichtean and Schellingian Systems of Philosophy* he attacks the "tendency to give and establish by grounds" (*Begruendungs- und Ergruendungstendenz*) in Reinhold's philosophy. Again, in the *Encyclopedia* and elsewhere Hegel attacks the Kantian project of critically investigating our faculty of knowledge in advance of applying it, resting the attack on the argument that "the examination of knowledge can only be carried out by an act of knowledge" and that "to seek to know before we know is as absurd as the wise resolution of Scholasticus, not to venture into the water until he had learned to swim."[16] This remark, it will be recalled, was one of Baillie's grounds for finding Hegel uninterested in epistemology. However, it will become clear that all these aspects of Hegel's work are to be understood not as signs of a general lack of interest in or hostility toward epistemology but at most as rejections of certain conceptions of how it should be done.

A glance at the *Phenomenology* suffices to raise some serious doubts about the adequacy of the common view that Hegel acknowledged no epistemological responsibilities toward his philosophical system. Schelling, whose philosophy of identity had a decisive and lasting influence on Hegel, really was guilty of being cavalier in matters epistemological in much the way that Hegel is often wrongly supposed to have been. Thus Schelling accepted his philosophy of identity in a crudely dogmatic manner as the gift of an alleged faculty of "intellectual intuition," understood as an unteachable, absolute precondition of philosophical insight the possession of which justified the philosopher in a complete disregard of all other viewpoints.[17] In the *Phenomenology* Hegel alludes to this dogmatic attitude disparagingly as "the rapturous enthusiasm which, like a shot from a pistol, begins straight away with absolute knowledge, and makes short work of other standpoints by declaring that it takes no notice of them."[18] And he criticizes such an attitude on the grounds that the standpoints which it dogmatically dismisses as the products of an inferior sort of cognition lacking its truth may with no less right turn round and dismiss *it* on the ground that it is inferior to *them* and lacks *their* truth, since "*one* bare assurance is worth just as much as another."[19] This dissatisfaction with Schelling's epistemological carelessness in fact antedates the *Phenomenology* by several years—going back to Hegel's early days in Jena, when he and Schelling were jointly developing the philosophy of identity. Again, Hegel in the *Phenomenology* writes dismissively of a strategy which, like that seemingly at work in his own earlier method of Critique, seeks to establish Philosophical Science over against alternative viewpoints by "appeal to whatever intimations of something better it may detect in the cognition that is without truth, to the signs which point in the direction of Science."[20] His objection is fundamentally that such a strategy, like Schelling's, relies on a dogmatic presupposition of the truth of Philosophical Science and has Philosophical Science "appealing to itself, and to itself in the mode in which it exists in the cognition that is without truth"—something which contrary viewpoints might quite well do too, and with no less right.[21] Again, Hegel refers to the *Phenomenology* as the place where he gives a *justification* of his Science or undertakes to *prove the necessity* of its philosophical standpoint.[22] Are we simply to dismiss all these concerns of the *Phenomenology* as the ephemeral stirrings of an otherwise dormant epistemological conscience? Surely not.

Hegel's impatience with Schelling's dogmatic appeal to intellectual intuition is part of a consistent pattern in his writings of rejecting such epistemological shortcuts. We might usefully mention a few of the other epistemological shortcuts offered by his contemporaries which Hegel explicitly rejects, for this will serve to reinforce the point that he is unlikely to have been guilty of epistemological carelessness himself. Hegel offers extended criticism of Jacobi's appeal to immediate knowledge, faith, or feeling as the guarantor of truth.[23] He is equally dismissive of the similar epistemological shortcuts of his Romantic contemporaries: Friedrich von Schlegel's appeal to an immediate knowledge of God, Novalis's conviction that the true infinite lies in the depth of the human soul, Schleiermacher's foundation of religion on a feeling of absolute dependence, an immediate consciousness of a relationship of immediate existence, and so forth.[24] Nor does Hegel accord any value to appeals to common sense of the kind which flourished in the Germany of his day as imports from the Scottish common sense philosophers.[25] The following are some of Hegel's most important objections to such epistemological shortcuts. First, he objects that merely labeling our firmest and dearest convictions products of intellectual intuition, immediate knowledge, common sense, and the like, or finding some special introspectible property of these convictions which we identify by such titles, does nothing to show that these convictions are actually true of the world.[26] Second, he points out that titles of this kind can be conscientiously applied by different people to quite different and indeed inconsistent propositions.[27] Third, he argues that the reliance on such epistemological shortcuts leads to an unrestrained, arrogant, self-righteous dogmatism.[28]

The common view that Hegel was careless about epistemology becomes still less plausible when one considers the space and energy which he devoted to the consideration of skepticism in its various forms from an early point in his philosophical career and the sophisticated and sympathetic understanding of large parts of the skeptical tradition at which he arrived.[29] Is it likely that someone in this position would have failed to do his utmost to ensure that his own philosophical system remained invulnerable to the epistemological difficulties which he saw arising out of skepticism? Once again the answer must be no.

Hegel's understanding of the skeptical tradition sketched in Part One provides a key with which to unlock his epistemological enterprise. Once we recognize which epistemological problems posed within the skeptical tradition were considered by Hegel to merit attention, we can find in his work an elaborate network of defenses erected to protect his philosophical system against them. This network of defenses was put in place early on in Hegel's career, but remained thereafter as a constant, if easily overlooked, aspect of his thought.

On the basis of Hegel's critical interpretation of the skeptical tradition considered in Part One and his account of the historical role of a skeptical culture considered in Part Two, we may reasonably predict that there will be two skeptical problems which he feels bound to answer on behalf of his own philosophical system above all: the ancient skeptic's problems of equipollence in general and concept-instantiation in particular. The interesting claim made by Hegel in *The Relation of Skepticism to Philosophy* and in the *History of Philosophy,* that the content of his own philosophical system is invulnerable to the attacks of even the genuine ancient form of skepticism, will mean specifically that his system is invulnerable to the problems of equipollence and concept-instantiation. He articulates that claim as follows in the *History of Philosophy:* "The operations of skepticism are undoubtedly directed against the finite. But however much force . . . its negative dialectic may have against the properly-speaking dogmatic knowledge of the Understanding, its attacks against the true infinite of the Speculative Idea are most feeble and unsatisfactory."[30]

On the same basis we can also predict that Hegel will *not* feel obliged to spend time defending his system against the difficulties distinctive of the modern skeptics, founded as these are on dogmatic presuppositions which themselves succumb to the genuine skeptical problems of the ancient skeptics. In particular, he will feel no need to answer modern skepticism's veil of perception problem since it is based on the various dogmatic assumptions which we considered in Part One. And this allows us to clear up one source of Scruton's misunderstanding of Hegel's attitude toward epistemology immediately. The fact that Hegel avoids "the first-person standpoint of Descartes," as Scruton correctly says he does, should not be seen as an indication that he abandons an interest in epistemology in general or in the task of confronting skeptical difficulties in particular, as Scruton wrongly infers. On the contrary, it is quite consistent with, and perhaps even a symptom of, Hegel's respect for and concern with skepticism—namely the radical skepticism of the ancients which, taken to its logical conclusion, undermines the Cartesian's dogmatic confidence in his own mental states or *cogitationes.*

If Hegel was concerned that his philosophical system should confront and withstand the skeptical problems of equipollence and concept-instantiation, as I have suggested, then we should be able to detect these specific concerns in his writings. And indeed once we know to look for them, they become readily apparent in texts from the Jena period on.

Consider first the problem of equipollence. Throughout his career Hegel was particularly concerned to deal with a special case of this problem—the special case in which an equal balance of arguments for and against a claim arises for the reason and in the sense that the claim is advanced *without any* supporting arguments and is then confronted by a contrary claim advanced in the same way.[31] Hegel gives an early and explicit statement of this special case of the equipollence problem when he discusses ancient skepticism in *The Relation of Skepticism to Philosophy.* There he says that the fourth of the five tropes of Agrippa "concerns *presuppositions (Voraussetzungen)*—against the dogmatists who in order to avoid being driven into an infinite regress posit something as simply first and unproven, and whom the skeptics immediately imitate by positing the opposite of that presupposition with just the same right."[32] It is crucial to note Hegel's concern with this special case of the skeptical equipollence problem if one is to recognize his elaborate attempts to answer skepticism in both earlier and later works for what they are.

In his later works, for example, Hegel often expresses a determination that his own philosophical system should not be or have *presuppositions*. Thus the very first paragraph of the *Encyclopedia* states that philosophy may not make "presuppositions and assurances (*Voraussetzungen und Versicherungen*)" and notes that this appears to cause a difficulty for the beginning of philosophy, "since a beginning, as an immediate, makes its presuppositions (*Voraussetzungen*) or rather is one itself."[33] The presuppositions which Hegel is concerned to avoid here and elsewhere are not simply claims put forward without further grounds, as interpreters have tended naturally enough to assume.[34] Hegel does not see the making of such claims as a problem *in itself*. Hence in early texts, as we saw, he dismisses the "tendency to give and establish by grounds" in philosophy and says of his own philosophy that "there is . . . no truth in the claim that the new philosophy attempts to ground the possibility of the identity presupposed in common life, for it does nothing but express and recognize that presupposed identity." And in the *Encyclopedia* he says that the beginning of his philosophical system, pure Being, "cannot be anything mediated or further determined."[35] No, the problem of presupposition with which Hegel is really concerned is the special case of the ancient skeptical equipollence problem which he early in his career identifies in the fourth trope of Agrippa: the problem of advancing a claim without further grounds *and having it confronted with an opposite claim advanced in the same way and therefore with equal right*. That this more specific problem of presupposition is the problem Hegel has in mind in the *Encyclopedia* is shown by the fact that shortly after his initial mention of the problem at the start of the work he explains that no provisional explication of philosophy is possible because it would be no more than "a tissue of presuppositions, assurances, and rationalizations (*Voraussetzungen, Versicherungen, und Raesonnements*)—that is, of contingent claims, over against which with the same right the opposite claims could be assured to hold (*versichert*)."[36]

Turning to earlier texts, the reader will recall that in the *Phenomenology* Hegel raises an objection both to a position like Schelling's, which simply asserts the truth of its own philosophy and the superiority of its form of cognition while dismissing the claims of other viewpoints as the products of an inferior sort of cognition, and to a position which seeks to establish its philosophy over against competing viewpoints by finding in them intimations of its philosophy's true account of things. Note, first of all, that both these positions are themselves oriented toward coping with the circumstance that there exist alternative viewpoints opposed to a philosophical viewpoint—a circumstance which threatens to give rise to an equipollence problem for that philosophical viewpoint. Second, note that Hegel objects to the former position explicitly, and to the latter implicitly, that they rest on a dogmatic assurance of the truth and superiority of their philosophical viewpoints which other alternative viewpoints might with no less right mimic on their own behalf, since "one bare assurance (*Versichern*) is worth just as much as another." This objection is an application of the special case of the equipollence problem found in the fourth trope of Agrippa, to which Hegel drew attention explicitly a few years prior to writing the *Phenomenology* in *The Relation of Skepticism to Philosophy*. In short, two positions which might be adopted in order to defend a philosophical viewpoint against the threat of equipollence skepticism succumb to it themselves. In the *Phenomenology* Hegel's proposal for answering the initial skeptical threat to his own Philosophical Science in such a way that the answer will *not* itself succumb to that threat is as follows. It will not prove necessary for Philosophical Science to assume its own truth and the superiority of its form of cognition in order to dismiss competing viewpoints as an inferior sort of cognition, or to assume its own truth and superiority in order to interpret and evaluate those competing viewpoints as mere intimations of its truth, either of which approaches itself falls victim to the kind of skeptical equipollence problem it was supposed to prevent. And this will not prove necessary because the alternative viewpoints which these approaches strive in vain to cope with in a sense condemn themselves even before Philosophical Science passes an extraneous verdict upon them; they show themselves to be self-defeating. This is Hegel's idea when he argues that Philosophical Science need not rely on applying an external criterion to these alternative viewpoints which they might not accept, since "consciousness [the alternative viewpoints] provides its own criterion within itself, so that the investigation becomes a comparison of consciousness with itself"—that is, a comparison in which it will always be found to be in conflict or contradiction with itself.[37]

Indeed five years before writing the *Phenomenology* Hegel was already expressing the same concern that the skeptical equipollence problem seemed to threaten his Philosophical Science and was already indicating a strikingly similar strategy for solving this problem. Thus in the 1802 essay *On the Nature of Philosophical Critique in General and Its Relation to the Present Condition of Philosophy in Particular* (hereafter *On the Nature of Philosophical Critique*) Hegel makes the point that his method of Critique cannot be applied to viewpoints which lack all traces of his own philosophical principle since it essentially consists in indicating such traces. He suggests that Critique's only recourse in these cases is therefore simply to discard the viewpoints in question. However, he points out that this generates a problem in that it leaves his philosophical principle and these discarded viewpoints facing one another with nothing in common:

> Because reciprocal recognition is hereby eliminated, there are only two subjectivities facing one another. Views which share nothing in common come forth just for this reason with equal right, and Critique has thus declared itself to be a nullity and turned itself into something subjective, by declaring the viewpoint to be judged to be anything but philosophy, while the viewpoint, on the other hand, claims to be nothing but philosophy, and its claim appears to be a one-sided decree . . . Its judgment is an appeal to the ideal of philosophy which, however, because it is not recognized by the adversary, becomes an alien court for the latter.[38]

Hegel first discusses the fourth trope of Agrippa version of the skeptical equipollence problem in *The Relation of Skepticism to Philosophy* at about the same date as this passage, and it is fairly clear that in this passage he is expressing concern about Philosophical Science's apparent vulnerability to such a version of the equipollence problem. This is the same concern which we have seen him to express a few years later in the *Phenomenology* and later still in the *Encyclopedia*. In *On the Nature of Philosophical Critique*, as in the *Phenomenology*, Hegel proposes to solve this problem for Philosophical Science by showing that the viewpoints opposed to Philosophical Science condemn themselves or are self-defeating in such a way that Philosophical Science has no need to apply an extraneous standard to them: "There is nothing to do but to recount how this negative side [i.e., the opposed viewpoints] expresses itself and confesses its nothingness (*Nichtssein*); and since it cannot fail to happen that what is nothing at the start in its development appears more and more as nothing . . . in this way Critique will, through this continuous construction proceeding from the first nullity, reconcile again even that incapacity which could see in Critique's initial claim nothing but high-handedness and arbitrariness."[39]

This makes it clear that Hegel's early method of Critique, understood as the presupposition of the truth of his own philosophical principle and the subsequent investigation of the extent to which it is anticipated in the philosophies of his contemporaries as a means to their evaluation, by no means testifies to a dogmatic and uncritical confidence in that principle on Hegel's part, as Haym takes it to. For the discipline of Critique was understood by Hegel from the start to be complemented by a discipline providing a solution to the skeptical problem of equipollence which seemed to afflict his philosophical principle because of the availability of competing viewpoints. This solution pursued the strategy of showing competing viewpoints to be self-condemning or self-defeating. While Hegel was actively committed to the project of Critique and throughout most of the Jena period the discipline which provided this solution was his early Logic. By the end of the Jena period it was his *Phenomenology*.

Turning to the skeptical problem of concept-instantiation, we can easily see that Hegel was concerned from his early years in Jena to answer this problem on behalf of his own philosophical principle. For example, in *The Relation of Skepticism to Philosophy* he offers extensive criticism of what is in effect an attempt to apply a dogmatic version of the skeptical problem of concept-instantiation to the content of his own philosophical principle. This attempt is Schulze's objection that all metaphysical or "rational knowing aims ... at *plucking out* a being from a thinking or existence from concepts."[40]

Hegel was, then, indeed concerned from the early Jena period on that his own philosophical principle should meet the epistemological standard of being invulnerable to the skeptical problems of equipollence and concept-instantiation. Having touched on one strategy by means of which he hoped to ensure this invulnerability with respect to the equipollence problem in general, we should now give a more comprehensive indication of the network of defenses which he erected in order to defend his own philosophical system against these two skeptical problems.

Roughly speaking, Hegel's attempt to defend his philosophical system against the skeptical problems of equipollence and concept-instantiation works on two fronts. First, Hegel has answers to these problems which focus directly on alleged special characteristics of the content of his philosophical system. These answers take the form indicated in Part One of exploiting the thought that there are certain natural presuppositions which skeptics must make about any given claim to which they apply these problems, but which do not in fact hold for the claim which articulates Hegel's own system. Hegel already embraces these answers unequivocally in *The Relation of Skepticism to Philosophy*. Thus, as we noted, application of the equipollence problem to a claim presupposes that the claim has a negation. But despite the naturalness of this presupposition, Hegel holds it to be false of the single claim which articulates his own philosophical system.[41] And for this reason he supposes the equipollence problem to be inapplicable to that claim. This, in essence, is the point of his argument in *The Relation of Skepticism to Philosophy* that the claim of his own system, the Rational, does not fall victim to the version of the equipollence problem found in the fourth trope of Agrippa, which holds that an ungrounded presupposition faces the difficulty that its opposite may be presupposed in an ungrounded way with equal right, because the claim of his own system or the Rational "has no opposite." [42] Again, application of the concept-instantiation problem to a given concept presupposes that that concept is distinct from the things in the world which instantiate it in such a way that it could exist without having any such instantiation. This presupposition, though again natural, is one which Hegel holds to be false of the single concept which articulates the claim of his system. [43] For this reason he supposes the concept-instantiation problem to be inapplicable to that claim. This is Hegel's line of thought when in *The Relation of Skepticism to Philosophy* he counters Schulze's attempt to raise a concept-instantiation problem about the claim of his system by observing that Schulze's attempt rests on the dogma, untrue of that claim, that "concept and object are not one." [44] We shall take a closer look at this first front in Hegel's defense of his own philosophical system against the skeptical problems of equipollence and concept-instantiation in Chapter Seven.

The second front on which Hegel seeks to defend his system against the skeptical problems focuses directly on alleged special characteristics of viewpoints *other than* the viewpoint of his own system. It would seem that an equipollence problem or anything like it could arise for the claim of Hegel's own system only if there were coherent alternative viewpoints. As we have seen, Hegel holds that one alternative viewpoint essential to any application of the equipollence problem as standardly conceived to the claim of his own system does not exist: that claim's negation. But Hegel goes further than this in his effort to show that neither the equipollence problem nor anything like it could arise for his own claim, by undertaking to demonstrate that *there are no coherent alternative viewpoints whatever.* This is the fundamental strategy for answering the equipollence problem which we found advocated in both the *Phenomenology* and *On the Nature of Philosophical Critique*—the strategy described in the former text as one of showing that "consciousness provides its own criterion from within itself," a criterion with which it always stands in internal contradiction, and in the latter text as one of showing "how this negative side expresses itself and confesses its nothingness." Hegel thus envisages a demonstration of the "nothingness" or incoherence of all alternative viewpoints as a solution to the threat of equipollence problems or similar problems facing his system. In *The Relation of Skepticism to Philosophy* such a destructive demonstration is said to be an essential side of any genuine philosophy. [45] During the Jena period this destructive demonstration was given first in the early Logic and later in the *Phenomenology*. Somewhat analogously, Hegel offers a solution to the problem of concept-instantiation apparently threatening the concept of his own system which focuses immediately on alleged special characteristics of concepts other than that of this system. His strategy appears to be to show by an examination of these other concepts both that they do not constitute genuine alternatives to the concept of his system because they are incoherent or self-contradictory and that they exhibit indirectly, in a way to be explained later, the fact that the concept of his system is not distinct from its instantiation (the fact whose direct assertion was one of Hegel's defenses on the first front). The execution of this strategy for solving the concept-instantiation problem occurs in the same disciplines as the execution of the destructive strategy for solving the general equipollence problem: the early Logic during the first part of the Jena period and the *Phenomenology* at the end of that period. We shall take a closer look at this second front in Hegel's defense of his philosophical system against the threat of skepticism in Chapter Eight.

Of the pieces of prima facie evidence mentioned earlier for Hegel's carelessness about epistemological problems in general and skeptical problems in particular, the appearance of shameless dogmatism in his early method of Critique has already been shown to be illusory. We are now in a position to account for the rest of the prima facie evidence as well. Consider first Hegel's rejection of the "tendency to give and establish by grounds" typified in Reinhold's philosophy and his insistence that his own philosophy, far from seeking to ground its principle of identity, "does nothing but express and recognize that presupposed identity." Hegel's rejection of the attempt to ground or furnish a foundation for his own philosophy, in the sense of finding some premise or premises distinct from the claim of his philosophy or less than that claim in its entirety from which to argue in its favor, has two major sources.[46] These sources show that his rejection of such a grounding of philosophy is not at all indicative of a general carelessness about epistemology. One source of this rejection was mentioned earlier: Hegel does not see the circumstance of advancing a claim without further grounds per se as epistemologically problematic. To this extent he could accept the later Wittgenstein's judgment that "justification comes to an end."[47] He therefore does not see any unconditional epistemological need to ground his philosophy. What he does find epistemologically problematic is the, in his eyes importantly different, circumstance of making ungrounded claims *against which opposite claims can be advanced in a similarly ungrounded fashion,* which gives rise to the equipollence problem in its fourth trope of Agrippa version. But as we saw, Hegel believes that the claim of his own philosophy, though resting on no deeper grounds, escapes this epistemological problem because it has no negation and indeed no coherent alternatives. The second source of Hegel's rejection of any attempt to ground the claim of his own philosophy on a premise distinct from or less than itself is that he sees no possibility of doing so. The reason for this is ultimately his conviction that all claims other than or less than the complete claim of his own philosophy which might be used to ground the latter are incoherent. This conviction receives early expression in a difficult passage from *The Difference between the Fichtean and Schellingian Systems of Philosophy*, where Hegel explains that we should not think of the "need for philosophy," or those divisions in the contemporary world-view which it is the function of Hegel's philosophy to overcome, as a *presupposition* of philosophy, "since in this way this need receives the form of Reflection. This form of Reflection appears as contradictory propositions . . . One can demand of propositions that they justify themselves; the justification of these propositions, as presuppositions, is supposed not yet to be philosophy itself. And so the activity of establishing by and giving grounds (*Ergruenden und Begruenden*) begins/comes undone (*geht los*) before and outside of philosophy."[48] Hegel's thought here is somewhat as follows. If we attempt to treat the "need for philosophy" as a presupposition of philosophy, as a claim distinct from or less than the complete claim of philosophy upon which philosophy's claim is grounded, then precisely by distinguishing this claim from philosophy's, we turn it into something self-contradictory and thus useless for such a grounding of philosophy, since any claim distinct from or less than the claim of philosophy is self-contradictory. Moreover, any further proposition adduced in support of this presupposition, since it too must be distinct from or less than philosophy's claim, will be in the same unhappy condition. Hence the whole business of establishing philosophy by grounds or giving grounds for it both *begins* and *comes undone* before and outside philosophy. (Hegel here puns on several senses of the verb *losgehen*: "to begin," "to go off," in the sense of being detonated unintentionally, and "to come undone," said of a loose button for example.) Hegel's conviction that any claim distinct from or less than the claim of his own philosophy is self-contradictory is a corollary of his destructive strategy for overcoming the skeptical problem of equipollence by demonstrating all claims other than the single claim of his own philosophy to be self-contradictory. Thus this second source of Hegel's rejection of the idea of grounding his philosophy is no more indicative of a general carelessness about epistemology than was the first.

The final piece of prima facie evidence for Hegel's carelessness about epistemology was his rejection of the Kantian demand for a critical investigation of our faculty of knowledge in advance of its application, on the grounds that "the examination of knowledge can only be carried out by an act of knowledge" and that "to seek to know before we know is as absurd as the wise resolution of Scholasticus, not to venture into the water until he had learned to swim." Hegel's criticism of Kantian epistemology here is not really the naive suggestion that Kant is engaged in the obviously incoherent project of attempting to find out about (and hence necessarily acquire knowledge of) our faculty of knowledge in advance of applying it to anything.[49] For Hegel recognizes that Kant only requires an investigation of our faculty of knowledge to precede any application of this faculty to *metaphysical* subjects and there is no obvious incoherence in *this* requirement.[50] Part of Hegel's point is rather the far from naive criticism that the professed a priori character of the results of Kant's critical investigation seems to leave them among those synthetic a priori claims which, like those of metaphysics but unlike those of, for example, mathematics, by Kant's own account require the critical investigation of their possibility as knowledge to be completed before they can be legitimately made. This part of Hegel's point is thus directed against a specific weakness which he perceives in Kant's way of doing epistemology rather than against epistemology per se.

A second part of Hegel's point may be approached via an objection which he often raises against Kantian epistemology. This is the objection that it essentially rests upon various *presuppositions*.[51] Hegel means by this in the first instance that it rests on various claims accepted without deeper grounds which might be confronted with opposite claims made in the same way and therefore with equal right, or in other words that it succumbs to the fourth trope of Agrippa version of the skeptical equipollence problem. For example, in the *Phenomenology* Hegel accuses Kantian epistemology of "presupposing something—a great deal in fact—as truth, supporting its scruples and inferences on what is itself in need of prior scrutiny to see if it is true."[52] Likewise, in the Heidelberg *Encyclopedia* he speaks of Kant's "critical procedure, which above all ought to have investigated its own presuppositions."[53] In the Berlin *Encyclopedia* he gives one of his more plausible examples of the kind of presupposition Kant is guilty of: "The critical philosophy has in common with empiricism that it assumes experience to be the sole foundation of knowledge."[54] This point, that Kantian epistemology essentially rests upon presuppositions which are themselves vulnerable to the equipollence problems raised by the ancient skeptics, is a plausible and important one (irrespective of the extent to which Hegel successfully identifies the presuppositions). By itself, this basic objection of Hegel's against Kantian epistemology is enough to show that in rejecting it he is not motivated by any general indifference toward epistemology, that on the contrary he is motivated by taking very seriously indeed certain epistemological problems, namely those of the ancient skeptics.

But Hegel's objection that Kantian epistemology essentially rests upon presuppositions also helps to explain and show consistent with an interest in epistemology a further part of his criticism that "to seek to know before we know is as absurd as the wise resolution of Scholasticus, not to venture into the water until he had learned to swim." As we saw from *The Difference between the Fichtean and Schellingian Systems of Philosophy*, it is for Hegel ultimately an implication of saying that a claim is a presupposition that it is incoherent or self-contradictory. His suggestion that Kantian epistemology rests on presuppositions therefore ultimately implies that it rests on self-contradictory claims.[55] And from this we can infer that Hegel's likening of Kantian epistemology to an attempt to avoid entering the water before learning to swim expresses the following thoughts. First, just as the only way to learn to swim is by actually entering the water, so the only way to conduct an investigation into our faculty of knowledge is by entering the "water" of metaphysics straightaway.[56] Second, this is so because only the complete metaphysical claim expounded in Hegel's own system is true, and any other or lesser claim is self-contradictory and untrue. Third, as a corollary of these points, any attempt in a Kantian spirit to conduct an investigation of our faculty of cognition which is prior to or less than an exposition of Hegel's indivisible metaphysical truth is bound to come to grief on self-contradictoriness and falsehood, just as any attempt to learn to swim prior to entering the water is bound to fail. This criticism of Kantian epistemology rests squarely on Hegel's belief that he can show all claims other than or less than the complete claim of his own metaphysics to be self-contradictory. Since, as we have seen, this belief is a reflection of Hegel's strategy for defending his metaphysics against the skeptical problem of equipollence, clearly the criticism which it supports is not an expression of epistemological indifference on his part.

In short, then, none of the prima facie evidence for Hegel's lack of concern with epistemological problems amounts to *more* than that. Rather, it must all be understood against the background of a clearly conceived and deeply cherished antiskeptical project which Hegel is pursuing.

So far we have noted that Hegel accepted as standards of epistemological respectability for a philosophical system its invulnerability to the skeptical problems of equipollence in general and concept-instantiation in particular. And we have noted that he attempted to ensure this invulnerability for his own system by working on two fronts—the one front focusing on special features of the viewpoint of his own system, the other on special features of other viewpoints. These aspects of Hegel's epistemological enterprise remained largely constant from early in his Jena period throughout the remainder of his career. For all its importance, though, Hegel did not regard the task of answering skepticism on behalf of his own philosophical system as *exhaustive* of the task of making this system epistemologically secure. The texts of the Jena period in particular reveal that he accepted and strove to meet an additional standard of epistemological respectability as well. This standard included the very exacting demand that the viewpoint of his own system be provided with a way of eliminating even the *appearance* of a vulnerability to the skeptical problems of equipollence and concept-instantiation. Hegel alludes to this standard in the *Science of Logic* when he writes that the beginning of the Logic "is neither something arbitrary and only provisionally accepted nor something which appears arbitrary (*noch ein als willkuerlich Erscheinendes*)."[57] To be more specific, Hegel understands this additional standard to comprise three extraordinarily rigorous conditions. First, the elimination of the appearance of Philosophical Science's arbitrariness must take the form of providing it with a way of demonstrating its nonarbitrariness for each nonscientific viewpoint. Second, this demonstration of nonarbitrariness for each nonscientific viewpoint must show it that all nonscientific viewpoints are inferior to Philosophical Science, so that Philosophical Science faces no equipollence problem; that Philosophical Science confronts no concept-instantiation problem; and that Philosophical Science is true. Third, there must be a *demonstration* of these circumstances *for* each nonscientific viewpoint in the sense of a proof which is completely compelling for each viewpoint entirely on the basis of views and criteria to which it is already committed. Let us for short refer to a procedure which satisfies these conditions as *a proof of Philosophical Science for all nonscientific viewpoints*.

This complex and demanding epistemological standard underlies Hegel's statements in the *Phenomenology* that "the intelligible form of Science is the way open and equally accessible to everyone, and consciousness as it approaches Science justly demands that it be able to attain to rational knowledge by way of the ordinary Understanding," and that "the individual has the right to demand that Science should at least provide him with the ladder to this standpoint [Science's], should show him this standpoint within himself."[58] These statements are the most explicit avowals of a commitment to the standard in question in Hegel's texts. Beyond them his commitment to this standard must be inferred from the fact that the details of his texts, above all of the *Phenomenology*, seem designed to meet it.

In coming to accept this standard of epistemological respectability during the Jena period, as in much of his epistemology, Hegel was sharply deviating from the views of his erstwhile philosophical ally Schelling. For Schelling did not see the construction of a bridge between nonscientific viewpoints and Philosophical Science as necessary or even desirable. Thus contrast with the preceding passages from the *Phenomenology* the following statement by Schelling in his *Further Presentations from the System of Philosophy*, written roughly five years before the *Phenomenology*: "It is unintelligible . . . why philosophy should have an obligation to be considerate of incapacity, it is rather appropriate to cut off the approach to [philosophy] sharply and to isolate it on all sides from common cognition in such a way that no path or pavement can lead from [common cognition] to [philosophy]. Here begins philosophy, and whoever is not already there or is afraid to reach this point—let him stay away or flee back." [59]

It is not entirely clear what considerations moved Hegel to embrace this demanding epistemological standard. Perhaps he was influenced by the reflection that the ancient skeptics did not assert that anyone's doctrines *really* fell victim to the problems of equipollence or concept-instantiation but only that they *appeared* to the skeptics to do so, with the result that his demonstration that his own Philosophical Science did not *really* succumb to such problems still left him with the task of eliminating the *appearance* that it did so. Perhaps the focus on the authority of viewpoints other than one's own which was involved in the equipollence problem made this additional epistemological ideal attractive to him. Whatever the exact origin of this epistemological standard may have been, it does have considerable intrinsic appeal and complements the other epistemological standards which Hegel accepts.

At the end of the Jena period, in the *Phenomenology,* Hegel made his most earnest and explicit attempt to meet this additional epistemological standard of providing a proof of Philosophical Science for all nonscientific viewpoints. During the Jena period as a whole his degree of commitment to this standard, his conception of what exactly would be required in order to meet it, and his strategy for meeting it underwent constant and rapid change. This is seen primarily by reading the *Phenomenology* alongside the several versions of the early Logic which preceded it. Such instability contrasts with the relative stability over the same years of the other parts of his epistemological enterprise. The trend during the Jena period was toward a deeper commitment to the standard in question, a more exacting conception of what would be required in order to meet it, and a correspondingly more scrupulous and ambitious strategy for doing so. Recognizing this trend enables one to make sense of many otherwise bewildering changes which Hegel's philosophy underwent at this time, particularly in the disciplines of the early Logic and the *Phenomenology.* They become intelligible as reflections of an unfolding epistemological enterprise having a coherent direction of development. We shall chart the course of Hegel's developing attempts to meet his additional epistemological standard in Chapter Nine.

How, in general terms, does Hegel propose to meet this additional epistemological standard on behalf of his own Philosophical Science? We can distinguish two major components of his strategy for doing so. First, he takes the systematic demonstration of the self-contradictoriness of all nonscientific claims and concepts which constitutes the core of his solution on one front to the skeptical problems of equipollence and concept-instantiation and he attempts to make this demonstration compelling for all nonscientific viewpoints themselves on the basis of their own views and criteria. We can detect this aim in two passages considered earlier where Hegel describes his destructive solution to the problem of equipollence. Thus the *Phenomenology* says that "consciousness provides its own criterion from within itself, so that the investigation becomes *a comparison of consciousness with itself.*"[60] And *On the Nature of Philosophical Critique* says that "there is nothing to do but to recount how this negative side expresses itself and *confesses* its nothingness" and that, in its development, this negative side "can be *pretty generally recognized* as [nothing]."[61]

The second component of Hegel's strategy is to demonstrate to all the self-contradictory nonscientific viewpoints in a way compelling for them on the basis of their own views and criteria that his Philosophical Science is true. This ambition is perhaps already expressed in the remark from *The Difference between the Fichtean and Schellingian Systems of Philosophy* that "the Absolute should be constructed for consciousness."[62] It receives more explicit expression, and is more clearly pursued, in the *Phenomenology*, where Hegel says that "the individual has the right to demand that Science should at least provide him with the ladder to this standpoint, should show him this standpoint within himself."[63] It was because Hegel accepted the realization of this proof of the truth of Philosophical Science for all nonscientific viewpoints as part of a standard of epistemological respectability that he could, notwithstanding his criticism of the "tendency to give and establish by grounds" that in attempting to prove Philosophical Science on the basis of something other than or less than itself this tendency would fall into the absurdity of attempting to prove Philosophical Science by grounding it on self-contradictions, claim that the method of the *Phenomenology* was "to begin from the first, simplest appearance of Spirit, the immediate consciousness, and to develop Spirit's dialectic up to the standpoint of Philosophical Science, the necessity of which is demonstrated by this process."[64] That is to say, the process referred to here of showing Philosophical Science to be somehow implied by lesser perspectives is not supposed to support the claim of Philosophical Science's truth, to "demonstrate" its "necessity," by grounding it on something other and more secure than itself. Rather it is supposed to do so by showing that the standard of epistemological respectability that the truth of Philosophical Science should be provable for all nonscientific perspectives on the basis of their own views and criteria can be met.

Much in Hegel's epistemological enterprise makes essential use of his notorious dialectical method. This is true, for example, of his demonstration that all nonscientific concepts and claims are self-contradictory, which is a central part of his response to the skeptical problems of equipollence and concept-instantiation. It is also true of both sides of his proof of Philosophical Science for all nonscientific viewpoints. Indeed the dialectical method was initially developed by Hegel in the early Logic of the Jena period largely because of the roles which it was to play within his epistemological project. After indicating more fully what these roles are during the coming chapters, I shall make a few remarks on the nature and value of the dialectical method itself in Chapter Ten. These remarks should serve as both a further clarification of Hegel's epistemological project and a first step toward its evaluation.

So Hegel was concerned with epistemology after all, and indeed from a very early date in his philosophical career. He had a set of clear, sensible, and rigorous standards of epistemological adequacy and made strenuous and original efforts to meet them on behalf of his own philosophical system. We may now turn to the details of the various parts of Hegel's epistemological project indicated in this chapter.

SEVEN

Two Defenses against Skepticism

W E HAVE seen that Hegel proposed in *The Relation of Skepticism to Philosophy* to solve the skeptical problems of equipollence and concept-instantiation for the claim of his own system, the Rational, by means of the doctrines that "the Rational has no opposite" and that it is untrue of the Rational that "concept and being are not one." In this chapter I propose to do three things. First, I shall say something about the influences which brought Hegel to adopt these enigmatic doctrines. Second, I shall show that while he originally adopted them as answers to skepticism in the context of his first confrontation with skepticism during the early Jena period, they were not given up later and remained fundamental tenets of his mature metaphysics. Third, I shall consider some questions and objections which might be raised concerning their ability to answer skepticism, with a view thereby to clarifying further the nature of Hegel's position.

Let us first consider how Hegel was influenced to adopt the doctrine that in the case of the Rational it is false to say that concept and being are not one—the doctrine that concept and being are in this case absolutely identical.[1] (More or less equivalent in Hegel's eyes are the doctrines that in the case of the Rational concept and object, thought and being, subject and object, and so forth are absolutely identical.) This doctrine is deployed in *The Relation of Skepticism to Philosophy* to thwart a range of skeptical opponents who share, and base one or another variant of the skeptical concept-instantiation problem upon, the assumption of a general distinctness of concepts from the things in the world which they depict of a kind making possible the existence of any concept in the absence of instantiation.[2] It is by no means a doctrine which Hegel artificially concocted solely for the purpose of having something to say in reply to the skeptics. In fact, it was not his invention at all but rather an implication of Schelling's philosophy of identity taken over by Hegel when he adopted that philosophy. Consider, for example, Schelling's slighting reference in his *Bruno* of 1802 to "finite cognition, which keeps object and concept . . . distinct from one another."[3] The original motives behind the philosophy of identity were diverse for both Schelling and Hegel. Something of this diversity is revealed in Hegel's description in *The Difference between the Fichtean and Schellingian Systems of Philosophy* of the various contemporary dualisms and divisions which constitute the "need for philosophy" and which the unifying principle of the philosophy of identity is supposed to overcome.[4] Epistemological motives seem initially to have played a very minor role for both Schelling and Hegel, and Hegel's achievement was to recognize quickly and exploit the antiskeptical resources of a theory already found attractive on other grounds.[5]

However, the credit for being the first to see the antiskeptical potential of a theory like the philosophy of identity belongs neither to Schelling nor to Hegel but to their friend Hoelderlin who developed the prototype of that philosophy in such pieces as *Judgment and Being*. Important in this connection is the following passage from a letter Hoelderlin wrote to Schiller in 1795: "I am trying to show that the indispensable demand which must be made of any system, the unification of subject and object in an absolute—self or however one wants to call it—is certainly aesthetically possible in intellectual intuition, but theoretically only in an unending approximation . . . I believe that I can thereby prove to what extent the skeptics are right and to what extent not."[6] Of special interest here is Hoelderlin's claim that he can show the skeptics to be partly mistaken as well as partly right. In order to interpret this sibylline statement, we must have recourse to a text written at about the same time and under Hoelderlin's immediate influence by his friend von Sinclair. In his *Philosophical Reasonings* von Sinclair characterizes skepticism as a standpoint which insists on holding apart the two sides of the oppositions subject-object, self-world.[7] He holds that the goal of philosophy is to achieve complete certainty, which would be to answer the skeptic.[8] If this certainty were achievable at all, he argues, it could be attained only by ceasing to hold apart the two sides of those oppositions on which the skeptic insists and instead recognizing just a unity.[9] This is impossible, however, since it involves the self-contradictory ideal of positing for a self a unity in which the self as such has been overcome.[10] For this reason the demand for certainty remains "an infinite task, the satisfaction of which, if one attempted it, would contradict itself."[11] These remarks of von Sinclair's allow us to understand Hoelderlin's letter and his suggestion that the skeptics are partly right but also partly wrong. For Hoelderlin, as for von Sinclair, the skeptics are partly right for the following reason. Their taunt that we cannot achieve certainty essentially rests on

an assumption of the subject-object opposition and could only be answered by a knowledge which overcame this opposition.[12] But this overcoming is impossible in *theoretical* knowledge because such knowledge
necessarily posits the opposition. So to this extent the skeptics' taunt
carries the day. How though are the skeptics partly wrong? For Hoelderlin at least there is an alternative to theoretical knowledge, namely
aesthetic knowledge or intellectual intuition, and this kind of knowledge
succeeds in overcoming the subject-object opposition in a unity and
thereby achieves the certainty which the skeptics challenge us to achieve.
So to this extent the skeptics' challenge is met, and the skeptics are answered. It is fair to assume that Hegel inherited from Hoelderlin certain
fundamental ideas guiding his own use against skepticism of the doctrine
of the absolute identity of concept and being or subject and object in the
unity of the Absolute, namely the ideas that skepticism presupposes a
division between subject and object, that a kind of knowledge which
overcame that division would therefore undermine skepticism, and that
we can have a knowledge of the Absolute which is of just this kind.

   Let us now consider what influenced Hegel to adopt the doctrine that
"the Rational has no opposite." Unlike the previous doctrine this one has
no exact precedent in Schelling's work. However, if we bear in mind the
influence which we have seen Hoelderlin's philosophy to have had on
Hegel perhaps we can trace its provenance. The metaphysical theory preserved in Hoelderlin's *Judgment and Being* bears a striking resemblance
to that found in Parmenides' poem and must have been developed in
conscious imitation of it. Thus, on the one hand, Hoelderlin's account
has an initially undifferentiated Being succumb to an original division
into the opposition between subject and object, which opposition von
Sinclair at least describes as a contradiction.[13] On the other hand, Parmenides' account holds that only an undifferentiated Being really is,
though mortals draw a distinction between what is and what is not, notwithstanding the incoherence involved in the notion of not-being, and
construct an imaginary world articulated out of this opposition they have
posited.[14] My suggestion is that Hegel's doctrine that the Rational has no
negation was probably influenced, at first via Hoelderlin's metaphysics,
by the Parmenidean doctrine of the incoherence of the notion of not-
being.[15] Supporting this hypothesis is the fact that in the *History of Philosophy* Hegel quotes and expounds Parmenides' argument for this
incoherence with evident approval: "The nothing, in fact, turns into
something, since it is thought or is said: we say something, think something, if we wish to think and say the nothing. 'It is necessary that saying
and thinking should be Being; for Being is, but nothing is not at all.'
There the matter is stated in brief.[16] Further supporting the hypothesis is
the clear influence of this Parmenidean argument for the incoherence of

the notion of not-being on Hegel's own argument for the self-contradictoriness of the category Nothing in his later Logic.[17] It is here, in Hegel's mature argument for the self-contradictoriness of the category Nothing (or Not-being), that his considered case for the principle that the Rational has no negation is to be found, if anywhere. We may suppose then that Hegel originally accepted Parmenides' doctrine of the incoherence of the notion of not-being, along with his argument for it, and that this formed the initial basis of Hegel's own doctrine that "the Rational has no opposite" and the inspiration of his mature argument in support of this doctrine.

Both of the Hegelian doctrines with which we are concerned made their first appearance in Hegel's thought early in the Jena period at about the time when he was most preoccupied with skepticism, and they were understood by him more or less from the start as bulwarks defending his philosophy against the skeptical problems of equipollence and concept-instantiation. However, they did not simply disappear from Hegel's metaphysics once this period of his greatest preoccupation with skepticism was past. Rather, they remained in place in later writings as part of a standing network of defenses against the skeptic.

Let us first consider a later formulation of the doctrine that "the Rational has no opposite." This doctrine's initial statement in *The Relation of Skepticism to Philosophy* reads in full: "The Rational has no opposite, it subsumes the finite items, of which one is the opposite of the other, together within itself."[18] A few years later in the *Phenomenology* Hegel, inveighing against the generally held view that the notions of truth and falsehood are determinate ones, wholly distinct and having nothing in common, argues that there is no such thing as the false, since "the false . . . would be the other, the negative of the substance, which as the content of knowledge is the true. But the substance is itself essentially the negative."[19] In other words, there is no negation of the substance or Absolute; negation is essentially subsumed within the substance, or is "itself directly present in the true as such."[20] This account in the *Phenomenology* expresses very much the same view as the passage from *The Relation of Skepticism to Philosophy*. In both texts Hegel denies that there is a negation of (the expression of) the Absolute, somehow restricting negation to relations of opposition between various elements, such as categories, which are synthesized and subsumed within the Absolute as its essential articulation. Thus the *Phenomenology* remains faithful to the doctrine of *The Relation of Skepticism to Philosophy* that "the Rational has no opposite."[21]

The presence in later texts of the doctrine that there is an absolute identity of concept and being, concept and object, thought and being, subject and object, and so forth in the Absolute is still more evident. Thus the *Science of Logic,* in which Hegel undertakes to unfold "the absolute, self-subsistent object, the logos, the reason of that which is, the truth of what we call things," is said to contain "thought in so far as this is just as much the object in its own self, or the object in its own self in so far as it is equally pure thought." [22] And in this text Hegel repeatedly emphasizes the overcoming of the distinctions between thought and object, thought and being, concept and being, concept and reality, and subject and object. [23] Again, in the *Encyclopedia* he states that in the system of categories which expounds the Absolute Idea in the Logic "the opposition between subjective and objective . . . vanishes." [24] The same doctrine plays a large role in the remarks in defense of the ontological argument which he makes in the *Lectures on the Proofs of God's Existence* shortly before his death. [25]

We should now consider certain questions and objections which might be raised concerning Hegel's two doctrines in their role as answers to skepticism in order to clarify Hegel's position further. The first question concerns the exact nature of the Rational which Hegel's two antiskeptical doctrines are supposed to characterize. So far we know little *more* about it than that it has the characteristics specified in these doctrines— namely of being a kind of philosophical claim lacking a negation and articulated by a concept absolutely identical with its object. The Rational, as understood in Hegel's final system, is the Absolute Idea expounded in his later Logic. Hegel understands this Absolute Idea to be the divine logos which is "the essential being of all [other matters]," in particular of natural and spiritual phenomena which are in some sense merely forms of its appearance, or "only a particular mode of expression for the form of pure thought." [26] In the Logic it is expounded in abstraction from its appearance in natural and spiritual phenomena, or in Hegel's words, as "God as he is in his eternal essence before the creation of Nature and a finite Spirit." [27] This Absolute Idea consists of a dialectically self-developing, ascending series of lesser categories, culminating in the Absolute Idea itself which, in addition to encompassing the sequence, recognizes itself within it. [28] The dialectically developing, ascending series of lesser categories begins with Being and the other relatively objective and inadequate categories which follow it in the Objective Logic and ascends through the relatively subjective and adequate categories found in the Subjective Logic, including, for example, the category of the Concept. The series is dialectically self-developing in the sense that the transition from one category to the next proceeds through steps of making explicit a self-contradiction contained within the first category and resolving it in a supposedly necessary transition to the next category. The lesser categories which constitute the content of the Absolute Idea have it as their foundation and arc implicitly one with it. [29] In the sense that the self-development of the content of the Absolute Idea concludes with the latter's recognition of itself in the whole course of that self-development, and so with a sort of review of that course of self-development, the end of this self-development returns us to its beginning, Being.[30] Such, then, is Hegel's conception of the Rational as articulated in his mature system. It is to the Rational in this sense that Hegel applies his two antiskeptical doctrines, claiming that it is neither conceptual nor objective, neither thought nor reality, but somehow the absolute identity of both, and that it subsumes negation within itself in the form of the self-contradictory categories which articulate it, but without itself having a negation.

Second, we might consider the objection to Hegel's two antiskeptical doctrines that they are simply too metaphysically extravagant and implausible to be interesting as answers to skepticism. As far as the doctrine of the absolute identity of concept and object in the Absolute is concerned, it is important to draw the following distinction in response to this objection. On the one hand, there are the insight into the nature of skepticism and the general strategy advocated against the skeptic in light of this insight which are involved in Hegel's deployment of this doctrine against skepticism. These might be interesting or persuasive even if the doctrine itself were not. On the other hand, there is the doctrine itself, as a means chosen by Hegel for the execution of that general antiskeptical strategy, but possibly replaceable in that role by some less extravagant and correspondingly more credible doctrine.

The basic insight into the nature of skepticism which Hegel exploits is that skepticism assumes a general distinction between concepts and their instances in the world of such a kind that any concept could exist in the absence of instances, that is, without having or ever having had instances. The general strategy against the skeptic which Hegel bases on this insight is to show that this assumption is false. Hegel proposes to do this by way of his doctrine of the absolute identity of concept and object in the Absolute, but the history of philosophy contains less grandiose and correspondingly more plausible views which equally imply the falsity of this skeptical assumption and which might therefore replace Hegel's doctrine in pursuit of the same antiskeptical strategy. For example, there is an Aristotelian tradition according to which it is in the very nature of the descriptive concepts or meanings which articulate thought and receive expression in language that they be analyzable into some basic stock of concepts or meanings which exist by virtue of applying to things, properties, relations, and the like *actually found in the world*. On this theory it is metaphysically impossible that a descriptive concept should exist which neither had instances nor was analyzable into concepts which had instances.[31] This Aristotelian view was recognized to have antiskeptical implications by Descartes, who appealed to it as part of a provisional response to his dream skepticism in the *First Meditation* (though only to sweep it aside by means of his next wave of skeptical argument, the hypothesis of an evil genius).[32] Thus, where Hegel will object to the skeptic who attempts to raise a general concept-instantiation problem that when one understands the nature of the concept of the Absolute, one sees that no concept-instantiation problem can arise concerning it because there is no distinction between the concept of the Absolute and the Absolute itself, the Aristotelian can object to the same skeptic that when one understands the nature of concepts or meanings *in general,* one sees that no general concept-instantiation problem can arise because the nature of concepts or meanings in general is such that at least the members of the basic stock of primitive concepts have instances in the world.

Third, let us consider an objection which might be raised against using either the Hegelian or the corresponding Aristotelian doctrine as an answer to skepticism.[33] It might be objected that these doctrines constitute extremely weak replies to the skeptic since, whatever kind of skeptic he is, when confronted with one of these doctrines, he will simply apply his own skepticism to it. The equipollence skeptic, for example, will just respond, "Well, these doctrines about the nature of the concept of the Absolute and about the nature of concepts in general are interesting, but I must tell you that I have at hand certain equally plausible, incompatible accounts of these matters, and once we have seen how your accounts and mine share equal strength, we shall realize that the only reasonable course of action is to suspend judgment." And the Cartesian skeptic will respond, "Yes, the doctrines are interesting, but I can think of grounds for doubting them which cannot be conclusively removed, and must therefore withhold my assent from them." Indeed this is effectively what Descartes' skeptic *does* say when the Aristotelian doctrine is brought forward against skepticism in the *First Meditation.*[34] However, Hegel and the antiskeptical Aristotelian have resources for meeting such a skeptical counterattack.

There is a feature of Hegel's doctrine of the absolute identity of concept and object, thought and being, in the Absolute which has not yet been mentioned and which becomes important in this connection. This is his claim that it is impossible to have a genuine grasp of the concept of the Absolute without recognizing the truth of this doctrine, that one cannot even have a genuine thought about the Absolute without recognizing the error in distinguishing between the concept of the Absolute and the Absolute's being. Thus in the *Lectures on the Proofs of God's Existence* Hegel notes with approval that "Spinoza defines the concept of God in such a way that He is that which cannot be conceived of without being," and both Spinoza and Descartes hold that "God as concept cannot be understood without being."[35] If asked to explain further this claim concerning the grasp of the concept of the Absolute, Hegel might follow Spinoza in drawing an analogy with such circumstances as the apparent impossibility of having a clear concept of a triangle without affirming that a triangle's internal angles must add up to the sum of two right angles.[36] But Hegel's explanation would go much further than merely using this kind of Spinozistic analogy. In the *Lectures on the Proofs of God's Existence* Hegel hints at the ultimate reason why in his view it is impossible to grasp the concept of the Absolute without recognizing its absolute identity with the being of the Absolute: "The determination of Being is in the Concept itself."[37] This is a reference to the essential structure of Hegel's concept of the Absolute—the Absolute Idea or the Concept, as he sometimes refers to it. (Although the Concept strictly occupies a lowlier position in the Subjective Logic than the Absolute Idea with which the Subjective Logic culminates, Hegel in practice rarely draws a sharp distinction between the two; hence, for example, he subtitles the whole Subjective Logic "The Doctrine of the Concept.") This essential structure is expounded in his later Logic, where the essential dialectical self-exposition of the Absolute Idea or Concept is ultimately seen, in the return to Being at the end of the work, to embrace, or articulate the Absolute Idea or Concept as, Being. At this point Being is presented as what it is in its truth: the Absolute Idea or "the Concept in the form of Being."[38] Since grasping the concept of the Absolute—the Absolute Idea or Concept—in Hegel's view just *is* grasping its self-exposition as presented in the Logic, it follows that it would be impossible for someone to possess the concept of the Absolute and yet fail to see its inclusion of or identity with Being.

Hegel's adherence to this claim about the concept of the Absolute being intelligible only to those who understand its absolute identity with the Absolute's being shows that he would not be in the least perturbed by the kind of response to his doctrine of the absolute identity of concept and object, thought and being, in the Absolute which we envisaged the equipollence or Cartesian skeptic making. For to the extent that such a response testifies to the skeptic's failure to believe the doctrine, it equally testifies in Hegel's view to his failure to have the concept of, to have a thought about, the Absolute at all, and therefore to his failure to understand Hegel's doctrine, since the articulation of this doctrine essentially employs the concept of the Absolute. The skeptic cannot even get as far as being skeptical about Hegel's doctrine, since in order understand it, he would have to believe it. What at first sight appeared to be a skeptical challenge to the doctrine turns out to be no more than the skeptic's falling into incoherence or talking at cross-purposes about something else.[39]

The Aristotelians might make a similar response to the skeptic's counterattack. They might argue that, in order to have a genuine concept of a thought, concept, or meaning, one has to recognize the fundamental aspects of the nature of thoughts, concepts, or meanings to which they have drawn our attention.[40] On this view, the skeptic who seemed to suspend judgment on the Aristotelian thesis that any descriptive concept must either have instances or be analyzable into concepts having instances would in fact not even be grasping the concept of a concept and so would not even be comprehending the Aristotelian thesis, let alone genuinely taking a skeptical attitude toward it.[41] It would seem, then, that Hegel and the Aristotelians are by no means defenseless against the skeptical counterattack which was intended to thwart the application of their antiskeptical doctrines.[42]

Fourth, let us consider another objection which might be raised against Hegel's two doctrines as answers to skepticism. Having followed his confrontation with the skeptic up to this point, someone might object that Hegel has unwittingly maneuvered himself into an unsavory dilemma. When he took up the cudgels against the skeptic it seemed as though Hegel, like the skeptic and the rest of us, was interested in *epistemological* issues. Epistemology is concerned in the first instance with knowledge and then with such matters as beliefs, propositions, concepts, how things really are, and truth. Given these circumstances, it seems that Hegel, in introducing his two doctrines about the absolute identity of concept and object in the Rational and about the Rational having no negation, faces the dilemma that he is either falling into incoherence or changing the subject and ceasing to address the epistemological questions in which the skeptic and the rest of us were initially interested. The reason is that his two doctrines violate certain principles essential to the concepts which constitute the discourse of epistemology. For example, it is part of the very concept of a proposition that it have a negation, part of the very concept of a belief or judgment that it be articulated by a proposition having a negation, and part of the very concept of knowledge that it involve a belief articulated in a proposition having a negation. Again, it is part of our very concept of a concept that it be something distinct from what it represents (except perhaps in a few unmysteriously self-referential cases, such as the concept of a concept), and it is part of our very concept of things really being a certain way that they be that way independently of the concepts we use to describe them.

Hegel's first response to this objection would, I think, be to impale himself willingly on one horn of the dilemma. Thus he is himself clearly aware of, and indeed insistent upon, the fact that he in the manner indicated violates principles belonging to the essence of the concepts we normally use in epistemology, and while he naturally denies that this leads him to incoherence, he is happy to accept the alternative that it leads him to change the subject.[43] But having in this way impaled himself on the latter horn of the dilemma, Hegel would go on to argue that this horn is not at all damaging to him, appearances notwithstanding. He would claim that his wholesale change of the meanings of key terms during the course of the investigation of epistemological matters is justified for two main reasons. On the one hand, he would argue, *some* such change of concepts is required because the concepts with which the epistemological discussion begins and to which our imaginary objector would have him remain faithful prove to be incoherent and therefore bad concepts to use.[44] On the other hand, he would argue, the particular new concepts which he introduces in place of the old incoherent ones have the merits, first, that they, unlike the old concepts and indeed unlike any thinkable alternatives, are alone self-consistent and, second, that they are analogous to the old concepts in various ways, the *Aufhebungen* of those concepts in the sense not only of being the results of their destruction and of the ascent to a higher conceptual level but also in the sense of being in some degree their *preservation,* so that their introduction into the epistemological discussion is not simply arbitrary.[45]

Faced with Hegel's bold response to the dilemma, the objector might of course change his objection somewhat, suggesting that Hegel is not really entitled to opt for the softer change-of-subject horn of the dilemma but belongs instead on the sharper horn of incoherence. The objector might say that Hegel is simply wrong to think that he has developed a set of new and self-consistent concepts with which to replace the old ones. Hegel's claims that thought and being, concept and object, are absolutely identical in the Rational and that the Rational has no negation rather involve just an incoherent use of the old familiar concepts and a mere illusion of new, coherent meaningfulness.[46] Such objections as this are among the most urgent that arise in connection with Hegel's philosophy. Without judging their merits, I would note that in the absence of much supporting argument they prove virtually impossible to evaluate due to the fact that our criteria for deciding in hard cases whether someone else possesses concepts which we ourselves lack, as Hegel in effect often says he does, rather than being merely a mangler of our own concepts or an utterer of meaningless sounds are complex, obscure, and vague. In sum, then, Hegel does have certain resources for answering the charge that he either falls into incoherence or else changes the subject during the course of the epistemological debate.

· E I G H T ·

Further Defenses against Skepticism

H EGEL answers the problems of equipollence and concept-instantiation not only by focusing directly on special characteristics of the Rational, the viewpoint of his own Philosophical Science, but also by focusing directly on special characteristics of the nonscientific viewpoints which appear to compete with Philosophical Science. In this chapter we shall be concerned with the latter focus, first as it bears on the equipollence problem, and then as it bears on the concept-instantiation problem.

The guiding idea behind Hegel's answer to the skeptical equipollence problem focusing on nonscientific viewpoints remained constant from his early Jena days until the end of his life. This idea, which we earlier identified in both *On the Nature of Philosophical Critique* and the *Phenomenology*, is that one can overcome the problem of equipollence on behalf of Philosophical Science by showing that all other viewpoints are self-contradictory or, as Hegel sometimes puts it, "nothing." Hegel articulates this idea about how the problem may be solved not only in the early texts mentioned but also, for example, in the *Lectures on the Proofs of God's Existence,* written shortly before his death.[1] It is an original Hegelian contribution to the history of epistemology.[2]

How, in general terms, does Hegel propose to realize this goal of showing all nonscientific viewpoints to be self-contradictory or nothing? His views on how this should be done once again exhibit a fundamental continuity from the early Jena period through the rest of his career. First, he sees that this goal cannot be achieved by focusing the attack directly on the infinitely expandable stock of nonscientific claims themselves. It is rather necessary to concentrate on the more manageable finite stock of *basic categories, forms of judgment, forms of inference, or similarly fundamental items* through which all nonscientific claims are and must be articulated. Hegel expresses this policy in the essay *On the Scientific*

Ways of Treating Natural Law from 1802–1803 when he says that the proof of the nullity of finite claims "is presented most convincingly by showing the unreal basis and ground from which they grow, and whose flavor and nature they absorb."[3] Thus in a sketch of his early Logic dating from 1801–2 Hegel proposes to consider and destroy the finite Understanding in respect of its "concepts, judgments, and syllogisms," while in *The Relation of Skepticism to Philosophy* he praises and takes as a model for his own destructive discipline Plato's *Parmenides* because it "encompasses the whole sphere [of finite cognition] through concepts of the Understanding and destroys it."[4] In the *Phenomenology* the fundamental items chosen for destruction are "shapes of consciousness" rather than the concepts, forms of judgment, and syllogisms mentioned in earlier texts, but they share with the latter items the property of being understood by Hegel as media through which all nonscientific claims are and must be articulated.

Second, Hegel insists that the destruction of nonscientific claims in this indirect manner must be *exhaustive,* covering not only those claims which we happen to have encountered or which we happen to have the mental power to imagine, but all the nonscientific claims there are or could be. Thus he says that the destructive treatment should be "exhaustive as regards the determinate," that it should encompass and destroy "the whole sphere [of finite cognition]."[5] He insists on this because he wants to eliminate even the possibility that Philosophical Science might find itself confronted by a coherent alternative viewpoint and so succumb to an equipollence problem. He is pursuing the epistemological equivalent of a scorched earth policy. Because of his indirect method of attacking nonscientific claims via the basic categories or similar items which are required in order to articulate them, this demand for the destruction of all actual and possible nonscientific claims becomes a demand for the destruction of all actual and possible nonscientific categories or similar items (i.e. not only those we have encountered or can imagine for ourselves).

Third, in pursuit of this ideal of demonstrating exhaustiveness Hegel wishes to show that the basic categories or similar items destroyed not only include all those which we can find or imagine to ourselves and which form the essential basis of all claims we can find or imagine to ourselves, but also constitute a complete, connected *system.* Thus in *The Relation of Skepticism to Philosophy* Hegel praises the Platonic *Parmenides* as a "system of genuine skepticism."[6]

Fourth, the destruction of all nonscientific claims via a destruction of all the nonscientific basic categories or similar items required in order to articulate them must take the form of showing the latter to be *self-contradictory* and therefore a guarantee of the self-contradictoriness of the former.[7] Such, then, is the general form of Hegel's attempts during various periods of his career to demonstrate the self-contradictoriness or nothingness of all nonscientific viewpoints in order to defend Philosophical Science against equipollence objections.

This general characterization of Hegel's destructive strategy prompts two questions. First, how does he propose to demonstrate the self-contradictoriness of the nonscientific basic categories or similar items? The concise answer to this question is: by means of his notorious dialectical method. A more informative answer would demand an examination of that method, and I defer this until Chapter Ten. Second, how exactly does he propose to demonstrate the exhaustiveness of the inventory of nonscientific basic categories or similar items which he destroys? In particular, how is the demonstration that they constitute a complete, connected system supposed to contribute to this, and how is it to be shown that they do in fact constitute such a system? A full answer to this second question would again demand an investigation of the dialectical method, but in advance of that we can usefully give an outline answer here.

Hegel's proposal to demonstrate the exhaustiveness of his inventory of basic categories or similar items by demonstrating their constitution of a complete, connected system rests on the following plausible idea. If the list of categories or similar items at which we arrive by examining the conceptual activity with which we are acquainted and by employing our imaginative estimation of conceptual possibilities can be shown to characterize such a system, then it is a reasonable assumption that we have listed all the basic categories or similar items there are and that the limits of our conceptual acquaintance and imagination coincide with the limits of conceptual possibility. We can be reasonably confident that we will not and could not at some future date find ourselves confronted by an additional category or similar item which we had missed or which was discovered or invented subsequently.

To this extent Hegel's solution to the problem of exhaustiveness reproduces a solution of Kant's to a similar problem. Thus in the *Prolegomena to Any Future Metaphysics* Kant explains how he began his investigation of the categories equipped with the traditional inventory of such items drawn up on the basis of contingent observations. This gave him a mere "aggregate" which he only "believed" to be "completely collected." In order to "know" of these categories, or of a list derived from them, that "just so many, neither more nor less, can constitute this kind of cognition," he had to derive them as a "system." For Kant, though not for Hegel, this was a matter of deriving them "from a principle a priori"— the principle in question being the logical forms of judgment.[8]

Reinhold adopted and adapted the Kantian ideal of showing the categories to form a complete system by deriving them from a higher, epistemologically secure principle which determined and made intelligible their organization as a system, giving it a central place in his conception of how Kantian philosophy should be presented as a systematic science. And Fichte, largely under the immediate influence of Reinhold, made Kant's strategy of demonstrating exhaustiveness by way of complete systematicity and complete systematicity by way of derivation from a higher, epistemologically secure principle into a basic component of his own philosophy.[9] Thus in *On the Concept of the Science of Knowledge* Fichte expresses the concern that in philosophy "human cognition in general should be exhausted," including not only "what man can know at his present level of existence but at all possible and thinkable levels of existence."[10] And he advocates as an essential means to the accomplishment of this end that philosophy be based on a "fundamental principle" (*Grundsatz*) which is demonstrably exhausted, having a "complete system built upon it."[11] Accordingly, in his *Science of Knowledge* itself Fichte professes to present an idealism which will "really deduce the system of the necessary modes [of the intellect] . . . from the fundamental laws of the intellect," and he attempts to deduce this system from the epistemologically secure fundamental principle of the deed or *Tathandlung* of the self's self-positing.[12] When Hegel writes in *The Difference between the Fichtean and Schellingian Systems of Philosophy* that Kantianism is "genuine idealism" by virtue of its "deduction of the categories" and that Fichte has emphasized this principle in "a pure and strict form," he has in mind a "deduction" of the categories in just this sense of a derivation of them as a system from a fundamental principle determining and making intelligible their systematic organization, not a "deduction" of the categories in Kant's usual technical sense of a justification of them.[13]

Hegel, in his pursuit of a demonstration of exhaustiveness via complete systematicity, borrowed and adapted from Fichte two crucial innovations introduced by the latter into the demonstration of complete systematicity which the *Science of Knowledge* was supposed to execute. First was the *dialectical method,* by means of which Fichte sought to exhibit the systematic connectedness of the categories and their derivability from the fundamental principle of the self's original act of self-positing.[14] This method was one of expounding a necessary development from each category to the next through successive stages of generating and resolving contradictions (contradictions which in Fichte's version of the method though not in Hegel's were supposed merely apparent). It became an essential part of Hegel's demonstration of complete systematicity and thereby of exhaustiveness, just as it was of Fichte's.

Hegel's second borrowing from Fichte was the *circularity* of the dialectical development. Fichte believed that in order to show that the dialectical derivation from philosophy's fundamental principle was complete or constituted a complete system of categories, it was necessary to show that the derivation not only began with that fundamental principle but also ended with it. As he puts the point in *On the Concept of the Science of Knowledge:* "Science is a *system* or complete when no further proposition can be deduced . . . We need a positive indicator that it is entirely and unconditionally impossible to deduce anything further. And this indicator could be no other than that the fundamental principle from which we began was the final result . . . It will turn out in the future construction of the science that it really does complete this circular course."[15] Hegel also takes the circular course of the dialectical development as a criterion of its completeness and hence of the completeness of the system of categories or similar items generated within it.

This second debt to Fichte was particularly important for Hegel because his strategy for demonstrating exhaustiveness by means of complete systematicity differed from the strategies of Kant, Reinhold and Fichte in one noteworthy respect. Unlike them, he could not begin the discipline within which complete systematicity was to be demonstrated from some true, epistemologically secure, explanatory principle, such as Kant's logical forms of judgment, Reinhold's proposition of consciousness, or Fichte's principle of the self's original act of self-positing were supposed to be. This was partly because of the insurmountable epistemological difficulties which Hegel saw confronting the presupposition of any such principle. But it was also partly because of the *destructive* nature of the discipline for which he wanted to demonstrate exhaustiveness via complete systematicity. Hegel's demonstration had to begin from a category or similar item which was not true, epistemologically secure, or capable of functioning as an explanatory principle, because it was *self-contradictory.*[16] For these reasons Hegel had to forgo any hope of beginning his demonstration of complete systematicity with a principle whose appropriateness as the foundation of the system would be self-evident and which might demonstrate or explain the organization and the completeness of the system of categories derived from it (as Kant, for example, envisaged the principle of the twelve logical forms of judgment demonstrating and explaining the organization and completeness of the system of twelve categories derived from it).

This peculiarity of Hegel's position could have posed a severe problem for his ambition of using a dialectical method of development from one category or similar item to the next as a means of demonstrating that all the categories or similar items he had collected in a contingent fashion constituted a complete system. For even if, using the dialectical method, he had succeeded in generating serially from some self-contradictory category or similar item taken as a starting point all of the categories or similar items so collected, thereby showing that they all belonged to the same system, how, in the absence of a true, explanatory principle governing the derivation, would this by itself have shown him that the system had been derived in its entirety? Thus even Fichte, with his belief that he did possess a true, epistemologically secure, explanatory principle on which to build his system, had been anxious that he would not be able to show that the items which he was able to derive from it dialectically constituted all those which *could* be so derived from it, and that he would therefore be unable to show that he had derived a complete system. His derivation might, unbeknownst to him, stop too early, leaving out further derivable items belonging to the system.[17] Hegel's failure to possess a true, epistemologically secure, explanatory principle as the starting point for his derivation could only make this problem of determining the proper end of the derivation more acute. Furthermore, it would appear to produce or at least exacerbate a corresponding problem concerning the proper *beginning* of the derivation: the problem of knowing that the principle from which the derivation begins is really the first in the series, that it is not itself derivable from something earlier which therefore also belongs to the system. In short, by beginning his derivation of the system from a mere self-contradictory category or similar item rather than a true, epistemologically secure, explanatory principle governing the system derived, Hegel seems to have denied us any hope of attaining the kind of insight into the nature of the system which we require in order to tell whether or not all its components are present.

Hegel's solution to this problem was to rely on the Fichtean suggestion that the circularity of the dialectical derivation may serve as the criterion of its completeness and hence of the completeness of the system derived. (This was Fichte's answer to his anxiety that his dialectical derivation might end too early as well.) Having forgone any appeal to a true, epistemologically secure, explanatory principle, Hegel used as the criterion of the proper start and finish of his dialectical derivation of categories or similar items, and hence of the completeness of the series or system of such items derived, the condition that *the derivation have a circular structure, eventually bringing us back to our starting point (having first gone through all the categories or similar items which we can contingently collect).*[18]

Summarizing Hegel's method of ensuring the exhaustiveness of the treatment of the basic categories or similar items discredited in his destructive discipline, he accepts the Kantian insight that the way to demonstrate exhaustiveness is to show that all the categories or similar items which have been collected constitute a complete system. He accepts the Fichtean suggestion that the demonstration that they do so should proceed by means of a necessary dialectical derivation of the categories or similar items out of each other—a dialectical derivation which for Hegel simultaneously shows the self-contradictoriness of the categories or similar items serially derived, thereby fulfilling the discipline's destructive function. He echoes Fichte once again in his idea that the criterion of the correctness of this derivation's finishing point and starting point, and hence of the completeness of the series or system derived, is to be the circular return of the derivation to its starting point (after going through all known and imaginable categories or similar items).[19]

We saw in Part One that Hegel's ideal for the discipline of his own which was to provide this destructive answer to the skeptical equipoll- ence problem—namely that it provide an *exhaustive* destruction of non- scientific viewpoints by way of demonstrating the *self-contradictoriness* of each member of a complete *system* of *categories* or similar items— was at times used by him as a standard against which to measure, and to some extent also as a model by means of which to interpret, ancient skepticism. Part of the reason for this was his concern, especially during the Jena period, to present his own destructive discipline embodying this ideal as itself a kind of skepticism. Consider, for example, his reference in *The Relation of Skepticism to Philosophy* to Plato's *Parmenides*, the text on which he at this time modeled his own early Logic, as the most complete and "self-standing document and system of genuine skepti- cism."[20] Consider his allusion in the *Encyclopedia* to his early Logic as "skepticism in the form of a negative science applied to all forms of finite cognition."[21] Consider his reference to the *Phenomenology* as "this self- completing skepticism."[22] Consider finally his statement in the *Encyclo- pedia* that his later Logic "includes the skeptical principle as a subor- dinate function of its own, in the shape of dialectic."[23] Each of these disciplines—the early Logic, the *Phenomenology*, and the later Logic— was at one time regarded by Hegel as the repository of the destructive answer to the skeptical equipollence problem which we have been con- sidering (and also the corresponding answer to the skeptical concept- instantiation problem which we have yet to consider). Thus Hegel was in the superficially paradoxical position of understanding as forms of skepticism the very disciplines whose function it was to defeat the threat of skepticism on behalf of his own Philosophical Science.

At least two features of Hegel's own destructive disciplines must have led him to think of them as forms of skepticism. First, they involved an exceptionless renunciation of the claims which they examined, as ancient skepticism did. Second, they endorsed, though in a qualified way, the ancient skeptics' raising of equipollence problems for all these claims as the motivation for renouncing them. For Hegel thought that the ancient skeptics were both right and in possession of an important insight when they recognized that one could always produce a balance of argument or justification for and against any nonscientific claim, and he reproduced this same insight in his own destructive disciplines. His only qualification of the position taken by the ancient skeptics on this score was that they overlooked the fact that there is a deeper characterization and explanation of the balance of justification for and against all nonscientific claims. The deeper account is, first, that the equal balance of justification consists in each such claim and its negation both being self-contradictory so that one can justify the claim by reducing its negation to absurdity and vice versa, and, second, that this self-contradictoriness is present because each finite claim and its negation are articulated by means of self-contradictory concepts.[24]

So far we have focused on what is more or less constant and fundamental in Hegel's destructive strategy for solving the problem of equipollence—the strategy which he sketches at quite different stages of his career in *On the Nature of Philosophical Critique*, the *Phenomenology*, and the *Lectures on the Proofs of God's Existence*.[25] However, each of these three works has a different discipline in view as the place where that more or less constant strategy is to be realized. Thus *On the Nature of Philosophical Critique* has Hegel's early Logic in view, the *Phenomenology* has itself in view, and the *Lectures on the Proofs of God's Existence* have Hegel's later Logic in view.[26] Having sufficiently emphasized continuity, we should now pay heed to differences. So let us consider each of these disciplines in turn.

The early Logic, which Hegel developed in the years 1801–1805, was a protean discipline. For example, in the 1801 essay *The Difference between the Fichtean and Schellingian Systems of Philosophy* it was modeled on Schelling's philosophies of the Self and Nature. In the 1801–1802 sketch transmitted by Rosenkranz it had more the general shape of a traditional logic such as Kant's. And in the 1802 essay *The Relation of Skepticism to Philosophy*, the 1802–1803 essay *On the Scientific Ways of Treating Natural Law*, and the 1804–1805 *Logic, Metaphysics, and Nature Philosophy* it followed the model of Plato's *Parmenides*. Throughout all these changes, the early Logic stayed faithful to the ideal of providing an *exhaustive* destruction of nonscientific claims by exhibiting a complete *system* of *self-contradictory categories* or similar items. However, the route by which Hegel strove to achieve this ideal varied from one version of the early Logic to another. Roughly speaking, he tried two alternative routes.

The first route is found in the sketch of the Logic transmitted by Rosenkranz, in the roughly contemporary fragment *The Idea of the Absolute Being*, and in *The Relation of Skepticism to Philosophy*. This route diverged from Hegel's more or less constant strategy outlined earlier in certain respects. In particular, the demonstration of the complete systematicity and the self-contradictoriness of the categories and similar items destroyed proceeded not by way of an immanent Fichtean dialectical development but by way of an application of certain extraneous information contained in the discipline which at this time constituted the beginning of Hegel's Philosophical Science proper, the Metaphysics—an application of Reason, as Hegel would sometimes describe it. Thus in the first of the three texts mentioned Hegel writes, "I believe that only from this speculative side can Logic serve as an introduction to philosophy."[27] In the second text he says that we must begin by recognizing "the simple Idea of philosophy itself" and that Logic "as a science of the Idea is itself Metaphysics."[28] And in the third text he claims that the destructive discipline "presupposes Reason immediately."[29] Traveling by this route, Hegel sought to demonstrate the self-contradictoriness of the nonscientific categories and similar items destroyed in the Logic by interpreting them from the standpoint of the Metaphysics as one-sided abstractions from the "self-standing . . . moments of the Idea" which received articulation in the Metaphysics—abstractions really existing only in synthesis with their opposites which therefore had to be added to them in order to see them as they were.[30] And he sought to demonstrate their constitution of a complete system by once again interpreting them from the viewpoint of the "self-standing . . . moments" of the Metaphysics in order to show that they formed a complete system of one-sided abstractions from the presupposed complete system of these moments.[31]

The second route taken by Hegel appears in the final version of the early Logic found in the *Logic, Metaphysics, and Nature Philosophy* and is anticipated, somewhat surprisingly, in the first version of the early Logic sketched in *The Difference between the Fichtean and Schellingian Systems of Philosophy*. This route followed Hegel's more or less constant strategy outlined earlier. Thus it did not essentially presuppose any information from the Metaphysics in order to demonstrate the self-contradictoriness or the systematicity of the categories and similar items destroyed, but instead made use of an immanent Fichtean dialectical method.[32] And at least in the case of the Logic of the *Logic, Metaphysics, and Nature Philosophy*, it employed the criterion of a circular dialectic in order to demonstrate complete systematicity. This route represents the considered method of the early Logic and was taken over by those disciplines which superseded the early Logic in the task of realizing Hegel's destructive ideal in order to solve the equipollence problem: the *Phenomenology* and the later Logic.

When Hegel abandoned the early Logic as a discipline shortly after writing its final version in the *Logic, Metaphysics, and Nature Philosophy*, the task of providing an exhaustive destruction of nonscientific claims in answer to the problem of equipollence passed in the first instance to the newly conceived discipline of the *Phenomenology*. Essentially the *Phenomenology* transposed the method used to achieve this goal in the final version of the early Logic out of the key of a destruction of categories, forms of judgment, and forms of syllogism and into the new key of a destruction of *shapes of consciousness*. Thus the Logic of the *Logic, Metaphysics, and Nature Philosophy* had sought to give an exhaustive destruction of nonscientific claims through exhibiting the self-contradictoriness of each member of a complete system of categories, forms of judgment, and forms of syllogism, and had sought to demonstrate self-contradictoriness and complete systematicity by means of a dialectical derivation of each member in turn taking a circular course. And now the *Phenomenology* sought to achieve the same exhaustive destruction by the same means, except that what were in question were no longer categories, forms of judgment, and forms of syllogism but rather shapes of consciousness.

The notion of a shape of consciousness at work in the *Phenomenology* calls for some explanation. It presupposes and builds upon a contemporary theory of the essential structure of selfhood or consciousness originally developed by Kant, Reinhold, and Fichte. According to this theory, selfhood or consciousness essentially involves three interdependent elements: consciousness of oneself as such, consciousness of something other than oneself as such, and consciousness of one's representation of this other something as such.[33] Hegel accepted this theory, but he made important additions to it which gave birth to his notion of a shape of consciousness.[34] The first addition was to see the theory's model of the structure of consciousness as only a general schema of numerous more specific models which could be identified. Each specific model would define a specific *kind* of consciousness as essentially involving a specific *kind* of each of the three elements identified in the general model (consciousness of self, of not-self, and of representation of not-self) in interdependence with one another. The second addition was to see the instantiation of each of these numerous specific models as belonging to a particular period of human history. These specific models associated with particular historical periods are what Hegel called shapes of consciousness.

Just as the concepts, forms of judgment, and forms of syllogism considered in the early Logic were supposed to constitute a necessary medium for the articulation of any nonscientific claim and therefore to be a suitable immediate target in an indirect attack upon all such claims, so too the shapes of consciousness considered in the *Phenomenology* were understood in this way.[35] Thus, in pursuing his exhaustive destruction of all nonscientific claims in the *Phenomenology*, Hegel had merely to transfer the dialectical method used in the final version of the early Logic to shapes of consciousness. This meant locating a self-contradiction within each shape in turn by finding two of its interdependent elements in contradiction with one another, and then developing the necessary resolution of this self-contradiction in the form of a new shape constituted by a new set of elements—thereby exhibiting both the self-contradictoriness of all shapes treated and their collective constitution of a necessarily connected series or system, whose completeness was manifested by the circular structure of the dialectical development.[36]

Did the execution of the strategy in the *Phenomenology* have any apparent advantages over its execution in the last version of the early Logic? There were, I think, two such advantages with respect to the proof given of the *exhaustiveness* of the destruction performed. We may indicate them briefly, since we shall consider them in more detail in Chapter Nine. First, the attempt in the last version of the early Logic to demonstrate the completeness of the system of categories and similar items covered by showing the dialectical derivation to have a circular structure had not worked. This was because the beginning of the derivation, the category of Unity, was only reached again in the Metaphysics, while the dialectical derivation did not extend as far as the Metaphysics.[37] In the *Phenomenology*, on the other hand, there was no such problem, since the dialectical derivation was understood to extend all the way to Philosophical Science proper, where the return to the beginning of the *Phenomenology* was made.[38] Second, the Kantian method of using complete systematicity to prove that all categories were present, on which the early Logic had entirely relied, was not a conclusive proof of this by any means. Even if it were demonstrated that all known categories constituted a complete system, this would not exclude the possibility that there existed an unknown second system of categories or some number of unknown additional categories lacking systematic connections.[39] In view of this weakness in the strategy of proving exhaustiveness solely by means of complete systematicity used in the early Logic, it is significant that the *Phenomenology* added a feature which reinforced that proof: its interpretation of human history as a teleological process having as its purpose the generation of the very system of shapes of consciousness which the *Phenomenology* presents and the culmination of that system in Hegelian Philosophical Science. If this part of the account in the *Phenomenology* could be made convincing, it would lend considerable support to the assumption that the complete system of shapes of consciousness which the *Phenomenology* exhibited was *the* system of such items and that there were none outside this system.

Finally, the later Logic is the discipline to which the task of destroying all nonscientific viewpoints in answer to the skeptical equipollence problem is assigned in the *Lectures on the Proofs of God's Existence*. It is also fairly explicitly designated as the successor of the abandoned early Logic in this function by the *Encyclopedia* itself. For the first paragraph of the *Encyclopedia* expresses Hegel's concern that his Philosophical Science should not be a presupposition, meaning that it should not fall victim to the fourth trope of Agrippa version of the skeptical equipollence problem. And further on in the text Hegel, offering his standard destructive solution to this problem, the solution that all "presuppositions and prejudices" are "to be given up at the time of beginning Science," remarks that, "Skepticism, as a negative science applied to all forms of cognition [i.e. the early Logic], would offer itself as an introduction in which the nullity of such presuppositions is presented. But it would be not only an uncomfortable but also a superfluous path for the reason that the dialectical is itself an essential moment of affirmative Science [i.e. the later Logic]." [40]

This assignment to the later Logic of the task of destroying all non-scientific viewpoints was made possible by a major change in Hegel's philosophy which occurred after the composition of the final version of the early Logic found in the *Logic, Metaphysics, and Nature Philosophy* and at about the same time as the *Phenomenology* came into being. Roughly speaking, Hegel's philosophy in the early Jena period comprised a negative, introductory early Logic and then a positive Philosophical Science which began with Metaphysics and proceeded to the Philosophies of Nature and Spirit. In this early philosophy the dialectical method found application only in the negative discipline of the early Logic, coming to an end before the start of positive Philosophical Science in the Metaphysics. [41] Hegel's later philosophy, on the other hand, consisted of a negative, introductory *Phenomenology* and then a positive Philosophical Science which began with the later Logic and proceeded to the Philosophies of Nature and Spirit. And in this later philosophy, in sharp contrast to the earlier, not only the negative introductory discipline (now the *Phenomenology*) was dialectical, but positive Philosophical Science (beginning now with the later Logic) was so too. This for the first time made it possible for positive Philosophical Science itself to present a systematic destruction through self-contradiction of all nonscientific categories, forms of judgment, and forms of syllogism. Hence the circular dialectical exposition of the positive nature of the Absolute Idea given in the later Logic is simultaneously a circular dialectical destruction and complete systematization of all the categories, forms of judgment, and forms of syllogism which nonscientific viewpoints use—that is, use by abstracting them from each other and from the whole dialectical movement which constitutes the Absolute Idea. [42]

This means that there was within Hegel's later philosophy a reduplication of the *Phenomenology* by the later Logic with respect to demonstrating the self-contradictoriness of all nonscientific viewpoints in order to protect Philosophical Science against the equipollence problem. The later Logic achieved this by focusing on categories, forms of judgment, and forms of syllogism; the *Phenomenology* achieved it by focusing on shapes of consciousness. However, more should be said about this reduplication (a reduplication which arises again and calls for a similar explanation in connection with the answer to the skeptical concept-instantiation problem to be considered below). For it would be strange if Hegel simply gave his destructive demonstration twice over. And indeed someone reading those passages from any of the editions of the *Encyclopedia* or from the *Lectures on the Proofs of God's Existence* in which Hegel refers to the later Logic as the place where this demonstration is to be performed might reasonably get the impression that, by the time of writing these texts, he understands the later Logic less as a *reduplication* of the *Phenomenology* in its pursuit of this task than as a *replacement* of it.[43]

This impression is correct in a certain sense, but not in the sense that the *Phenomenology* was simply abandoned, on grounds of superfluousness or unsuitedness to the destructive task, as the early Logic was.[44] The important point to note is that, however the later Logic replaced the *Phenomenology* in its destructive role, the fact that the *Phenomenology* would be superseded in this manner was already quite clear to Hegel at the time when he wrote it and belonged to the self-understanding of the work. We can read Hegel's comments in the *Encyclopedia* and the *Lectures on the Proofs of God's Existence* as expressions of a preference for the later Logic over the *Phenomenology* as a destructive discipline, or of the supersession of the *Phenomenology* by the later Logic in its destructive function, so long as we recognize and understand this circumstance.

The circumstance in question is visible from the fact that the *Phenomenology* describes itself as only the "appearance" of Philosophical Science which "is not yet Science in its developed and unfolded truth," so that one must make an "advance from this system [i.e. the *Phenomenology*] to the Science of the true in its true shape."[45] This "Science of the true in its true shape" is, of course, the later Logic along with the Philosophies of Nature and Spirit based upon it. By saying that the *Phenomenology* is an *appearance* of this Philosophical Science, Hegel means roughly that it expresses the same truths as Philosophical Science but only in an impure or distorted form.[46] For example, whereas he understands the later Logic to articulate the natures of categories and their necessary dialectical development in a pure and undistorted manner, he understands the *Phenomenology* to articulate them in the distorted form of shapes of consciousness and the necessary dialectical development of shapes of consciousness.[47] Because of its distortedness, the *Phenomenol-*

ogy ultimately suffers a Hegelian *Aufhebung* (annihilation through self-contradiction, elevation to a higher conceptual level, and preservation in a changed meaning), finding re-expression at the higher conceptual level of Philosophical Science. This is why the *Science of Logic* refers to the *Phenomenology* as the "*Aufheben* of itself," and why the *Phenomenology* itself, near its conclusion, gestures forward to a scientific retreatment of its own content, which is in fact found in the section of the *Encyclopedia* bearing the same name.[48]

It is an implication of this conception of the *Phenomenology* as ultimately subject to an *Aufhebung* that the work is not only distorted but actually self-contradictory. In Hegel's eyes this does not have the disastrous consequences for the work that one might expect because it is a constant assumption of his, even from the first versions of the early Logic, that self-contradiction *comes in degrees,* in the sense that some types of it are more adequate as means for expressing philosophical truths than others.[49] Calling the *Phenomenology* an *appearance* of Philosophical Science signifies for Hegel that it is the most adequate type of self-contradiction, the best expression of philosophical truth of which a self-contradictory viewpoint is capable. This Hegelian doctrine that self-contradiction comes in degrees and can at its best give a relatively adequate expression of philosophical truths is essential for the coherence of the project to be considered in Chapter Nine: the project of proving Philosophical Science to all the—thoroughly self-contradictory!—nonscientific viewpoints on the basis solely of their—thoroughly self-contradictory!—views and criteria.

Since the presentation of a necessarily developing series of self-contradictory shapes of consciousness found in the *Phenomenology* is ultimately, according to the very self-understanding of the *Phenomenology,* a distorted version of the undistorted presentation of a necessarily developing series of self-contradictory categories found in the later Logic, the destruction of all nonscientific viewpoints in pursuit of a defense of Philosophical Science against the equipollence problem which occurs in the *Phenomenology* is supposed, even at the time of its writing, to be a distorted version of the destruction in pursuit of the same end which occurs in the later Logic. Thus it belongs to the very self-conception of the *Phenomenology* that if one wishes to give the destructive solution to the problem of equipollence in an undistorted form, "in its true shape," one must set aside the *Phenomenology* and give the version of that solution articulated in the later Logic. The *Phenomenology* itself consciously gives quite adequate grounds for the preference indicated in some of Hegel's later texts for the version of the destructive solution found in the later Logic.

Does this not just mean, though, that the destructive solution to the equipollence problem given in the *Phenomenology* was, and was understood by the *Phenomenology* itself to be, straightforwardly superfluous? It does not for two reasons. The first reason concerns the function of the *Phenomenology* to be discussed in the next chapter—its provision of a proof of Philosophical Science for all nonscientific viewpoints. This requires that it construct its defense of Philosophical Science in a way which is compelling for these nonscientific viewpoints at their own level and hence in a way which is less than undistortedly true. The second reason is that at the time when the *Phenomenology* was written, the articulation of "the Science of the true in its true shape" which would make the destructive solution to the equipollence problem provided in the *Phenomenology* superfluous was not yet possible, it being one of the essential functions of the *Phenomenology* to make this Science possible.[50]

Nor does this account mean that the *Phenomenology* was, or was understood by itself to be, simply unsuited to the task of giving a destructive solution to the equipollence problem. The work's status as an *appearance* of Philosophical Science meant that the version of the destructive solution found in it was supposed to express the same truths as the version found in the later Logic. The self-contradictoriness, the necessary connections, the circularity, and hence also the complete systematicity exhibited in the version of the destructive solution in the *Phenomenology* were exhibited equally in the version in the Logic and were genuine. The only shortcoming of the version in the *Phenomenology,* and its only divergence from the version in the Logic, was its presentation of all these aspects of its solution in a distorted form.

Providing these important qualifications are borne in mind though, we can say that the later Logic represents Hegel's considered, preferred execution of his strategy of showing all nonscientific viewpoints to be self-contradictory in order to demonstrate the invulnerability of Philosophical Science to the skeptical problem of equipollence.

Just as Hegel tackles the skeptical problem of equipollence facing his Philosophical Science in two ways, once by a direct consideration of the viewpoint of Philosophical Science itself and once by a direct consideration of nonscientific viewpoints, so he also answers the skeptical problem of concept-instantiation in these two ways. The first answer, focusing on the viewpoint of Philosophical Science, is that concept and object are absolutely identical in the case of the concept which articulates Philosophical Science. This answer was examined in the preceding chapter. We should now consider the second answer, which focuses on nonscientific viewpoints.

Hegel's texts seem designed to cope with a concept-instantiation problem raised against Philosophical Science within the framework of the equipollence method and composed of two parts: the observations (a) that any concept, and in particular the concept which articulates Philosophical Science, might exist without possessing instantiation in reality, and (b) that for any concept, and in particular for the concept which articulates Philosophical Science, one can find alternative, competing concepts which appear to have as good a claim to represent how things really are. The first of Hegel's two answers to this problem, that which focuses on the viewpoint of Philosophical Science and tells us that concept and object are absolutely identical in the case of Philosophical Science's concept, seeks to overthrow the problem by refuting observation (a). His second answer, that which focuses on nonscientific viewpoints, tackles the problem by attempting to refute both observation (a) and observation (b). Let us consider how.

The way in which this second answer attempts to refute observation (b) has in fact already been explained. For this is to be done just by exhibiting the self-contradictoriness of each member of a complete system of nonscientific basic categories—and thereby, on some fairly plausible assumptions, the self-contradictoriness of all nonscientific concepts. We saw earlier in this chapter that and how Hegel proposes to accomplish this, since it is an essential component of his strategy for showing all claims other than Philosophical Science's to be self-contradictory in order to defend Philosophical Science against the general problem of equipollence. The demonstration in the early Logic, the *Phenomenology*, and the later Logic that no claims are genuine alternatives to that made by Philosophical Science thus functions simultaneously as a demonstration that no concepts are genuine alternatives to that used by Philosophical Science, and hence as a refutation of observation (b).

The manner in which Hegel's second answer seeks to refute observation (a) requires more extended explanation. Ultimately the reason for rejecting (a) will be the same as that given in the first answer, namely that concept and object are absolutely identical in the case of Philosophical Science's concept. But whereas in the first answer this claim was presented more or less as an unargued assertion about the concept which articulates Philosophical Science, in the second answer Hegel attempts to prove it in an indirect fashion by exhibiting certain characteristics of nonscientific concepts.[51] The general strategy of this proof, whose details vary from one period to another, is perhaps clearest from the early Logic—several versions of which, particularly those alluded to or expounded in *The Relation of Skepticism to Philosophy, On the Scientific Ways of Treating Natural Law,* and the *Logic, Metaphysics, and Nature Philosophy,* consciously imitate Plato's *Parmenides* as a model of the strategy.

In the last, and only fully expounded, version of the early Logic, that of the *Logic, Metaphysics, and Nature Philosophy,* the procedure of the proof is as follows. First, Hegel sets up an assumption of the *distinctness* of the items he wishes to prove absolutely identical: the assumption that the concept of Unity (Philosophical Science's concept) is distinct from the many (its instantiation). He then seeks to show by means of a dialectical derivation that this assumption leads to entanglement in a series of self-contradictions throughout all our fundamental categories which cannot be satisfactorily resolved so long as the assumption is retained. The aim is in effect a reductio ad absurdum of the original assumption, which is then taken as demonstrative of the need to identify (absolutely) the items which that assumption posited as distinct.[52]

Let me illustrate just how this strategy appears in the Logic of the *Logic, Metaphysics and Nature Philosophy*. This Logic begins with the concept of Unity. Thus, although the relevant pages at the beginning of the work have been lost, Hegel remarks later that "the Logic began with Unity itself."[53] But this concept of Unity is posited in abstraction from and opposition to the many—"multiplicity remains opposed to it" and "Unity and multiplicity [are] . . . still independent existents (*noch fuer sich Bestehende*)."[54] It is posited in the context of an assumed opposition between the real and the ideal, the objective and the conceptual, and is posited on the ideal or conceptual side of this opposition: "The ideal activity simply means the same as Unity."[55] The very fact that the concept of Unity at the start of the Logic is a concept of Unity in opposition to the many distinguishes it from *absolute* Unity, that is, the Absolute in which concept and object are absolutely identical: "One of the things in opposition is necessarily Unity itself; but this Unity is because of this very fact not absolute Unity."[56] The opposition between the concept of Unity and the many is the principle underlying the whole of the Logic—"the general principle of the logic of the Understanding."[57] And it is the source of the dialectical, self-contradictory character of the concepts posited in the Logic, including the concept of Unity considered in abstraction from the many itself—the Logic being through and through dialectical (unlike the Metaphysics which is not at all so—the transition to the Metaphysics is "the overcoming of the Logic itself, as of dialectic").[58] Thus in *On the Scientific Ways of Treating Natural Law*, where essentially the same distinction between absolute Unity and the concept of Unity taken in abstraction from the many is drawn, Hegel says of the concept of Unity in abstraction from the many that it has as "its essence . . . nothing but to be the unmediated opposite of itself," and that "it shows itself in its essence to be its own opposite."[59] And in the *Logic, Metaphysics, and Nature Philosophy* he says that the abstract concept of Unity or "negative Unity . . . abolishes its own determinacy and that of its opposite" and that it infects all concepts based upon it with self-contradictoriness, so that in the Logic "in the realization of a concept always something other than itself arose." [60] It is by being shown to lead unavoidably to the self-contradictions of the Logic that the principle of a concept of unity in opposition to the many "is recognized as not ultimately valid (*nicht fuer sich seiend*), and by this means is overcome (*aufgehoben*)." [61] The positive moral drawn from all this is the need to posit an absolute Unity which is a concept not abstracted from but rather in absolute identity with the many, in order to restore self-consistency. Hegel thus contrasts this absolute or "pure Unity" as self-consistent, as something which "remains the same as itself in its totality," with the abstract concept of Unity which is self-contradictory and the source of self-contradictoriness in concepts based upon it. [62] Accordingly, at the beginning of the Metaphysics this principle of absolute Unity, Unity not posited in abstraction from the many and therefore not self-contradictory in character, is established: Unity or "the in-itself posits itself here as a self-sameness," as something which "has destroyed the possibility of the many, of being different." [63]

When it replaced the early Logic, the *Phenomenology* inherited the task of refuting observation (a) by demonstrating the absolute identity thesis through an examination of nonscientific viewpoints. However, it went about accomplishing this task in a slightly different way. First, the thesis which Hegel set out to reduce to absurdity in the *Phenomenology* concerned the distinctness of subject and object *in general*—or equivalently for Hegel, the distinctness of concept and instance *in general*—rather than the distinctness of the concept of Philosophical Science (Unity) and its instantiation (the many) in particular. The refutation of the former thesis was understood, reasonably enough, to imply the refutation of the latter.

A second difference between the approach taken in the early Logic and that taken in the *Phenomenology* concerns the general structure of the demonstration. In the early Logic, as we saw, the demonstration took the form of beginning with the assumption of the distinctness of Philosophical Science's concept from its instances and reducing this assumption to absurdity by generating dialectically from it a series of self-contradictions which could not be resolved. The step from these unresolved self-contradictions to self-consistent Philosophical Science was, to use the term employed in *The Difference between the Fichtean and Schellingian Systems of Philosophy,* a dialectically underived "postulate." [64] The demonstration in the *Phenomenology,* by contrast, did not begin with an explicit assumption of the distinctness of Philosophical Science's concept from its instantiation, but instead exhibited in serial fashion that each possible way in which the distinctness of a subject and an object might be articulated (each shape of consciousness), and hence each way in which the distinctness of a concept and its instance might be articulated, was self-contradictory. And instead of having the dialectical derivation in the course of which this was shown come to an end with an unresolved self-contradiction, as in the early Logic, Hegel had it proceed to the self-consistent viewpoint of Philosophical Science, at the point where the attempt to articulate a distinction between a subject and an object, and hence a concept and its instance, was given up. The main reasons for the difference between the structures of the demonstrations in the early Logic and the *Phenomenology* are the following. First, as noted, the *Phenomenology*, unlike the early Logic, seeks to refute the thesis of the distinctness of Philosophical Science's concept from its instantiation by the indirect route of showing *all* attempts to articulate the distinctness of a concept from an instance to be self-contradictory, not by the direct route of giving a reductio ad absurdum of that thesis in particular. This explains why the *Phenomenology* need not follow the procedure found in the early Logic of beginning with the explicit assumption of the distinctness of Philosophical Science's concept from its instantiation and striving to end a derivation from this assumption with an unresolved self-contradiction. Second, the *Phenomenology*, in order really to show that *all* ways of articulating the distinctness of a subject and an object, and hence of a concept and an instance, are self-contradictory, requires a *circularity* in its dialectical derivation of these ways—circularity being necessary in order to show that they constitute a complete system and hence are exhausted, in accordance with a strategy discussed earlier in this chapter. But, as was pointed out earlier, the manner in which the early Logic ended its dialectical derivation on an unresolved self-contradiction before reaching self-consistent Philosophical Science prevented its derivation from achieving circularity. Circularity is only achieved once the derivation is extended right into self-consistent Philosophical Science in the manner of the *Phenomenology*.

Despite these differences between the structures of the demonstrations in the early Logic and the *Phenomenology*, the fundamental strategy of the demonstrations is more or less the same: to show that once, and so long as, we make the assumption of a distinction between a subject and an object, and hence a concept and its instance, in general or the assumption of a distinction between Philosophical Science's concept (Unity) and its instantiation (the many) in particular, self-contradictoriness inevitably results. This is understood as, first, a refutation of the distinction posited in the assumption and, second, an indication of the need to make an absolute identification of the items posited as distinct in the assumption.

A third novelty in the *Phenomenology* is that the continuation of its dialectical derivation all the way to the self-consistent standpoint of Philosophical Science, by and of which the absolute identity thesis is articulated, allows Hegel to bolster the strategy of demonstration just described as more or less common to the early Logic and the *Phenom-*

enology. It does so by enabling him to offer in addition a demonstration that all the viewpoints which posit as distinct the items he wishes to prove absolutely identical, and which therefore fall into self-contradiction, are themselves implicitly committed to the truth of his absolute identity thesis concerning Philosophical Science, this being demonstrated by the possibility of developing them in a necessary, dialectical fashion to the standpoint of Philosophical Science, which expresses that thesis about itself.

Finally, the later Logic, whose general relation to the *Phenomenology* we discussed earlier, also attempts to refute observation (a) through a demonstration of the absolute identity thesis founded on an examination of nonscientific viewpoints. This is perhaps clearest from the *Lectures on the Proofs of God's Existence,* which were written, as Hegel reports, in connection with the later Logic.[65] In these lectures Hegel expresses approval of the ontological proof of God's existence, which he understands as a statement of his own thesis of the absolute identity of concept and existence in the case of the Absolute. However, he points out the inadequacy of merely *presupposing* this thesis of absolute identity, as he thinks traditional proponents of the ontological proof do, and the need actually to demonstrate it instead: "But there is here the following circumstance which makes the proof unsatisfactory. That most perfect and real being is a presupposition, measured against which being by itself and concept by itself are one-sided. With Descartes and Spinoza God is defined as cause of himself; concept and existence are an identity, or God as concept cannot be grasped without being. That this is a presupposition is what is unsatisfactory."[66] We saw earlier that at one level Hegel, understanding this problem as the threat that the absolute identity thesis will succumb to the fourth trope of Agrippa version of the equipollence difficulty, offers as a solution to it his demonstration in the later Logic that all alternative viewpoints are incoherent. But what interests us here is another level of his solution to the problem. This is his (in practice hard-to-distinguish) demonstration in the later Logic that all viewpoints for which a concept and its instance are not absolutely identical but distinct—all of the categories of the later Logic when these are conceived as the ordinary Understanding, the nonscientific viewpoint, conceives them, namely in abstraction from objective reality—fall inevitably into self-contradiction.[67] This demonstration proves the absurdity of positing such a distinctness and shows indirectly the need to posit instead an absolute identity of concept and instantiation in order to restore self-consistency. Hegel alludes to this by now familiar strategy in the passage which responds to the above problem:

> The finite and subjective is however not only a finite measured by the standard of that presupposition: it is finite in itself and therefore the oppo-

site of itself; it is the unresolved contradiction. Being is said to be different from the concept, one believes one can hold onto the latter as something subjective, as something finite, but the determination of being is in the concept itself. This finitude of subjectivity is abolished (*aufgehoben*) in the concept itself, and the unity of being and the concept is not a presupposition over against it by which it is measured.[68]

The later Logic, having in this way shown the need to posit an absolute identity of concept and instantiation, in its role as an exposition of Philosophical Science furnishes us with a concept which *is* thus absolutely identical with its instantiation, namely the Absolute Idea, and hence meets this need.

To complicate matters a little further, Hegel in the passage just quoted also seems to have in mind another kind of demonstration of the absolute identity of concept and being or concept and instance which he has provided in the later Logic through a consideration of nonscientific viewpoints. This is the demonstration that the categories Concept and Being treated in the Logic, when taken as the Understanding or the nonscientific viewpoint takes them, that is, in abstraction from each other or "outside of their unity," develop into one another in a necessary dialectical fashion.[69] In the preceding passage Hegel has particularly in mind the dialectical development of the category Concept into the category Being, something which happens in the later Logic because before returning to its beginning, the category Being, the dialectical development of the work goes through all subsequent categories, including the category Concept. But the structure of the Logic gives him equal reason to point out in addition, as he elsewhere does, the converse development of the category Being into the category Concept.[70] This necessary dialectical development into one another of the categories Concept and Being when they are taken in abstraction from one another is supposed to provide an additional demonstration from the consideration of nonscientific viewpoints that concept and being or concept and instance are absolutely identical in the true view of things.

Hegel thus sought to solve the skeptical problem of concept-instantiation facing his Philosophical Science by refuting the two observations (a) and (b) which constitute that problem through a consideration of features of nonscientific viewpoints. And he pursued this goal in a succession of different disciplines spanning most of his philosophical career: the early Logic, the *Phenomenology*, and the later Logic. This solution complemented his more direct and dogmatic answer to the concept-instantiation problem by means of the doctrine of absolute identity which we discussed in the preceding chapter.

NINE

The Proof for Nonbelievers

HAVING considered those parts of Hegel's epistemological enterprise in which he seeks to provide solutions on behalf of his own Philosophical Science to the skeptical problems of equipollence and concept-instantiation, we must now consider his efforts to meet the one remaining standard of epistemological respectability which he accepts. This standard requires that Philosophical Science be free even of the *appearance* of vulnerability to such skeptical problems or of falsehood, or equivalently that Philosophical Science be furnished with a way of proving to each nonscientific viewpoint, on the basis solely of views and criteria which that viewpoint already accepts, that it is superior to all such viewpoints and so never succumbs to equipollence difficulties, that it faces no concept-instantiation problems, and that it is true. In brief, the standard requires a proof of Philosophical Science for all nonscientific viewpoints. Hegel's attempts to meet this epistemological standard grew increasingly determined and sophisticated over the course of the Jena period, culminating in the attempt found in the *Phenomenology,* and many of the changes in his philosophy during this period, particularly in the area of the early Logic and the *Phenomenology,* first become intelligible in this light. In the present chapter we shall follow this development in some detail. However, a number of qualifications or complications must be made explicit before we explain the steady and methodical progress Hegel made in pursuit of this epistemological standard during his Jena years.

First, in the *Phenomenology* this *epistemological* goal is not sharply distinguished from at least two different goals which are pursued by means of the same procedure of giving a proof of Philosophical Science for all nonscientific viewpoints compelling in the light of views and criteria already accepted by those viewpoints. These additional goals are the *pedagogical* goal of establishing a way of teaching Philosophical Science to willing pupils (a goal not demanding but nevertheless satisfied by a procedure rigorous enough to satisfy the epistemological goal), and what one might, for want of a better term, call the *metaphysical* goal of establishing a way of welding together a contemporary consensus in favor of Philosophical Science in order to constitute its truth, in accordance with an implicit assumption that truth is somehow constituted by society's collective judgment.[1] These epistemological, pedagogical, and metaphysical goals are also at work and are even less distinguishable in texts prior to the *Phenomenology*. Hence it would be an oversimplification to attribute advances in the sophistication of the proof of Philosophical Science for all nonscientific viewpoints made in the texts of the Jena period *solely* to Hegel's interest in attaining the epistemological goal.

Second, previous Hegel scholarship has put a number of obstacles in the way of seeing the progressive response to the epistemological ideal of providing a proof of Philosophical Science for all nonscientific viewpoints which is to be found in successive versions of the early Logic and in the ultimate replacement of that discipline by the *Phenomenology*. Although I shall not here rehearse the detailed spadework necessary to remove these obstacles, their prominence requires that they be mentioned and that the views which should replace them be indicated. One obstacle consists in a popular conception of the development of the relation between the early Logic and the Metaphysics in the Jena period. This conception appears in a fuller form in Baillie, and in a more curtailed form in Poeggeler.[2] According to Baillie, Logic and Metaphysics start out as strictly separate disciplines in the Frankfurt period, Metaphysics being a discipline embodying Reason and beyond the ken of the ordinary Understanding, while Logic is a discipline directed exclusively toward the Understanding and involves no presupposition of Reason or Metaphysics. But the distinction between Logic and Metaphysics begins to break down at the start of the Jena period when Logic comes to presuppose an application of Reason or the contents of Metaphysics. According to both Baillie and Poeggeler, the artificiality of the distinction between Logic and Metaphysics at the beginning of the Jena period leads inevitably to the disappearance of the distinction between the two disciplines and their replacement by the later Logic, which combines fundamental traits of both. I believe it to be the case, and my account of the development of the early Logic and the *Phenomenology* as manifesting a progressive attempt to meet the epistemological standard with which we are concerned in this chapter will presuppose it to be the case, that this Baillie-Poeggeler view of the developing relation between the early Logic and the Metaphysics almost precisely *reverses* the truth. What in fact happens is the following. Early in the Jena period, particularly in the sketch of the Logic transmitted by Rosenkranz and in *The Idea of the Absolute Being*, the distinction between Logic and Metaphysics is indeed artificial in the way claimed by Baillie and Poeggeler. Somewhat later in the Jena period, in the *Logic, Metaphysics, and Nature Philosophy*, the two disciplines become genuinely separated into a Metaphysics embodying Reason and a Logic directed exclusively toward the ordinary Understanding and not presupposing Reason or Metaphysics. (This is the situation Baillie sees in the Frankfurt period, not because of any misinterpretation of the texts, but simply because, following nineteenth century tradition, he wrongly attributes the *Logic, Metaphysics, and Nature Philosophy* to the Frankfurt rather than to the later Jena period.) Finally, this separation is maintained after the radical revision of Hegel's philosophy which occurs toward the end of the Jena period, and which leads (roughly) to the replacement of the early Logic by the *Phenomenology* and of the Metaphysics by the later Logic. It is retained in the form of a division between the later Logic as a discipline embodying Reason and the *Phenomenology* as a discipline directed exclusively toward the ordinary Understanding and not presupposing Reason or the later Logic.

Another obstacle lies in the faulty interpretation of the early Logic of the *Logic, Metaphysics, and Nature Philosophy* found in Haym, Trede, and Poeggeler, according to which that discipline's dialectical course essentially involves an application of Reason, or is only intended to be fully intelligible and convincing from the philosophical vantage point of the Metaphysics.[3] My account of Hegel's steady progress toward his epistemological ideal presupposes that this Logic is rather intended to be fully accessible and convincing to the ordinary Understanding, to a viewpoint which is not in possession of a knowledge of Reason or Metaphysics. This is Baillie's interpretation of the text, and it is correct (though in need of more proof than Baillie offers).[4]

The final obstacle is a widespread and rather natural reading of the *Phenomenology*, found in Fulda, for example.[5] According to this reading, Hegel's considered understanding of the work is that it presupposes the later Logic in at least the sense that the necessary development from one shape of consciousness to the next which appears within the *Phenomenology* is to be identified with the necessary development from one logical category to the next in the later Logic, so that an understanding and acceptance of the former necessity requires a prior understanding and acceptance of the latter necessity. This reading of the *Phenomenology* is made natural by, among other things, the passages near the end of its Introduction where Hegel says that the necessity of the transition from one shape of consciousness to the next or the origination of the new object for consciousness, as part of the process depicted in the *Phenomenology*, occurs "behind the back of consciousness," and that this makes the *Phenomenology* "itself already Science."[6] Nevertheless, the account I shall give of the way in which the *Phenomenology* serves the epistemological goal we are concerned with in this chapter assumes that the *Phenomenology* does not presuppose the later Logic in this sense. It assumes that the whole course of the proof of Hegel's system given in the *Phenomenology,* including the necessary development from one shape of consciousness to the next, is intended to be available to the ordinary Understanding, to a viewpoint which is neither acquainted with nor accepts the scientific standpoint of the Logic. I believe this to be the correct account of Hegel's considered view of the work, though naturally the case demands considerable argument. These, then, are the three obstacles set down by Hegel scholarship in the way of the interpretation I want to give of Hegel's early works as increasingly determined efforts to provide a proof of Philosophical Science for all nonscientific viewpoints. The interpretation will be presented as though they had been removed.

The third and final qualification is that the pleasing picture to be painted of a steady progress over time in Hegel's early works toward the provision of a proof of Philosophical Science for all nonscientific viewpoints is clouded by one minor exception, namely the very first model of the early Logic found in *The Difference between the Fichtean and Schellingian Systems of Philosophy.* This is quite different from the models of the early Logic found in the slightly later sketches in Rosenkranz and in *The Idea of the Absolute Being,* and it anticipates in several ways which make it somewhat better able to serve as a proof of Philosophical Science for all nonscientific viewpoints the character of both the early Logic of the *Logic, Metaphysics, and Nature Philosophy* and the *Phenomenology.*[7] Having mentioned this minor exception, I shall disregard it in what follows.

With these qualifications and complications noted, we may now chart Hegel's progressive, cumulative pursuit of the epistemological goal of providing a proof of Philosophical Science for all nonscientific viewpoints. Phase one in this course of development is represented by the model of the early Logic found in the sketch transmitted by Rosenkranz and in *The Idea of the Absolute Being,* which stem from the period 1801–1802. As we saw in the preceding chapter, this model makes the demonstration given in the Logic depend essentially on an application of Reason or the contents of the Metaphysics. This observation is valid both for the negative demonstration of the worthlessness of nonscientific viewpoints and for the positive demonstration of the truth of Philosophical Science given in the Logic. Thus we saw in the preceding chapter that on this model the negative demonstration presupposes a knowledge of the system of the pure moments of the Metaphysics in order to show that its collection of nonscientific categories and similar items constitutes a complete system and is therefore exhaustive. And we saw that the negative demonstration presupposes this knowledge of Metaphysics again in order to show that the nonscientific categories and similar items are all self-contradictory. As for the positive demonstration, Hegel says that in the Logic we show that the Understanding strives to imitate Reason, but that in doing so, we must "always hold before us the original model which [the Understanding] copies, the expression of Reason itself."[8] Thus the Logic shows that the Understanding in certain respects attempts to express the deeper rational truth of the Metaphysics, but this demonstration rests entirely on a presupposition of the rational truth of the Metaphysics itself. The nonscientific viewpoint which the Logic is to raise to Philosophical Science is therefore to be given no proof convincing for it in the light of its own views and criteria. It is simply supposed, in its despair at seeing its own viewpoint condemned as self-contradictory, to accept on authority Hegel's claims that the truth is rational in nature and that the Understanding contains merely a pale reflection of rational truth, and then to raise itself to the rational viewpoint by the intermediate step of concentrating on those aspects of its own thought which it is told constitute this pale reflection (hence the Logic "holds forth the image of the Absolute so to speak in a reflection and thereby makes people familiar with it").[9] In short, the nonscientific viewpoint being instructed by the Logic of phase one must first accept the claims of the Metaphysics on authority if it is to find either the negative or the positive demonstration compelling. It cannot find them compelling solely on the basis of views and criteria to which it is already committed. This deprives these demonstrations of the character of proofs for nonscientific viewpoints in the sense at issue in this chapter. Phase one aspires to give no more than a negative and positive teaching of the nonscientific viewpoint, appealing essentially to views and criteria which are not already the pupil's own but which he must accept on authority. In what follows we shall see Hegel striving with increasing determination and ingenuity to turn this mere negative and positive teaching into a negative and positive proof completely compelling on the basis of the views and criteria which the nonscientific viewpoint already possesses.

Phase two begins with the publication of *On the Nature of Philosophical Critique* early in 1802. The attitude during phase one had essentially been that because nonscientific viewpoints were thoroughly incoherent, any self-understanding which they might come to from their own resources was of no value or importance. All that mattered was to find a way of communicating to them the scientific insights which would enable them to see their own incoherence and ascend to the perspective of Philosophical Science. *On the Nature of Philosophical Critique* marks a significant shift in attitude. Thus Hegel writes that the only proper response for genuine philosophy to make to completely nonscientific viewpoints is "to recount how this negative side expresses itself and confesses its nothingness." [10] That is, Hegel now thinks it important that the non-scientific viewpoints whose self-contradictoriness is to be demonstrated should *themselves* furnish this demonstration, that the demonstration should be one which their own resources bring them to. Again, Hegel shows a more pronounced concern than at phase one that this negative demonstration should be compelling for *all* nonscientific viewpoints. Thus he remarks of this negative demonstration that "it cannot fail to happen that what is nothing at the start in its development appears more and more as nothing, so that it can be pretty generally *(ziemlich allgemein)* recognized as such." [11] In both these respects *On the Nature of Philosophical Critique* hints at an emerging commitment to give at least the negative side of a proof of philosophical Science for *all* nonscientific viewpoints *compelling in the light of their own views and criteria*—a proof of the kind with which we are concerned in this chapter.

However, a much more concrete step in the direction of giving such a proof is found in the essay *The Relation of Skepticism to Philosophy* from 1802, which accordingly constitutes the major event in phase two. This essay does not make progress in the direction of giving a proof of Philosophical Science for all nonscientific viewpoints by virtue of any revision it makes in the discipline of Logic, but in a different way. The conception of Logic it presents indeed differs from that of either phase one or the still earlier essay *The Difference between the Fichtean and Schellingian Systems of Philosophy,* in that it for the first time takes Plato's *Parmenides* as its model. However, unlike the later versions of the early Logic which are based on this model, namely those found in *On the Scientific Ways of Treating Natural Law* and the *Logic, Metaphysics, and Nature Philosophy,* this version is still thought of in the same way as the Logic of phase one in the respect that it is understood essentially to presuppose and apply the rational truth of Metaphysics.[12] This prevents it from being any more of a proof for all nonscientific viewpoints, in the sense of a demonstration completely compelling in the light of their own views and criteria, than was the Logic of phase one.

If, then, the Logic conception of *The Relation of Skepticism to Philosophy* makes no progress toward giving such a proof, how *does* the essay make progress in this direction? It does so by virtue of what it says not about the kind of skepticism which is *one* with genuine philosophy in the manner of the Platonic *Parmenides* or Hegel's own Logic but about "the skepticism which is separated from [philosophy]." [13] Hegel has strong praise for this kind of skepticism when it is directed only against the Understanding and not against genuine philosophy, and he finds it epitomized in the equipollence method articulated in the ten tropes of Aenesidemus. This version of skepticism constitutes a way in which the

Understanding can both be brought to recognize its own inadequacy by being given a genuine proof of this and be brought to do so without first having to accept esoteric philosophical assumptions, the proof being accessible and compelling to the Understanding in the light of views and criteria to which it is already committed. By thus embracing "the skepticism which is separated from [philosophy]," Hegel in effect provides himself with the negative side of a proof of Philosophical Science for all nonscientific viewpoints *outside* of the early Logic—a negative demonstration which does not, in the manner of that given in the Logic, require a prior acceptance of philosophical assumptions on authority as a precondition of being found intelligible or compelling. Thus Hegel emphasizes the prooflike character of the destruction effected by this skepticism: he says it "knows how to prove, when some fact is set up as certain, that that certainty is nothing." [14] But at the same time he emphasizes that this skepticism proceeds from the views and criteria of the nonscientific viewpoints themselves and does not presuppose philosophical truths: he says that it is "turned against the common human Understanding or the common consciousness in a manner which is precisely not philosophical but popular," and that it shows the common consciousness the uncertainty of its alleged certainties "in a way which likewise is manifest to the common consciousness." [15] This, then, constitutes Hegel's first serious attempt to provide at least the negative side of a proof of Philosophical Science for all nonscientific viewpoints—a discrediting of all nonscientific viewpoints which is compelling to these viewpoints themselves on the basis of their own views and criteria.

To describe this change in other terms, at phase one the main obstacle to giving the negative side of a proof of Philosophical Science for all nonscientific viewpoints which would be completely compelling in the light of their own views and criteria was that, although Hegel had a standard for the respectability of claims which he could reasonably ascribe not only to himself but also to all nonscientific viewpoints, namely self-consistency, he had no generally shared basis for a demonstration that this standard was violated by all nonscientific viewpoints. His insight into the self-contradictoriness of all nonscientific categories, based as it was on recognizing them to be one-sided abstractions from their opposites in the light of an acquaintance with the pure moments of the Metaphysics in which the two sides were synthesized, was hardly something that he could expect nonscientific viewpoints to emulate. In *The Relation of Skepticism to Philosophy* he finds a hopeful solution to this problem. He assumes with some plausibility that in addition to self-consistency it is a generally accepted condition of a claim's respectability that it not succumb to equipollence objections. But then he can also suppose with some plausibility in connection with the latter condition unlike the condition of self-consistency that along with himself each nonscientific viewpoint can be brought to recognize, merely by having the fact pointed out to it and without first having to accept any alien assumptions, that all nonscientific viewpoints fail to meet the condition because they succumb to equipollence objections. Thus the equipollence method seems to offer an opportunity for discrediting all nonscientific viewpoints in a way completely compelling to them on the basis of their own views and criteria.

We saw in the preceding chapter that although Hegel believes the phenomenon of equipollence afflicting nonscientific claims to be genuine, he also believes that it is a result of deeper facts which the equipollence skeptic does not clearly perceive, namely the self-contradictoriness of the claims involved and, deeper still, the self-contradictoriness of the categories by means of which the claims are articulated. At phase two this deeper view of things is still only available to a viewpoint which has attained the rational insights of the Metaphysics and is thus able to grasp the destructive demonstration in the Logic that the Understanding is constituted by a system of categories and similar items all of which are self-contradictory, thereby infecting all of the Understanding's claims with self-contradictoriness. The trend in Hegel's thought after phase two is toward making the equipollence version of the negative side of the proof of Philosophical Science for all nonscientific viewpoints superfluous by in effect turning the whole Logic—and thereby the deeper explanation of the phenomenon of equipollence, with its still greater power to discredit those claims to which it is seen to apply—into a demonstration which any nonscientific viewpoint is bound to acknowledge on the basis of its own views and criteria without first having to accept any philosophical insights. Thus the peculiar two-tier character of Hegel's introduction to Philosophical Science at phase two—one tier constituted by equipollence skepticism's destructive demonstration, the other by the Logic with its essential presupposition of the Metaphysics—is only a temporary phenomenon. It disappears once the need which gives rise to the additional skeptical tier, namely the need to give the negative side of a proof of Philosophical Science for all nonscientific viewpoints compelling in the light of their own views and criteria, comes to be met by a new conception of the Logic itself, thus making the supplementation of the Logic by the additional skeptical tier superfluous.

The task of providing a proof of Philosophical Science for all nonscientific viewpoints in the full sense required, it will be recalled, that it be proved to all these viewpoints, on the basis solely of views and criteria to which they are already committed, that Philosophical Science is superior to them all and hence invulnerable to equipollence problems, faces no concept-instantiation difficulties, and is true. Viewed as an attempt to accomplish this task, the strategy of using equipollence skepticism in the manner of *The Relation of Skepticism to Philosophy* could be no more than a small step in the right direction. Some of its shortcomings as a way of attaining this goal, even supposing it to work optimally well, are the following. First, it does not actually discredit the propositions to which it is applied but only the grounds on which or the way in which they are accepted. Second, it leaves Hegel's assertion that Philosophical Science is invulnerable to equipollence difficulties as a mere assurance which nonscientific viewpoints must accept on trust. Third, it does not give a systematic or demonstrably complete discrediting of nonscientific viewpoints.[16] Fourth, it does nothing to dispel concept-instantiation worries about Philosophical Science. And fifth, it is only negative in character, offering no positive reasons for accepting Philosophical Science.

We can understand the development of the early Logic and the *Phenomenology* after phase two as a series of responses designed to remedy shortcomings such as these in order to achieve the goal of giving a proof of Philosophical Science for all nonscientific viewpoints in the full sense. In what follows I shall present such shortcomings in the form of a series of objections and queries which a nonscientific viewpoint might raise as rational grounds for continuing to doubt Philosophical Science's validity even if it accepts all that Hegel purports to have shown it so far by way of proof of Philosophical Science (for example, at phase two, that all known nonscientific claims succumb to equipollence objections). In this way we shall be able to understand the development of the early Logic and the *Phenomenology* after phase two as a cumulative introduction of a succession of innovations designed to provide answers to more and more of these objections and queries—answers of a kind compelling for the nonscientific viewpoint which might raise these objections and queries purely on the basis of its own views and criteria. This development will thus become intelligible as a cumulative attempt to exclude all reasonable grounds which nonscientific viewpoints might offer for withholding the acknowledgment that Philosophical Science is superior to all other viewpoints and so succumbs to no equipollence problems, faces no concept-instantiation problems, and is true. If Hegel achieved this, he could reasonably claim to have provided a proof of Philosophical Science for all nonscientific viewpoints in the full sense.

Phase Three is represented by the Logic conception of the essay *On the Scientific Ways of Treating Natural Law* from 1802–1803. We can introduce the innovation by means of which this text advances the cause of giving a proof of Philosophical Science for all nonscientific viewpoints by considering two queries which might still worry a nonscientific viewpoint which had accepted phase two's discrediting by equipollence skepticism of all nonscientific claims encountered so far. Such a viewpoint might ask: (i) Even if, as we may agree, it has been shown that we have no better reasons for believing any of the nonscientific claims we believe than we have for disbelieving them, or in short that they succumb to equipollence, does this not only discredit our grounds for believing them or the way in which we believe them while leaving open the possibility that many of them might nevertheless be *true*? And it might further ask: (ii) Since there are any number of nonscientific concepts we can think of which stand in competition with that of Philosophical Science, how are we to know that Philosophical Science's concept rather than these nonscientific concepts, is the right one to use in order to capture genuine features of the world?

The crucial innovation in the Logic conception of *On the Scientific Ways of Treating Natural Law* which provides an answer to these queries is the introduction of a new technique for demonstrating the self-contradictoriness of nonscientific categories. It will be remembered that at phase one the demonstration was achieved by comparing the nonscientific categories with the pure moments of the Metaphysics from which they and their opposites had been abstracted, in order to show that each nonscientific category only really exists in unity with its opposite and is therefore implicitly self-contradictory. And generally, prior to phase three Hegel appears to have had no method of demonstrating the self-contradictoriness of nonscientific categories without essentially presupposing esoteric knowledge in such a fashion. As a consequence, he had no way of compelling all nonscientific viewpoints to recognize this self-contradictoriness on the basis of their own views and criteria. The innovation of *On the Scientific Ways of Treating Natural Law* is to dispense with demonstrations of self-contradictoriness based on esoteric information and to replace them with arguments for the self-contradictoriness of each category which are designed to be intelligible and convincing for nonscientific viewpoints.

This innovation may be illustrated by an argument from *On the Scientific Ways of Treating Natural Law* in which Hegel attempts to show the incoherence of the concept of reciprocal action.[17] The argument goes somewhat as follows. If reciprocal action is understood to be of unequal strength, then the action is not really reciprocal, since only one side is under compulsion.[18] But if the action on both sides is supposed equally strong, then the two sides are in equilibrium, so that there is no action on either side, and this is so even if the equal action supposed on both sides is indirect.[19] Hegel in the same text gives several similar arguments designed to show the incoherence of other categories, such as attraction and repulsion or freedom and coercion.[20] Aside from the question of the merit of such arguments, it is clear that they are intended to rely on no esoteric assumptions, so that if they are convincing at all, they will be so for a nonscientific viewpoint which has not yet accepted such assumptions. That Hegel intends these arguments to be compelling for the ordinary nonscientific viewpoint which uses the categories discredited by them is implied in his warning that the "positive science" of the Understanding "runs the risk of having every specific detail *prove to it* to be the opposite specific detail."[21]

Thus, whereas in *The Relation of Skepticism to Philosophy* the negative side of the proof of Philosophical Science for all nonscientific viewpoints was restricted to a demonstration of the equipollence difficulties facing nonscientific claims, here Hegel has extended that negative proof deeper, revealing to nonscientific viewpoints the self-contradictoriness afflicting the categories through which such claims are made and giving rise to the self-contradictoriness and hence susceptibility to equipollence of those claims.[22] The fact that he has done so and has done so within the scope of the Logic means that the skeptical tier of the two-tier introduction to Philosophical Science envisaged at phase two has become superfluous: there is no longer any need of a proof for nonscientific viewpoints of their vulnerability to equipollence difficulties *outside* the Logic, since the proof for them of this and still worse defects is now effected within the Logic itself.

This innovation allows Hegel to give an answer to any nonscientific viewpoint that raises the two queries mentioned earlier. He should now be able to demonstrate to that viewpoint in a way compelling to it on the basis of its own views and criteria in response to query (i) that nonscientific claims could not possibly be true because they are articulated by self-contradictory categories which make them self-contradictory, and in response to query (ii) that nonscientific concepts do not constitute a genuine alternative to that of Philosophical Science because they are self-contradictory. In principle, then, Hegel has at phase three offered a stronger negative proof of Philosophical Science for all nonscientific viewpoints than he achieved at phase two. However, this is still not his strongest proof of Philosophical Science for all nonscientific viewpoints by a long way.

The innovation just considered was a major step toward turning the early Logic as a whole into a proof for nonscientific viewpoints compelling in the light of their own views and criteria. It might be asked whether the Logic at work in *On the Scientific Ways of Treating Natural Law* did not take even further steps in this direction. Did it not, for example, attempt to give an exoterically compelling demonstration of a necessary development from each category to the next, making the complete systematicity and therefore exhaustiveness of the set of categories destroyed evident for nonscientific viewpoints on the basis of their own views and criteria (rather than something compelling only for a person who had made certain esoteric philosophical assumptions, as in the Logic of phase one)? Although the textual evidence on this point is thin, Hegel seems not yet to have gone this far. Instead, the Logic at work in *On the Scientific Ways of Treating Natural Law* seems to have begun by setting up the categories as a system using esoteric information from the Metaphysics in the manner of the Logic of phase one, only then giving its publicly convincing demonstration of the incoherence of each category in turn.[23] This fact leaves obvious room for a strengthening of the negative side of the proof of Philosophical Science for all nonscientific viewpoints in later texts.

Phase four is represented by the Logic of the *Logic, Metaphysics, and Nature Philosophy*, dating from 1804–1805. We can understand this text as attempting to answer three queries which a nonscientific viewpoint might still raise as grounds for withholding assent to Philosophical Science even if it had fully accepted the demonstration of the vulnerability to equipollence difficulties of all known nonscientific claims offered at phase two and the stronger demonstration of the self-contradictoriness of all known nonscientific categories offered at phase three. The queries are as follows. (i) Even if all the nonscientific categories encountered *so far* are self-contradictory, so that all the nonscientific claims encountered or conceivable *so far* are self-contradictory as well, might it not still be the case that there are other nonscientific categories waiting to be discovered or invented which are self-consistent and which could therefore articulate self-consistent nonscientific claims, claims which might then compete with and be as convincing as or even superior to that of Hegel's Philosophical Science? (ii) In the same way, might it not be the case that self-consistent nonscientific categories are waiting to be invented or discovered which will constitute genuine competition for the concept of Philosophical Science? (iii) Even disregarding the issue of the existence of competing concepts, which only serves to make the problem more acute, how are we to know that Philosophical Science's concept corresponds to anything in reality?

Clearly what the nonscientific viewpoint needs to be shown if queries (i) and (ii) are to be dispelled is that the nonscientific categories whose incoherence was demonstrated at phase three exhaust all the nonscientific categories there are, not merely all those which have been discovered or invented so far. The Logic of the *Logic, Metaphysics, and Nature Philosophy* recognizes the legitimacy of these queries and attempts to answer them by demonstrating exhaustiveness to the nonscientific viewpoint. Two innovations in this Logic are designed to make this goal attainable. First, Hegel introduces an immanent, necessary dialectical development from each category to the next of a kind which is supposed to be compelling for the nonscientific viewpoint. Second, he introduces the kind of circularity in this dialectical development whose role in proving complete systematicity and therefore exhaustiveness we considered in the preceding chapter, and he intends this circularity to be something which the nonscientific viewpoint is bound to recognize when it follows the dialectic. Thus, in the *Logic, Metaphysics, and Nature Philosophy* the dialectic begins from (abstract) Unity at the start of the Logic and returns to (pure) Unity where the Logic ends and the Metaphysics begins. It is of central importance that both of these new aspects of the Logic are supposed to be compelling for the nonscientific viewpoint working without the benefit of esoteric assumptions. Given this fact, Hegel can hope by their means to prove to the nonscientific viewpoint on the basis of its own views and criteria, in accordance with the strategy explained in the preceding chapter, that the collection of nonscientific categories whose self-contradictoriness is demonstrated in the Logic constitutes a complete system and therefore all the nonscientific categories there are. In this way he can hope to dispel queries (i) and (ii) by convincing the nonscientific viewpoint that there are no nonscientific categories except those which have been shown to be incoherent, and therefore none which might be used to articulate coherent nonscientific claims in competition with the claim of Philosophical Science or which might themselves be a self-consistent alternative to Philosophical Science's concept.

The Logic of the *Logic, Metaphysics, and Nature Philosophy* also provides an answer to query (iii). Since the whole discipline is supposed to be accessible and compelling for the nonscientific viewpoint, the reductio ad absurdum of positing the concept of Philosophical Science (Unity) as distinct from its instantiation in reality (the many) and the consequent indirect proof of their absolute identity, which we saw in the preceding chapter the Logic is designed to effect, are supposed to be compelling for the nonscientific viewpoint.[24] Thus the worry expressed in query (iii) should be eliminated by proving to the nonscientific viewpoint which raises it that the assumption on which it rests, namely that the concept of Philosophical Science is distinct from its instantiation in reality and might therefore exist without the latter, is false, for the reason that the concept of Philosophical Science is absolutely identical with its instantiation in reality.

In attempting to answer the three queries in the ways described, the Logic of the *Logic, Metaphysics, and Nature Philosophy* aspired to provide a stronger and considerably more ambitious proof of Philosophical Science for all nonscientific viewpoints than Hegel had previously given. It could do so largely because it was the first version of the Logic since phase one which did not in any way presuppose a knowledge of the Metaphysics, being intended instead to be wholly accessible to nonscientific viewpoints and wholly compelling for them in the light of their own views and criteria. This is why the claim which I made earlier against Haym, Trede, and Poeggeler but with Baillie—that the Logic of the *Logic, Metaphysics, and Nature Philosophy* is intended in its entirety to be compelling for the Understanding or the nonscientific viewpoint and not to presuppose a knowledge of Metaphysics—is important for my account.

Phase five is represented by the *Phenomenology* of 1807. This is Hegel's final, most interesting, and in principle strongest attempt to provide a proof for all nonscientific viewpoints compelling in the light of their own views and criteria of the superiority of Philosophical Science over all other viewpoints and hence its invulnerability to equipollence problems, its immunity to concept-instantiation difficulties, and its truth.

We should begin by noting some points of continuity between the *Phenomenology* and the Logic of the *Logic, Metaphysics, and Nature Philosophy*. For it is important that, notwithstanding the shift from the medium of categories and similar items in the early Logic to the medium of shapes of consciousness in the *Phenomenology*, the answer given at phase five to the challenge of providing a proof of Philosophical Science for all nonscientific viewpoints builds on the answer given at phase four, just as each earlier answer built on that which preceded it. Thus the *Phenomenology* aims to dispel all three of the queries which were dealt with in the Logic of the *Logic, Metaphysics, and Nature Philosophy*, and it employs a similar strategy in order to do so. In close analogy to the latter work, it aims to dispel queries (i) and (ii) by exhibiting in a way compelling for nonscientific viewpoints the self-contradictoriness of each member of a complete system of nonscientific shapes of consciousness and thereby showing that *all* nonscientific concepts and claims are self-contradictory, in order to remove any suspicion a nonscientific viewpoint might have that self-consistent nonscientific claims or concepts in competition with those of Philosophical Science remain to be discovered or invented. Again in analogy to the Logic of the *Logic, Metaphysics, and Nature Philosophy*, it seeks to realize this design by, on the one hand, offering a dialectical development through the shapes of consciousness treated which is compelling for nonscientific viewpoints and which demonstrates both the self-contradictoriness and the systematic connectedness of those shapes and, on the other hand, giving this dialectical development a circular structure as a means to exhibiting the completeness of the system. Again in analogy to the Logic of the *Logic, Metaphysics, and Nature Philosophy*, the *Phenomenology* seeks to dispel query (iii) by giving a publicly compelling proof of the absolute identity of Philosophical Science's concept and the reality instantiating it. And as we saw in the preceding chapter, the general strategies of the proofs given in the two texts are very similar, namely in revolving around the attempt to give a reductio ad absurdum of positing Philosophical Science's concept as distinct from its instantiation, although the *Phenomenology* attempts to effect this reductio ad absurdum indirectly by showing quite generally that positing a subject as distinct from an object or a concept as distinct from an instance always leads to self-contradiction, whereas the Logic of the *Logic, Metaphysics, and Nature Philosophy* attempts to effect it directly. This continuity between phase four and phase five is possible only because, as was urged earlier in opposition to a popular reading, the whole demonstration presented in the *Phenomenology* is intended, like that presented in the Logic of the *Logic, Metaphysics, and Nature Philosophy*, to be compelling for a nonscientific viewpoint which has not yet encountered or accepted any assumptions from Philosophical Science.

So much for continuity. We should now consider a new set of queries—or rather, two objections and two queries—which a nonscientific viewpoint confronted with the proof offered to it at phase four might raise as reasonable grounds for still withholding assent to Hegel's Philosophical Science. Considering these objections and queries will enable us to see that the *Phenomenology* makes certain innovations in an effort to answer them. In doing so the *Phenomenology* attempts to remove the last reasonable grounds which a nonscientific viewpoint might give, in the face of the proof of Philosophical Science Hegel has offered it, for refusing to acknowledge that Philosophical Science is superior to all other viewpoints and hence invulnerable to equipollence problems, faces no concept-instantiation difficulties, and is true. The objections and queries are as follows:

(i) It might be objected that the proof of Philosophical Science found in the Logic of the *Logic, Metaphysics, and Nature Philosophy* is simply too difficult or obscure to function as a proof for *all* nonscientific viewpoints.

(ii) There is a more specific objection to the negative proof of Philosophical Science for all nonscientific viewpoints—and indeed to the negative proof of Philosophical Science simpliciter, with which we were concerned in the preceding chapter—as given in the Logic of the *Logic, Metaphysics, and Nature Philosophy*. This objection concerns a flaw not in the strategy of the proof but in its execution, a flaw which, it seems, Hegel later recognized and attempted to correct. The flaw is that the Logic fails to prove that the categories it destroys constitute a complete system, as it is supposed to, because its dialectic stops short of the pure Unity of the Metaphysics, which it would have to reach if the demonstration of a circular structure in the dialectic on which the proof of the completeness of the system depends (a structure beginning with abstract Unity and ending with pure Unity) were to succeed. The failure of the Logic of phase four to satisfy the circularity criterion of complete systematicity and its consequent failure to prove complete systematicity have the effect on its proof of Philosophical Science for all nonscientific viewpoints of invalidating its answers to queries (i) and (ii). Let us take a closer look at this flaw. In the Logic of *The Difference between the Fichtean and Schellingian Systems of Philosophy* the dialectic stopped short of the content of the Metaphysics, ending on an unresolved contradiction or set of contradictions, from which a step of *postulating* intuition (*Anschauung*), or the synthesizing operation which turns the self-contradictory content of the Logic into the rational content of the Metaphysics, had to be made in order to reach the Metaphysics. This step of postulation was not determined by any dialectical necessity. In the Logic of the *Logic, Metaphysics, and Nature Philosophy* the situation is similar, despite the fact that Hegel has now, unlike in the earlier work, formed an ambition to construct a circular dialectic leading from the abstract Unity with which the Logic begins to the pure Unity with which the Metaphysics begins, and despite the fact that the transition from the Logic to the Metaphysics is in some ways modeled on the dialectical developments found within the Logic. In both works the Metaphysics is reached not by a dialectical transition from the Logic but by a postulation or an intellectual leap which leaves behind and is unregulated by the dialectic of the Logic. This can be seen from several passages in the *Logic, Metaphysics, and Nature Philosophy*. Consider, for example, Hegel's claim there that in his Logic, as in Fichte's system, "becoming absolutely one (*das absolute Einswerden*) remains only a *should*, that is, it remains a beyond in opposition to the Unity of the boundary [that is, the abstract Unity with which the Logic begins]." [25]

The failure of the dialectic of the Logic in the *Logic, Metaphysics, and Nature Philosophy* to reach the Metaphysics was no mere slip on Hegel's part but was forced on him by his conception of how the Logic was supposed to work as a proof of the absolute identity of Philosophical Science's concept and its instantiation, so that the obstacle to giving the dialectic a circular course which this failure represented was not one which could simply be overcome by inserting the missing dialectical transition. [26] This is because, as we have seen, the Logic followed the strategy for proving this absolute identity of beginning with an explicit assumption of the distinctness of the items to be absolutely identified and then showing by means of a dialectical derivation that the result of this assumption was a series of self-contradictions which could not be resolved so long as the assumption was retained, the moral of this being directly the reduction of the assumption to absurdity and indirectly the need to posit as absolutely identical those items which were originally posited as distinct in the assumption. This strategy made it essential that the Logic, founded through and through on the assumption of distinctness, should end on an unresolved self-contradiction. And this would not have been the case if its dialectical development had reached the standpoint of the Metaphysics, distinguished as this was by its lack of self-contradictions. It was therefore for reasons lying deep in Hegel's understanding of how the Logic was supposed to work as a proof of the absolute identity thesis that he stopped its dialectic short of the Metaphysics and thereby doomed his newly conceived aspiration of using a circular dialectic as the means of demonstrating the completeness of the system of categories treated in the work. The circle could not be completed. I would suggest that Hegel's criticism in the *Encyclopedia* that "skepticism in the form of a negative science applied to all forms of finite cognition"—by which he means his own early Logic—would have to "find the finite forms in a merely empirical and unscientific fashion, and accept them as given" should be read in part as a record of his realization that the attempts he had made within the early Logic to demonstrate the complete systematicity of the categories dealt with there, and in particular the final attempt in the Logic of the *Logic, Metaphysics, and Nature Philosophy,* had failed for reasons of the kind just considered.[27] Within the conception of the early Logic it had proved impossible to give a destructive demonstration which was substantially better than the historical skepticism which "exercises its dialectic contingently, for just as the material comes up before it, it shows in the same that implicitly it is negative."[28] A major task for the *Phenomenology,* if it is to make progress toward giving a proof of Philosophical Science for all nonscientific viewpoints, will therefore be to make the proof of complete systematicity via a circular dialectic, which the Logic of the *Logic, Metaphysics, and Nature Philosophy* aspired to but was unable to perform, actually work.

(iii) There is a query which might be raised even by a nonscientific viewpoint which had been convinced by the proof of a complete system of categories which was intended at phase four. Such a viewpoint might seek to keep queries (i) and (ii) from phase four alive despite this proof by pointing out that, even if all known nonscientific categories have been shown to constitute a complete system each of whose members is self-contradictory, it is still not beyond the bounds of reasonable hope that some *new* system of nonscientific categories or some *new* systemless nonscientific categories might be found which are self-consistent and are therefore genuine alternatives to the concept of Philosophical Science and make it possible to articulate self-consistent claims in competition with that of Philosophical Science. Certainly, it might be conceded, the demonstration that all the categories known so far constitute a complete system makes this possibility seem rather remote. Nevertheless, it might be insisted, this possibility does not seem so remote that it would be unreasonable cautiously to withhold assent from Hegel's Philosophical Science, which is after all very unfamiliar and extravagant, in the hope that it might be realized.

(iv) Even if the nonscientific viewpoint could be given a proof which would persuade it of the futility of holding onto the ground for withholding assent to Philosophical Science just indicated in (iii), and could thereby be made to recognize that Philosophical Science is the only coherent view of things and that Philosophical Science's concept is the only coherent concept, still it might withhold assent from Philosophical Science, or refuse to infer from Hegel's demonstration of the incoherence of positing the concept of Philosophical Science as distinct from its instantiation the positive moral that they are absolutely identical, on another ground. This ground is that Philosophical Science has major flaws other than self-contradictoriness—in particular, artificiality or arbitrariness—which make it more attractive to give up altogether the attempt to find any truth or any coherent concept and maybe just try to avoid believing anything or learn to live with one's own incoherence, than to accept Philosophical Science, or posit the absolute identity of the concept of Philosophical Science with its instantiation.

Hegel seeks in the *Phenomenology* to dispel these objections and queries by means of three innovations. The first innovation is the attempt to provide a demonstration which is easier for nonscientific viewpoints of many different levels of sophistication to follow and to find convincing than the difficult and obscure demonstration given in the Logic of the *Logic, Metaphysics, and Nature Philosophy.* Thus the demonstration in the *Phenomenology* is consciously graduated to respond to the different abilities of different viewpoints. It constitutes in Hegel's metaphor a "ladder" onto which the nonscientific viewpoint can climb at a level corresponding to its initial intellectual resources. In addition, Hegel is generally at pains in the *Phenomenology* to make the dialectic easier to follow, more adapted to comprehension by nonscientific viewpoints. In these ways he hopes to remedy the weakness of his proof of Philosophical Science for all nonscientific viewpoints pointed out in objection (i).

The second innovation is that the dialectic of the *Phenomenology* extends all the way to Philosophical Science, no longer stopping short and leaving the final step to Philosophical Science one of dialectically unguided postulation as in the early Logic. Thus Hegel writes in the *Phenomenology* that "the individual has the right to demand that Science should at least provide him with the ladder to this standpoint [i.e. Science's]," and he writes in the *Encyclopedia* that the *Phenomenology* develops its dialectic "up to the standpoint of Philosophical Science." [29] Hegel was able to make this change because of a modest revision in his strategy for proving the absolute identity of the concept of Philosophical Science and its instantiation. In the early logic, as we have seen, this proof obstructed the extension of the dialectic all the way to Philosophical Science by requiring it to end on an unresolved self-contradiction. By the time of writing the *Phenomenology* Hegel seems to have realized that if the circular structure of the dialectic could really be established and the completeness of the system of shapes of consciousness treated thereby be demonstrated, it would be possible to dispense with the early Logic's direct approach of reducing to absurdity the postulation of Philosophical Science's concept as distinct from its instantiation by beginning with that postulation explicitly and then showing it to lead to an unresolved self-contradiction. Instead one would be able to reduce the thesis of the distinctness of Philosophical Science's concept from its instantiation to absurdity indirectly by showing that *all possible* ways of articulating a distinctness of concepts from their instances—all possible shapes of consciousness, or ways of positing a subject in opposition to an object—led to self-contradiction, thereby showing by implication that positing Philosophical Science's concept as distinct from its instantiation did so too. In this way the *Phenomenology* could avoid beginning with Philosophical Science's concept taken in abstraction from its instantiation and, more importantly, could avoid ending with an unresolved self-contradiction, while still offering a proof of the absolute identity thesis. This new strategy for proving the absolute identity thesis both *made possible* the extension of the dialectic of the *Phenomenology* all the way to Philosophical Science and hence the completion of its circular course, and also *required* this. It made it possible by removing the need to end the dialectic on a self-contradiction and therefore short of self-consistent Philosophical Science. It required it because it was essential to the new strategy that the coverage of *all possible* ways of articulating the subject-object opposition, all possible shapes of consciousness, be demonstrated, and this required a demonstrated coverage of "the *entire system* of consciousness," which in turn required a demonstration of the circular course of the dialectic.[30]

The third innovation is the historical dimension of the *Phenomenology*. The *Phenomenology* not only exhibits a necessarily developing series of self-contradictory shapes of consciousness and their necessary development into self-consistent Philosophical Science, but also interprets history as a teleological process having as its purpose the generation in sequence over time of just this necessary series and its culmination in Philosophical Science. The dialectical development of the work thus becomes the key to an interpretation of the nature and purpose of history. This projection of the dialectical development into the dimension of history is something quite new in the *Phenomenology*, having no precedent in the early Logic.

We can now return to the remaining objection and two queries in order to see how the second and third innovations enable Hegel to answer them. We begin with objection (ii), the objection that the Logic of phase four failed to demonstrate the complete systematicity and therefore exhaustiveness of the list of categories and similar items which it discredited because it failed to establish a dialectic having a circular course. This shortcoming is remedied in the *Phenomenology* by means of its second innovation, the extension of the dialectic all the way to Philosophical Science. Thus compare the failure of the Logic of the *Logic, Metaphysics, and Nature Philosophy* to make its dialectic extend all the way from the abstract Unity at its start to the pure Unity of the Metaphysics with the way in which the *Phenomenology* by its own account succeeds in giving its dialectic a circular course. As we have seen, the *Phenomenology* extends its dialectic, which begins from Sense-Certainty and then goes through the other shapes of consciousness, into Philosophical Science. Once Philosophical Science is reached, it "contains the passage of the Concept into consciousness"—by which Hegel means a process of returning by means of an unbroken course of dialectic to Sense-Certainty and the other contents of the *Phenomenology*.[31] This process, Hegel tells us, is ultimately realized in the dialectical development within Philosophical Science which, via the Philosophy of Nature, "reinstates the subject" of the Philosophy of Spirit.[32] And sure enough, if we examine the *Encyclopedia* version of the Philosophy of Spirit, we find that it does return us to Sense-Certainty and the other shapes of consciousness in a section bearing the same title as the *Phenomenology*.[33] In this way the extension of the dialectic of the *Phenomenology* into Philosophical Science allows it to be given a circular structure. And this enables the *Phenomenology* to offer a demonstration of the complete systematicity and therefore exhaustiveness of the shapes of consciousness which it treats.[34] Thus the nonscientific viewpoint which is to be convinced of the exhaustiveness of the discrediting of shapes of consciousness effected in the *Phenomenology* is first made to consider, regardless of its initial level of sophistication, the most primitive shape treated there.[35] It is then shown the necessity of the dialectical development from this shape through the subsequent shapes, which include all those that it knows or can imagine already and its own shape, and eventually the necessity of this development's arrival at Philosophical Science. Once it reaches Philosophical Science, it sees that the necessary dialectical course has taken it in a circle, since within Philosophical Science this course brings it back to the most primitive shape from which it began. This shows it that the shapes considered constituted a complete system, so that it can be sure that they exhaust all the shapes there are. The strategy envisaged at phase four as a means of dispelling queries (i) and (ii) raised there by the nonscientific viewpoint thus at last finds its proper execution in the *Phenomenology*.

The innovations of the *Phenomenology* also make possible an answer to query (iii), the query whether, even if all known nonscientific categories constitute a complete self-contradictory system, there might not still be a second system of nonscientific categories or individual nonscientific categories outside any system, which are innocent of self-contradictoriness. This query was already a rather weak ground for withholding assent from Hegel's Philosophical Science. The third innovation aims to make even this weak ground untenable by proving to the nonscientific viewpoint that it has been the whole purpose of history to generate precisely that complete system of self-contradictory shapes of consciousness, culminating in Philosophical Science, which is known, so that to hope that other shapes outside this system remain to be discovered or invented would be vain. In this way the proof of exhaustiveness by way of complete systematicity is reinforced by the demonstration that the genesis of exactly this complete system, culminating in Philosophical Science, has been the very purpose of history.[36]

Finally, the innovations of the *Phenomenology* make possible an answer to query (iv). The second innovation in itself promises a powerful reply to the suggestion that Philosophical Science is arbitrary or artificial. So far we have been mainly concerned with the *negative* side of the proof of Philosophical Science for all nonscientific viewpoints as this developed in the early Logic and the *Phenomenology*. The second innovation, the extension of the dialectic of the *Phenomenology* all the way to Philosophical Science, marks a major attempt to strengthen the *positive* side of the proof. This positive side already received fairly clear expression as an ideal in *The Difference between the Fichtean and Schellingian Systems of Philosophy*, where Hegel made it a task of the Logic that "the Absolute should be constructed for consciousness."[37] No version of the early Logic went very far in pursuit of this goal, though. To be sure, the versions of the Logic in *The Difference between the Fichtean and Schellingian Systems of Philosophy* and the *Logic, Metaphysics, and Nature Philosophy* tried to derive dialectically the content of Philosophical Science in a way compelling for nonscientific viewpoints. But this content was derived only in a distorted, abstract, oppositional form, and a dialectically underived leap to Philosophical Science had to be performed before it could be grasped in its true, synthesized form.[38] The *Phenomenology* certainly retains this kind of derivation of the content of Philosophical Science in an imperfect form as part of what it attempts to make compelling to nonscientific viewpoints. It even aims to perform this derivation of Philosophical Science as an *appearance* much more exhaustively than the early Logic, aspiring to derive *all* parts of Philosophical Science in this way.[39] But the *Phenomenology* can, by virtue of its innovation of a dialectic which leads all the way into Philosophical Science, hope also to accomplish the task expressed in the injunction that "the Absolute should be constructed for consciousness" in a more perfect way. It can hope by means of its dialectic not only to develop the content of Philosophical Science as an *appearance* in a way compelling for the nonscientific viewpoint but also eventually to supersede this derivation of Philosophical Science in an imperfect form by a derivation of Philosophical Science "in its true shape" which is compelling for the nonscientific viewpoint, namely at the point where the dialectic of the *Phenomenology* culminates in Philosophical Science.[40]

By thus strengthening the positive side of his proof of Philosophical Science for all nonscientific viewpoints, Hegel makes possible a powerful answer to query (iv). He can now hope to demonstrate to any nonscientific viewpoint which raises the suggestion that Philosophical Science is arbitrary or artificial on the basis of views and criteria to which that viewpoint is already committed that its views and criteria compel it to develop all the way from its self-contradictory viewpoint into the self-consistent viewpoint of Philosophical Science, and moreover that all other nonscientific viewpoints are compelled likewise. In this way the ambition would be realized with respect to each nonscientific viewpoint that Philosophical Science be able to "show [the individual] this standpoint within himself," and with it the even higher ambition that Philosophical Science be able to show each individual its own standpoint within *everyone*.[41] By thus making demonstrable to each nonscientific viewpoint on the basis of its own views and criteria that "all roads lead to Rome"—that all nonscientific viewpoints are implicitly committed to the truth of Philosophical Science in the sense that they can all be compelled to develop into Philosophical Science simply by drawing out consequences of the views and criteria which they already accept—the *Phenomenology* would effectively dispel any suggestion that Philosophical Science is arbitrary or artificial. The *Phenomenology* aims to show that, on the contrary, in this special but strong sense Philosophical Science is a necessary viewpoint. Hence Hegel's statement in the *Encyclopedia* that the method of the *Phenomenology* is "to begin from the first, simplest appearance of Spirit, the immediate consciousness, and to develop Spirit's dialectic up to the standpoint of Philosophical Science, the necessity of which is demonstrated by this process."[42]

Thus the second innovation of the *Phenomenology* by itself allows Hegel to make a powerful reply to query (iv) offered as a last-ditch ground for withholding assent from Philosophical Science. This answer to query (iv) is made still more powerful by the addition of the third innovation, the historical dimension of the *Phenomenology*. For what, Hegel may ask, could be less arbitrary or artificial than a viewpoint which is not only the sole self-consistent viewpoint and the necessary outcome of all other viewpoints, but also the very telos of history, which has been working to achieve it by first serially generating all the other, self-contradictory viewpoints in order to have them then develop into it as their self-consistent and necessary culmination?

The *Phenomenology* is Hegel's last attempt to provide a proof of Philosophical Science for all nonscientific viewpoints. It is safe to assume that he regards this discipline as the successful culmination of his quest for such a proof. And in particular, we may assume that he believes himself to have removed in the *Phenomenology* the last reasonable grounds nonscientific viewpoints might advance for withholding assent from Philosophical Science in the face of the proof with which he has furnished them.

TEN

The Dialectical Method in
Hegel's Epistemology

ET US review briefly the epistemological standards which Hegel accepts and the strategies which he develops in order to meet them on behalf of his Philosophical Science. The standards are: (a) that Philosophical Science be invulnerable to the skeptic's equipollence problems, (b) that it be invulnerable to the skeptic's concept-instantiation problems, and (c) that it be provable to all nonscientific viewpoints solely on the basis of their own views and criteria as superior to them all and hence invulnerable to equipollence problems, as immune to concept-instantiation problems, and as true. The strategies for meeting these standards are: for (a) the doctrine that the claim of Philosophical Science has no negation and the discrediting of all nonscientific viewpoints through self-contradiction; for (b) the doctrine that Philosophical Science's concept and its instantiation are absolutely identical, the proof of this doctrine via a reductio ad absurdum of the thesis of their distinctness and the discrediting of all competing, nonscientific concepts through self-contradiction; and for (c) the complex proof of Philosophical Science for all nonscientific viewpoints described in the preceding chapter.

The purpose of this part of my book has been to explain rather than to evaluate the epistemological, and in particular antiskeptical, enterprise based on these standards and strategies. However, the first task of an evaluation of the enterprise would, it seems to me, be to examine Hegel's dialectical method more closely with a view to estimating its ability to play the several crucial roles assigned it within the enterprise. The original development of the dialectical method during the Jena period, initially in connection with the early Logic, was motivated largely by its perceived suitedness for just these roles. And certainly very little of Hegel's epistemological enterprise could succeed if the dialectical method were to fail. While a proper explanation or evaluation of the dialectical method would require a book unto itself, we may at least take a first step toward this goal by concluding with a few remarks about the method written, like the rest of this part, in a spirit of sympathetic exegesis.

First, though, let us briefly recapitulate the crucial roles played by the method within the epistemological enterprise. We saw in Chapter Seven that it was by means of a particular application of the destructive part of the dialectical method modeled on an argument of Parmenides' that the category Nothing (or Not-being) was shown to be self-contradictory and the claim of Hegel's Philosophical Science thereby shown to have no negation. And we saw in the same chapter that it was through an essential dialectical self-exposition that the Absolute Idea or Concept of Philosophical Science embraced, or expressed itself as, Being, thereby making the absolute identity of the concept of Philosophical Science and its reality or object recognizable for anyone who understood this concept. We saw in Chapter Eight that the dialectical method played the roles of destroying through self-contradiction all the nonscientific viewpoints which might have competed with the viewpoint of Philosophical Science and of displaying their exhaustiveness by articulating them as a complete system. We also saw in Chapter Eight that it was the dialectical method that effected the destruction of all concepts which might have competed with the concept of Philosophical Science and demonstrated the complete systematicity and hence exhaustiveness of the collection of nonscientific concepts so destroyed. And we saw there that it was the dialectical method that gave an indirect proof of the thesis of the absolute identity of Philosophical Science's concept and its instantiation by reducing to absurdity the assumption of the distinctness of Philosophical Science's concept from its instantiation in particular (the early Logic) or the assumption of the distinctness of a concept from its instance in general (the *Phenomenology* and the later Logic). Finally, we saw in Chapter Nine that the dialectical method played a number of essential roles in Hegel's undertaking of giving a proof of Philosophical Science for all nonscientific viewpoints compelling for them in the light of their own views and criteria.

The dialectical method is supposed to expound a necessary development through a series of categories (or similar items) by means of alternate steps of generating self-contradictions in earlier categories and resolving them in later categories. As an illustration of the character of these steps, consider the textbook example found at the start of the later Logic of the transition from the category Being to the category Becoming. The method begins with an implicitly self-contradictory category— in this case Being—and makes the self-contradiction explicit by demonstrating how the category implies or develops into a contrary category— in this case Nothing.[1] The converse implication or development—in this case of Nothing into Being—is demonstrated similarly. This negative result is then shown to have a positive outcome, which is understood to be as necessary as the negative result was, namely a new, higher category which Hegel refers to as "the negative of the negative" and which somehow unites the two contrary categories involved in the preceding self-contradictions—in our example the new category is Becoming.[2] The whole procedure then repeats itself, beginning from this higher level.

The negative side of the dialectical method is in principle least problematic. Hegel is not the only or the first major philosopher to have suggested that fundamental concepts of ours are implicitly self-contradictory—consider, for example, Kant's explanation of the Mathematical Antinomies as arising from a self-contradiction in our concept of the world. And there seems nothing inherently suspect in the suggestion.

The plausibility of this negative side of Hegel's dialectical method may be enhanced at a general level by reflecting on certain features which it shares with Socratic elenchus. The later Hegel was fond of seeing anticipations of his own dialectical method and its philosophical purposes in the late Platonic dialogues, in particular the *Parmenides,* the *Sophist,* and the *Philebus.*[3] These works themselves prove to be largely a dead end for the purpose of illuminating the character of his own dialectic because he radically misunderstands them, reading into them his own dialectical method and its purposes in a very unconvincing way.[4] However, his misinterpretation of the late Platonic dialogues does not *simply* involve reading into them his own dialectical method and its purposes. It also in various ways involves reading into them the method of Socratic elenchus and its purposes, as these are portrayed in the early Platonic dialogues. For this reason, despite Hegel's hints to the contrary, it is to the early rather than the late Platonic dialogues that we should turn if we would throw light on his own dialectic.

An illustration of Hegel's mistaken assimilation of the methods and purposes of late to those of early Platonic dialogues is found in his notorious mistranslation of the *Sophist,* 259c–d.[5] In this passage the Eleatic stranger in fact speaks sharply against those who, failing to distinguish carefully the different senses of terms, insist on the genuineness of what are merely apparent contradictions. And he says that what is by contrast worthwhile is to "follow our statements step by step and, in criticizing the assertion that a different thing is the same or the same thing is different in a certain sense, to take account of the precise sense and the precise respect in which they are said to be one or the other." According to Hegel's mistranslation in the *History of Philosophy,* on the other hand, the Eleatic stranger says here that what is important is to grasp "that that which is different is the same and that which is the same is different, and in one and the same respect."[6] This mistranslation involves two misassimilations of the methods and purposes of late to those of early Platonic dialogues. First, the mistranslation shows Hegel reading the late dialogues as though they were concerned to demonstrate contradictions in our ordinary beliefs or concepts. This is not a major ambition of the late dialogues and is quite opposed to the spirit of the passage from the *Sophist*. But it *is* a major concern of the early dialogues, in which Socrates is at work verifying the Delphic oracle's pronouncement that he is the wisest of men, despite his knowledge of his own ignorance, by demonstrating the self-contradictoriness of other people's fundamental beliefs and definitions.[7] Second, and for our purposes more importantly, the mistranslation shows Hegel reading the late dialogues as insisting on the sameness of the senses of words involved in apparent contradictions in order to preserve the genuineness of these contradictions. This is quite contrary to Plato's intentions in the passage from the *Sophist,* where he is insisting on *distinguishing* the different senses of words in order to *avoid* paradox. And it is equally contrary to the detailed arguments of the *Sophist,* which follow this policy scrupulously. But once again Hegel's misinterpretation echoes a theme which really is pervasive in early Platonic dialogues. For in the early dialogues Socrates manifests a high degree of sensitivity toward what he perceives as the common impropriety of positing ex post facto a merely invented or imagined distinction of senses with the more or less eristic purpose of avoiding the acknowledgment that one has been shown by Socratic cross-examination to be guilty of a genuine self-contradiction. Socrates invariably associates this impropriety with the name of Prodicus, the Sophist renowned for his art of drawing fine distinctions of sense.[8]

The characteristic of Socratic elenchus just mentioned proves helpful in illuminating the negative side of Hegel's own dialectical method. So too does a further characteristic of Socratic elenchus. As is well known, Socrates and Plato share a pronounced preference for the spoken over the written word. One of Socrates' reasons for this preference is an implicit assumption that the meaning of a given term or assertion employed by someone is in part constituted by, and hence only determinable by investigating, a large network of related assertions which that person would be prepared to make. Such a network of assertions, though not adequately communicable by a person in a written text, may be elicited from him by careful cross-examination.[9] This assumption that the meaning of a given term or assertion is in part constituted by a large network of related assertions which the person using it would be prepared to make helps to explain how Socrates can understand elenctic arguments as demonstrations of the self-contradictoriness of the interlocutor's initial hypothesis, despite the appearance that these arguments merely demonstrate a contradiction between two or more independent propositions advanced by the interlocutor, only one of which is the interlocutor's initial hypothesis. Socrates thinks of the apparently independent propositions which are in contradiction with one another as all belonging to the network of propositions which constitutes the meaning of the initial hypothesis.[10]

These two characteristics of Socratic elenchus—Socrates' assumption that a large network of assertions which a person would be prepared to make is always constitutive of what that person means by a given term or assertion, and his strict prohibition on the retroactive positing of invented or imagined distinctions of sense in order to avoid acknowledging a self-contradiction—both have a bearing on the negative side of Hegel's dialectical method. The first characteristic, Socrates' assumption that a large network of assertions which a person would be prepared to make is internal to the meaning of any given term or assertion used by that person—that is, a network larger than most of us today would acknowledge—is by no means foolish or easily refutable. Including a broader network of accepted propositions among our criteria of meaning-identity would perhaps give us a somewhat different, a more fine-grained concept of meaning than that which we normally employ. But it is not at all obvious that it would be an inferior concept of meaning. To the extent that one finds Socrates' assumption attractive, and in proportion as one broadens the network of meaning-internal assertions, one will, like him, find it plausible to impute a high incidence of implicit self-contradictoriness to people's concepts and claims. For in order to find such implicit self-contradictoriness in a concept or claim, one need only find a contradiction between two or more of the assertions which belong to the network constitutive of its meaning—and the larger the network, the easier this will be. Now Hegel, like Socrates, works on the assumption that a broad network of beliefs is internal to the meaning of the concepts which he is attempting to discredit. For example, in a passage belonging to an argument designed to prove the self-contradictoriness of the concepts of attraction and repulsion Hegel assumes that Newton's third law of motion, the law that to every action there is an equal and opposite reaction, is internal to the meaning of these concepts. He writes: "If the increased density or specific weight of a body is explained as an increase in the force of attraction, the same phenomenon can be explained with equal ease as an increase in the force of repulsion, for there can only be as much attraction as there is repulsion . . . the one has meaning only with reference to the other. To the extent to which the one were greater than the other, to that same extent it would not exist at all."[11] Hegel's assumption that a broad network of beliefs is internal to the meaning of the concepts which he is attempting to discredit helps to make intelligible—and, to the extent that the assumption is reasonable, helps to make reasonable—his expectation that he will be able to unearth by means of the negative side of his dialectical method a large amount of self-contradictoriness in these concepts.

The other characteristic of Socratic elenchus, its strict limiting of the conditions under which it is legitimate to postulate retroactively distinctions of sense, is also by no means foolish or indefensible. A plausible case could be made for such strictly limited conditions by arguing in something like the following fashion: Meaning a term in a given sense necessarily involves intending to use it in that sense. Consequently, in order to have meant a term X in two different senses at a given time, a person must have intended to use it with those two senses at that time. But since intention necessarily involves a consciousness of what one intends, the person must also have been conscious of the intention of using term X in those two senses at that time. And finally, it is unclear how a person could have been conscious of this without simultaneously being conscious of the difference between the two senses intended. The strict limitation which follows from this argument for legitimately imputing to someone two or more different senses in his use of a term at a given time is that he must have been conscious at that time of intending to use the term in those different senses. To the extent that one imposes strict conditions on the retroactive postulation of distinctions of sense as Socrates does—that is, somewhat stricter conditions than most of us are in the habit of imposing—this enhances the ease of sustaining the charge that certain beliefs a person has contradict one another, and hence that any concept or belief to whose network of meaning-constituting beliefs they both belong is self-contradictory. For there is less room to explain away contradictions between beliefs as merely apparent on the ground that, contrary to appearances, key terms involved in them are being used in distinct senses. Now Hegel, like Socrates, imposes strict conditions on the retroactive postulation of distinctions of sense. And for reasons just sketched, this again helps to make intelligible, and to the extent that the strict conditions involved are plausible, it helps to make plausible, the assumption supporting the negative side of Hegel's dialectical method that a high degree of self-contradictoriness is to be found among our concepts and beliefs.

An example of Hegel's imposition of such strict conditions is his criticism in the *Science of Logic* of Kant's reaction to the Antinomies expounded in the *Critique of Pure Reason*. Hegel takes the view that the Antinomies exhibit genuine contradictions.[12] According to him, Kant's reaction to the Antinomies was on the contrary to distinguish two senses in which reality was being talked about in the two opposed propositions making up each Antinomy—reality qua thing-in-itself in the one proposition and reality qua appearance in the other—and to argue on this ground that their inconsistency was merely apparent. Kant then claimed that we were in possession of a knowledge of the one of these two seemingly contradictory propositions which referred to reality qua *appearance*.[13] This interpretation of Kant's reaction focuses on and is convincing for the Third and Fourth Antinomies (the Dynamical Antinomies). Thus in the Third Antinomy Kant seeks to dispel the apparent contradiction between our belief in universal natural causation and our belief in human freedom by distinguishing two senses in which reality is at issue on the two sides of this apparent contradiction. Our belief in universal natural causation concerns reality qua appearance, while our belief in human freedom concerns reality simpliciter or qua thing-in-itself, and so the contradiction between the two beliefs is merely apparent. In addition, while our belief in human freedom cannot constitute knowledge because if it is true it must concern reality qua thing-in-itself, our belief in universal natural causation, since it concerns reality qua appearance, can and in fact does constitute knowledge. Hegel objects to Kant's attempt to dispel the genuine contradictions of the Antinomies in this way that reacting to these discovered contradictions among our fundamental beliefs by thus distinguishing ex post facto two different senses of reality in play on the two sides of each contradiction, in order to dispel the appearance of contradiction and make room for our knowledge of one side of what is adjudged a merely illusory contradiction, is "like attributing to someone a correct perception, with the rider that nevertheless he is incapable of perceiving what is true but only what is false."[14] To spell out Hegel's point: just as when we praise someone for having a correct perception of things, we do so not in the bizarrely qualified sense that he has a correct perception only of what is false, but in the sense that he has a correct perception simpliciter, likewise the beliefs which we have in (our knowledge of) universal natural causation and human freedom are not beliefs about (our knowledge of) reality in some dramatically qualified sense of reality, such as reality qua appearance, but about (our knowledge of) reality simpliciter. If, upon attributing a correct perception to someone, we were to discover a difficulty in this attribution, such as that the person's perception was in fact incorrect, and were to seek to protect our original attribution in the face of this difficulty by introducing retroactively the qualification that what was perceived was not the true but only the false, we would be deceiving ourselves, since at the time when we made the attribution we in fact had no such qualification in mind. Similarly, if, when confronted with the contradiction between our beliefs in (our knowledge of) universal natural causation and human freedom, we suddenly, like Kant, introduce dramatic qualifications to their meanings retroactively in an effort to show the contradiction merely illusory, we are deceiving ourselves, since we in fact had no such qualifications in mind. Thus Hegel's criticism of Kant's reaction to the Anti-

nomies reflects a strict prohibition on the retroactive positing of invented
or imagined distinctions of sense in order to avoid acknowledging a genuine contradiction which is similar to the Socratic prohibition found in
the early Platonic dialogues.

Having considered these two ways in which one might hope to make
more intelligible and plausible the negative side of Hegel's dialectical
method we may now turn to its positive side. This, it will be remembered,
consists in a necessary transition at each stage of the dialectic beyond the
self-contradiction demonstrated to a new category, "the negative of the
negative"—or to use our example from the later Logic, a necessary transition beyond the self-contradictory categories of Being and Nothing to
the new category of Becoming.[15] This positive side of the dialectical
method is as indispensable for much of Hegel's epistemological enterprise as is its negative side. For example, it is essential to his strategy of
demonstrating that the nonscientific categories or similar items treated
in his destructive disciplines not only are self-contradictory but also constitute a complete system, and hence all the nonscientific categories or
similar items there are, so that the very possibility of an equipollence
problem arising for Philosophical Science is eliminated.

As Inwood has pointed out, the positive side of the dialectical method
is particularly difficult to make sense of or accept.[16] A clue to understanding Hegel's conception of the necessary transitions which it involves lies,
perhaps, in his remark that, "It is . . . in the grasping of opposites in their
unity or of the positive in the negative, that speculative thought consists."[17] For this statement suggests that the necessary transition from the
"negative" of two mutually implying contrary categories, like Being and
Nothing, to the "positive" of a new category, like Becoming, for Hegel
just consists in the two mutually implying contrary categories being
somehow preserved and unified in this new category. To spell out this
suggestion more fully: if, having shown that two contrary categories imply one another, we can find a new category which, alone among categories, in some sense preserves and unifies those contrary categories, then
we will have shown that the transition to this new category is necessary
in the sense of "necessary" with which Hegel is concerned. The necessity
of these transitions should therefore be thought of as sui generis. In particular, it should not be confused with or assimilated to the necessity of
logical or other types of implication. Such a sui generis kind of necessary
transition, if it could really be discovered in particular cases, would seem
quite capable of playing at least the more important roles which Hegel
assigns to it within his epistemological project, such as its role in the
demonstration that the categories or similar items treated in Hegel's destructive disciplines are not only self-contradictory but also constitute a
complete system. And it would arguably be capable of playing the most

important nonepistemological roles assigned to it within Hegel's Philosophical Science as well.

This kind of sui generis necessary transition may be illustrated by reference to our example from the beginning of the later Logic. Hegel's thought seems to be somewhat as follows. Having shown the two contrary categories Being and Nothing to be mutually implying and therefore self-contradictory, we find that the category Becoming in a way preserves and unifies those mutually implying contrary categories. It does so because a state of becoming, while a unified state, is essentially a transition from a state of nothing (or not-being) to one of being, or vice versa. If we take some other new category at random, we will find that it does not preserve and unify the contrary categories Being and Nothing in any analogous way. There is, for example, no analogous sense in which the category Substance could be said to preserve and unify them. Indeed, Hegel supposes, if we were to examine methodically all our categories beside Becoming, we would find none which preserved and unified the categories Being and Nothing in any analogous way. In Hegel's view, these circumstances justify him in ascribing to the transition from the mutually implying contrary categories Being and Nothing to the category Becoming that sui generis necessity which consists in Becoming being the only category which preserves and unifies the mutually implying contraries Being and Nothing.

In this way it is possible to make reasonably good sense, at least at a general level, of the positive side of Hegel's dialectical method, the idea that the outcome of a self-contradiction in a category is a necessary transition to a new category, to "the negative of the negative." To this extent the positive side of the dialectical method should not be branded as its Achilles' heel too quickly. This is not to suggest that the positive side of the method is free of problems, though. For example, it is unclear in precisely what sense and under precisely what conditions transitions such as that from the two categories Being and Nothing to the new category Becoming are to count as unifications and preservations of the first two categories in the third category. And more seriously, it is unclear to what extent the supposition is plausible that this unification and preservation, even if it can be defined with sufficient rigor and identified in specific cases, is performed only by a *single* category in each case. For example, the categories "Was" or "Will be" might be advanced in competition with the category Becoming as equally plausible unifiers and preservers of the contrary categories Being and Nothing. Merely being something that was or will be is a unified state, while what merely was or will be in one sense has being and in another sense is nothing. Still, my purpose here has not been to give a conclusive evaluation of Hegel's dialectical method but rather to illuminate its general character and sug-

gest some ways in which it may be more defensible than a first examination would suggest. This will suffice as an elucidation of this essential
component of Hegel's epistemological, and in particular antiskeptical,
enterprise and as a step toward the estimation of its ability to play the
roles assigned to it within that enterprise.

In conclusion, I would like to say that whether Hegel's crusade on the
field of epistemology ends in defeat or victory—and doubtless only a
rather optimistic or reckless ally would join him in expectation of the
latter—it is one of the nobler endeavors in this area and deserves to be
recognized as such. It is noble, on the one hand, because of the clarity
with which it understands the nature of the skeptical foe, and in general
the rigor of the epistemological challenges which it accepts. And, on the
other hand, because of the ingenuity, originality, and persistence with
which it struggles to cope with these challenges. In both respects Hegel's
epistemology compares favorably, I would suggest, with the epistemolo-
gies of more familiar figures in the lists against skepticism such as Descartes.

Selected Bibliography

Notes

Index

Selected Bibliography

The following is a list of some literature dealing with Hegel's views on skepticism in particular or epistemology in general. Texts which I have found particularly helpful are marked with an asterisk.

Baum, M. "Zur Methode der Logik und Metaphysik beim Jenaer Hegel." *Hegel-Studien,* supplementary vol. 20.

Buchner, H. "Zur Bedeutung des Skeptizismus beim jungen Hegel." *Hegel-Studien,* supplementary vol. 4.*

Duesing, K. "Die Bedeutung des antiken Skeptizismus fuer Hegels Kritik der sinnlichen Gewissheit." *Hegel-Studien,* 1973.

Fischer, K. *Hegels Leben, Werke, und Lehre.* 2 vols. Heidelberg, 1901.

Fulda, H. F. *Das Problem einer Einleitung in Hegels Wissenschaft der Logik.* Frankfurt am Main: Vittorio Klostermann, 1975.*

Habermas, J. *Erkenntnis und Interesse.* Frankfurt am Main: Suhrkamp, 1968. Tr. *Knowledge and Human Interests.* Boston: Beacon Press, 1971.*

Hasler, L. "Skepsis und Natur: Zur philosophischen Funktion des Skeptizismus beim fruehen Hegel." *Hegel-Jahrbuch,* 1976.

Haym, R. *Hegel und seine Zeit.* Hildesheim: Georg Olms Verlagsbuchhandlung, 1962.

Hyppolite, J. *Genèse et structure de la phénoménologie de l'esprit de Hegel.* Paris: Aubier, Éditions Montaigne, 1946. Tr. *Genesis and Structure of Hegel's Phenomenology of Spirit.* Evanston: Northwestern University Press, 1974.

Inwood, M. J. *Hegel.* London: Routledge and Kegan Paul, 1983.*

Phalén, A. *Das Erkenntnisproblem in Hegels Philosophie.* Upsala, 1912.

Rockmore, T. *Hegel's Circular Epistemology.* Bloomington: Indiana University Press, 1986.

Solomon, R. C. "Hegel's Epistemology." *American Philosophical Quarterly,* 1974.

Verneaux, R. "L'essence du scepticisme selon Hegel." *Histoire de la philosophie et métaphysique: Recherches de philosophie, I.* Paris: Editions Desclée de Brouwer, 1955.*

Notes

Introduction

1. For the role of skepticism in Hegel's history of philosophy in the narrow sense see R. Verneaux, "L'essence du scepticisme selon Hegel," *Histoire de la philosophie et métaphysique: Recherches de philosophie I* (Paris: Editions Desclée de Brouwer, 1955), especially the overview of the role of skepticism in Hegel's history of ancient philosophy on p. 150.
2. G. W. F. Hegel, *Phenomenology of Spirit*, tr. A. V. Miller (Oxford: Oxford University Press, 1979), no. 78.
3. Thus three of the more helpful studies treating the role of skepticism in Hegel's thought—H. F. Fulda, *Das Problem einer Einleitung in Hegels Wissenschaft der Logik* (Frankfurt am Main: Vittorio Klostermann, 1975), esp. pp. 36–37, 164; H. Buchner, "Zur Bedeutung des Skeptizismus beim jungen Hegel," *Hegel-Studien*, supplementary vol. 4; Verneaux, "L'essence du scepticisme selon Hegel," esp. pp. 147–148—focus on the fact that Hegel's philosophy includes its own "skeptical" procedure, but they do not recognize, or at least fail to investigate, the skeptical source and nature of the problems which this procedure is in part designed to solve.
4. The method was originally introduced and developed in Hegel's Jena Logic. See K. Duesing, "Spekulation und Reflexion: Zur Zusammenarbeit Schellings und Hegels in Jena," *Hegel-Studien* (1969), p. 128.

1. The Superiority of Ancient to Modern Skepticism

1. On the subject of this chapter, cf. Verneaux, "L'essence du scepticisme selon Hegel," pp. 140–142.
2. See Hume, *An Enquiry Concerning Human Understanding* (Oxford: Clarendon Press, 1975), sec. 12, pt. 2, which contrasts Pyrrhonism unfavorably as a "popular" form of skepticism with the skepticism which raises "philosophical objections" in the manner of Hume himself. However, Hume's attitude to Pyrrhonism is ambivalent. He also says, for example, that in bringing us to correct judgment, "nothing can be more serviceable, than to be

once thoroughly convinced of the force of the Pyrrhonian doubt" (sec. 12, pt. 3). Interpretation thus becomes more complicated than my text might suggest.

3. J. G. Fichte, *The Science of Knowledge,* tr. P. Heath and J. Lachs (Cambridge: Cambridge University Press, 1982), p. 118. English translations of German and Greek works are cited where possible and convenient. In such cases I have often revised the cited translation in various ways or substituted my own translation.

4. G. W. F. Hegel, *The Relation of Skepticism to Philosophy* (*Verhaeltnis des Skeptizismus zur Philosophie*), in *Jenaer Schriften* (Frankfurt am Main: Suhrkamp, 1977), p. 214.

5. Only a few major philosophers in the modern period either before or since Hegel have recognized this method as the core of skepticism. One of the few is Kant. Consider for example the following statement from the *Critique of Pure Reason,* tr. N. Kemp Smith (London: Macmillan Press, 1978): "A skeptical objection sets assertion and counter-assertion in mutual opposition to each other as having equal weight, treating each in turn as dogma and the other as the objection thereto. And the conflict, as the being thus seemingly dogmatic on both the opposing sides, is taken as showing that all judgement in regard to the object is completely null and void" (A388–389). For a helpful discussion of Kant and this form of skepticism, see G. Tonelli, "Kant und die antiken Skeptiker," in *Studien zu Kants philosophischer Entwicklung,* ed. H. Heimsoeth, D. Henrich and G. Tonelli (Hildesheim: Georg Olms Verlagsbuchhandlung, 1967).

6. Sextus Empiricus, *Outlines of Pyrrhonism,* in *Sextus Empiricus I,* tr. R. G. Bury (London: Loeb Classical Library, 1976), bk. 1, ch. 6. Bury translates *logos* here simply as "proposition," but there are reasons for preserving the ambiguity of the Greek between "argument" and "proposition." On the one hand, Sextus Empiricus's method of bringing about a suspension of judgment is almost invariably in practice one of balancing opposed *arguments,* not merely propositions, so that this sense of *logos* must surely be involved in his definition of Pyrrhonist procedure. On the other hand, any opposition of arguments is of course at the same time an opposition of the propositions which are their conclusions, and more important, Sextus does not quite *always* advocate a balancing of opposed arguments. For example, in the fourth trope of Agrippa opposed propositions are balanced against one another without any supporting arguments on either side as the means of inducing a suspension of judgment. See *Outlines of Pyrrhonism,* bk. 1, ch. 15: "If . . . our disputant . . . should claim to assume as granted and without demonstration some postulate . . . then the trope of hypothesis will be brought in . . . For if the author of the hypothesis is worthy of credence, we shall be no less worthy of credence every time that we make the opposite hypothesis." To complicate the situation further, though, it is reasonable to assume that even in the case of the fourth trope of Agrippa the idea of an equal balance of arguments is at work in addition to the idea of an equal balance of propositions. For even here there is an equal balance of arguments for the propositions opposed to one another in the special sense of

there being no arguments for either proposition. And this is presumably the reason why the two propositions are assumed to be put forward with equal plausibility and therefore to be capable of inducing a suspension of judgment.

7. G. W. F. Hegel, *History of Philosophy* (*Lectures on the History of Philosophy*), tr. E. S. Haldane and F. H. Simson (New York: Humanities Press, 1974), vol. 2, p. 345.

8. *Outlines of Pyrrhonism*, bk. 1, ch. 12; Sextus Empiricus, *Against the Ethicists*, in *Sextus Empiricus III*, tr. R G. Bury (London: Loeb Classical Library, 1968), ch. 4, 112–113. Sextus Empiricus's views on these matters are less unambiguous than one might have wished and expected. Two ambiguities are: first, while he at times suggests that only evaluative beliefs cause *tarachē* (*Against the Ethicists*, ch. 4, 112–113; *Outlines of Pyrrhonism*, bk. 1, ch. 12, 27–28), at other times he implies that the search for or possession of any beliefs does so (*Outlines of Pyrrhonism*, bk. 1, ch. 12, 26; see also Sextus Empiricus's practice of striving for *epochē* on all subjects, not just ethical ones, which seems predicated on the assumption that all beliefs cause *tarachē*). Second, while he at times suggests that only beliefs can produce *tarachē* (*Against the Ethicists*, ch. 4, 112–113), at other times he suggests that a degree of disquietude will unavoidably be left even after the elimination of all beliefs (*Outlines of Pyrrhonism*, bk. 1, ch. 12).

9. Hegel rightly emphasizes the difference here between ancient skepticism, which uses its equipollence method in order to induce a suspension of belief that it thinks positively desirable because of the otherwise elusive quietude (*ataraxia*) this affords, and modern skepticism, which values firm belief and knowledge of the truth so highly that it finds anything which forces a suspension of belief a source of mental discomfort. For this reason he objects to the association of the word "doubt" with ancient skepticism, since this connotes the modern skeptic's mental anguish at arriving at a condition—suspension of belief—which the ancient skeptic not only did not find undesirable but had an overriding ambition to attain. See *History of Philosophy*, vol. 2, pp. 332–333.

10. For an example of the former kind of modern skepticism, see Hume, *An Enquiry Concerning Human Understanding*, pp. 152–153: "By what argument can it be proved that the perceptions of the mind must be caused by external objects, entirely different from them, though resembling them . . . ? Here experience is and must be entirely silent. The mind has never anything present to it but the perceptions, and cannot possibly reach any experience of their connexion with objects." For an example of the latter kind of modern skepticism, see Hume, *Dialogues Concerning Natural Religion* (New York: Hafner, 1966), pp. 9–10: "So long as we confine our speculations to trade, or morals, or politics, or criticism, we make appeals every moment to common sense and experience, which strengthen our philosophical conclusions . . . But in theological reasonings, we have not this advantage, while at the same time we are employed upon objects which, we must be sensible, are too large for our grasp." (The words are those of Philo, the work's most radical skeptic.)

11. *The Relation of Skepticism to Philosophy*, pp. 237–238. In leveling the charge of dogmatism against modern skepticism in this essay, Hegel is primarily thinking of the contemporary soi-disant skeptic "Aenesidemus" Schulze. Thus the quoted passage continues: "Schulzean skepticism unites with the crudest dogmatism." And Schulze is the only example of a modern skeptic explicitly considered in the essay. This raises a problem, for if Schulzean skepticism were the *only* target in Hegel's criticism of modern skepticism as dogmatic, then while this criticism would be justified, it would be of relatively little interest. This is because Schulze's skepticism is of a very timid variety indeed, being cast essentially within the framework of the Kantian distinction between the phenomenal and the noumenal in such a way as to subject only the noumenal to skeptical attack while according certainty and immunity from skeptical attack to the phenomenal. Thus Schulze describes his skepticism as the view that "in philosophy nothing can be decided on the basis of incontestably certain and universally valid first principles concerning the existence or non-existence of things-in-themselves and their properties or concerning the limits of man's capacity for knowledge." G. E. Schulze, *Aenesidemus* (Berlin, 1911), p. 18. And Hegel reports with contempt that Schulze accords immunity from rational doubt not only to facts of consciousness but even to the doctrines of modern physics and astronomy. *The Relation of Skepticism to Philosophy*, pp. 225–226. Thus the question arises whether Hegel intends his charge of dogmatism leveled at Schulze to have a broader target as well, whether he intends it to apply to modern skepticism in general in addition to this one feeble limb of it. Is his charge intended, for example, to apply to Hume or to the Descartes of the *First Meditation*?

That Hegel *does* intend his critique of modern skepticism in *The Relation of Skepticism to Philosophy* to have this broader application is made clear from remarks in other texts. Thus the Berlin *Encyclopedia* clearly brings Hume within the scope of this critique. Hegel writes there: "The skepticism of Hume ... should be clearly marked off from Greek skepticism. Hume assumes the truth of the empirical element, feeling and sensation, and proceeds to challenge universal principles and laws, because they have no warranty from sense-perception. So far was ancient skepticism from making feeling and sensation the canon of truth, that it turned against the deliverances of sense first of all." And he goes on to refer the reader to his *The Relation of Skepticism to Philosophy* for further information on the difference between ancient and modern skepticism. G. W. F. Hegel, *Encyclopedia*, tr. W. Wallace (Oxford: Oxford University Press, 1978), no. 39; cf. no. 81, Zusatz. Again, there are passages which make it clear that Hegel would include Cartesian skeptics among the modern skeptics guilty of dogmatism, because of their exemption of their own *cogitationes* from skeptical doubt. Thus the *Phenomenology* unfavorably contrasts Cartesian skepticism, the resolve to "accept only one's own deed as what is true," with the skeptical method of the *Phenomenology* itself (no. 78). And *The Relation of Skepticism to Philosophy* implicitly criticizes Cartesians for the limitation they seek to put on an unrestricted skepticism when they observe that if the skeptics "doubt everything, nevertheless this 'I doubt,' 'it seems to me,' and so forth is certain, thus pointing out in objection the reality and objectivity of the activity of thought" (p. 248). We may conclude, then, that when Hegel criticizes Schulze in *The Relation of Skepticism to Philosophy* for being dogmatic in his skepticism, his target is really modern skepticism as a whole. And we should accordingly expect the details of Hegel's case to be such as to support this more general charge of dogmatism. My text is primarily concerned with this more general charge, and therefore to a considerable degree transposes criticisms which Hegel wrote primarily with Schulze in mind into the more accessible and interesting key of a criticism of the modern skepticism expounded or advocated by Descartes, Hume, and its other more familiar spokesmen.

12. *Outlines of Pyrrhonism*, bk. 2, ch. 7.
13. *The Relation of Skepticism to Philosophy*, pp. 253–254.
14. The "facts of consciousness" assumed as certain by modern skeptics are the focus of one of Hegel's most pervasive and persistent complaints against modern skepticism. When he criticizes the assumption of the certainty of facts of consciousness in *The Relation of Skepticism to Philosophy*, he is thinking in the first instance of the treatment of them as certain in Schulze's skepticism. In *Aenesidemus* Schulze writes: "No skeptic denies that there are in man intuitions, concepts or ideas . . . This is a matter of fact." In *Between Kant and Hegel*, tr. G. di Giovanni and H. S. Harris (Albany, N.Y.: State University of New York Press, 1985), p. 108. But beyond Schulze Hegel is also thinking of the role facts of consciousness play as the indubitably known mental states assumed in Cartesian and Empiricist epistemology, under such names as "cogitationes," "ideas," and "impressions." In note 11 above we saw that Hegel in various texts takes Descartes and Hume to task for making this assumption. That there is such a limit to skepticism in Descartes is clear, since it is on the basis of his allegedly indubitable mental states that he infers, or more exactly intuits, his own existence and from there re-establishes most of the system of beliefs about which his methodical doubt has obliged him to suspend judgment. Equally, Hume never, even in his most skeptical moods, questions his currently experienced ideas and impressions.
15. *Outlines of Pyrrhonism*, bk. 1, ch. 10.
16. For Sextus Empiricus's general acknowledgment of this qualification, see *Outlines of Pyrrhonism*, bk. 1, ch. 1. For a specific application of it to the skeptic's own formulae, see the same work, bk. 1, ch. 7. Please note that my use of the pronouns "he," "him," etc., in this paragraph and in other similar contexts is not gender-specific but generic.
17. *Outlines of Pyrrhonism*, bk. 1, ch. 11.
18. *History of Philosophy*, vol. 2, p. 331; cf. pp. 332, 343.
19. *The Relation of Skepticism to Philosophy*, p. 248: Ancient skepticism absolutely refuses "to express any certainty and being," and this holds good for appearances as well.
20. *The Relation of Skepticism to Philosophy*, p. 248.
21. M. F. Burnyeat, "Can the Skeptic Live his Skepticism?" in *The Skeptical Tradition*, ed. M. F. Burnyeat (Berkeley: University of California Press,

1983). I have quoted continuously material from Burnyeat's main text together with material from a connected footnote. Cf. M. F. Burnyeat, "Idealism and Greek Philosophy: What Descartes Saw and Berkeley Missed," in *Idealism Past and Present,* Royal Institute of Philosophy Lectures, no. 13 (1982), pp. 26–27.

22. Sextus Empiricus, *Against the Logicians,* in *Sextus Empiricus II,* tr. R. G. Bury (London: Loeb Classical Library, 1983), bk. 1, 190–200.

23. Hegel was probably influenced in his suggestion that for the ancient skeptics a correct assertion about how things appeared to one was not a description of reality or a bearer of truth by his acquaintance with a more contemporary philosophical position, that of Fichte. When discussing Cartesian skepticism in the *Phenomenology,* Hegel refers to the subject's mental contents or appearances as his own "deed" (*Tat*) (no. 78). In *The Relation of Skepticism to Philosophy* he refers to these same Cartesian stopping points for skepticism as the "activity of thought" (*Denktaetigkeit*) and as "expressed activity" (*ausgesprochene Taetigkeit*) (p. 248). This striking choice of language suggests that when Hegel attributes to the ancient skeptics the view that appearances do not constitute part of reality, he has in mind Fichte's metaphysics in which the self's free act of self-positing enjoys metaphysical priority over existence or reality. Fichte writes in the *Science of Knowledge:* "When all existence of or for the subject is taken away, it has nothing left but an act" (p. 33). Applied to the ancient skeptics, this Fichtean view will have suggested to Hegel that they could coherently conceive of their expressions of appearances as expressions of mental acts metaphysically prior to reality rather than as descriptions of bits of mental reality.

24. *History of Philosophy,* vol. 2, p. 332. Cf. p. 343: The skeptics' appearances "did not have the significance of a truth for them, but only of a certainty."

25. *The Relation of Skepticism to Philosophy,* p. 248.

26. *The Relation of Skepticism to Philosophy,* p. 238.

27. *Outlines of Pyrrhonism,* bk. 1, ch. 10.

28. *Outlines of Pyrrhonism,* bk. 1, ch. 11.

29. *Outlines of Pyrrhonism,* bk. 1, ch. 10.

30. *Outlines of Pyrrhonism,* bk. 1, ch. 7.

31. *Outlines of Pyrrhonism,* bk. 1, ch. 29.

32. Sextus Empiricus's occasional deference to what is believed by all men in common may be something casually inherited from Aenesidemus. For Aenesidemus seems to have espoused the principle (officially rejected by Sextus) of the truth of those views which are held in common by all men—probably as one of the Heraclitean components of his skepticism. See J. M. Rist, "The Heracliteanism of Aenesidemus," *Phoenix,* no. 24 (1970).

33. Cf. *Outlines of Pyrrhonism,* bk. 1, ch. 13, where Sextus Empiricus warns against the acceptance of an argument which presently appears sound on the ground that someone might later furnish an equally plausible counterargument.

34. *Outlines of Pyrrhonism,* bk. 2, ch. 6, 57. A more familiar kind of argument found in Sextus Empiricus for the invulnerability of claims about our own current appearances to skeptical attack holds that such appearances, since

they lie in our affection, *necessitate* our recognition of them. At *Outlines of Pyrrhonism*, bk. 1, ch. 11 Sextus argues that the sense-presentation which is virtually identical to the appearance "since [it] lies in feeling and involuntary affection . . . is not open to question." Cf. bk. 1, ch. 7, 13. This argument is essentially the same as the argument from the Cartesian principle of *evidence* considered below as a defense of claims about our own current mental states against skepticism, and my unfavorable comments on the latter argument will apply equally to the former.

35. See e.g. P. Feyerabend, "Explanation, Reduction, and Empiricism," *Minnesota Studies in the Philosophy of Science III*.

36. Although Hegel does not give details of how he thinks the skeptics argued or could have argued for equipollence on the issue of their own current mental states, it is worth noting that his own philosophy, in designating only that viewpoint as true for which the distinction between the subject or self and the object has been overcome, implies the denial of literal truth to all first-person statements, such as "I believe, feel, desire X," so that it constitutes what one might call a kind of "eliminative idealism." Perhaps this feature of his own philosophy alerted Hegel to the possibility that the skeptics might generate a case against the existence of mental states tout court and, by implication, against the existence of their own current mental states.

37. *Outlines of Pyrrhonism*, bk. 1, ch. 33, 226. My emphasis.

38. C. G. Kuehn, *Galeni Opera Omnia* (Leipzig, 1821–1833), vol. 8, p. 711: "Of these people then some say that they do not even know their own affections (*pathē*) surely, whom they reasonably call rustic Pyrrhonists." Cf. vol. 14, p. 628.

39. The relevant passage is to be found in K. Deichgraeber, *Die Griechische Empirikerschule* (Berlin, 1930), p. 133: "Let them then accept this as agreed upon by us as well—for I wish to grant them every favor—even that we know neither whether there really is a sun or moon or earth, nor a sea, nor whether we are awake, nor even whether we think (*phronoumen*) or are alive, nor really concerning anything how it is by nature."

40. *The Relation of Skepticism to Philosophy*, p. 254.

41. *The Relation of Skepticism to Philosophy*, p. 249.

42. Sextus Empiricus indicates that *every* statement in which the skeptic expresses his own view of things is merely an expression of how things appear to him. For example, the *Outlines of Pyrrhonism* begins with the qualification: "Of none of our future statements do we positively affirm that the fact is exactly as we state it, but we simply record each fact, like a chronicler, as it appears to us at the moment" (bk. 1, ch. 1). Thus *all* of the statements which the skeptic makes in propria persona should be susceptible if any are to Hegel's analysis of the skeptic's acceptance of appearances as an acceptance which avoids any claim about reality or truth. This partly explains Hegel's claim that ancient skepticism "is founded on an elaborately thought out annihilation of everything which is held to be true and existent" and that within it "the form of an existent . . . quite disappears as form." *History of Philosophy*, vol. 2, pp. 332, 328. It also partly explains Hegel's puzzling claim that ancient skepticism "does not flit to and fro with thoughts that

leave the possibility that something may still be true, but it proves with certainty the untruth of all." *History of Philosophy,* vol. 2, p. 333. At first sight this claim seems to involve a total misunderstanding of the ancient skeptic's position, since the ancient skeptic does not seek to *prove* anything, let alone with certainty, and does not seek to show the *untruth* of anything, but instead suspends judgment on all questions. We can, though, partly understand Hegel's claim as an overdramatic statement of a consequence of his analysis of the skeptic's own statements, for the skeptic, in giving up all pretensions to describe reality or state truths, in a sense rejects the notion of truth altogether.

Someone might object to this that the skeptic's confinement of himself to appearance statements only involves a rejection of the notion of truth in the sense of a refusal to predicate truth of those statements with which he himself identifies, but that he retains the usual presupposition that there are true descriptions of reality, only ruefully renouncing any pretension to determine which these are. This objection is misleading for two reasons. First, it overlooks the fact that Sextus Empiricus questions skeptically whether or not anything true exists at all (*Outlines of Pyrrhonism,* bk. 2, ch. 9). Second, it suggests incorrectly that the ancient skeptic places some positive value on the continued use of the notion of truth and regards it as desirable that we should discover which descriptions are true. Such a suggestion may be valid for the modern skeptic, who finds limitations on his ability to identify the truth a source of discomfort, but it is not valid for the ancient skeptic, who regards the suspension of judgment (*epochē*) as the means to quietude (*ataraxia*) and happiness. The ancient skeptic thinks it a good thing to remain in a state of suspended judgment and strenuously works to sustain this state by maintaining a balance of opposed arguments. He sees no need to ascertain the truth and much misery in the attempt to do so. This is part of Hegel's point in the passage from which the puzzling claim quoted before was drawn: "The function of skepticism is wrongly termed the inculcation of proneness to doubt ... This supposes a deep interest in a content, and the desire of the mind that this content should either be established in it or not, because it desires to find its rest either in the one or the other. Such a doubt is said to betoken a keen and sharp-witted thinker, but it is only vanity ... This skepticism has nowadays entered into our life ... But the older skepticism does not doubt, being certain of untruth, and indifferent to the one as to the other; it does not flit to and fro with thoughts that leave the possibility that something may still be true, but it proves with certainty the untruth of all. Or its doubt to it is certainty which has not the intention of attaining to truth, nor does it leave this matter undecided, for it is completely at a point, and perfectly decided, although this decision is not truth for it. This certainty of itself has as result the rest and security of the mind in itself." *History of Philosophy,* vol. 2, pp. 332–333.

43. This may be the *only* way to generate a sane general doubt about one's own current mental states.

44. Descartes, *Principles,* sec. 9, in *Descartes—Philosophical Writings,* tr.

G. E. M. Anscombe and P. T. Geach (London: Nelson's University Paperbacks, 1971). My emphasis.

45. Consider also Hume's skepticism about the self which is based on the supposed coherence of the suggestion that, "What we call a *mind* is nothing but a heap or collection of different perceptions." *A Treatise of Human Nature* (Harmondsworth: Pelican Books, 1969), bk. 1, sec. 2. Here the supposed *objecthood* of mental states lends an appearance of coherence to the idea that they might exist without there being some thing or person having them as its properties.

46. *The Relation of Skepticism to Philosophy*, p. 248.

47. *The Relation of Skepticism to Philosophy*, pp. 253–254.

48. Sextus Empiricus, *Against the Physicists*, in *Sextus Empiricus III*, bk. 1, 49. Cf. *Outlines of Pyrrhonism*, bk. 2, ch. 1, 10. Skeptical arguments following a similar pattern in the *Outlines of Pyrrhonism* include those concerned with the existence of the intellect (bk. 2, ch. 6, 57) and the existence of the Stoic *lekton* (bk. 2, ch. 11, 107). I distinguish from this pattern of argument arguments in which the existence of a kind of thing is called into question by adducing a case for the *incoherence* of its concept or definition as one side of the equipollence procedure. See for example the arguments concerning cause, motion, space, and time in the *Outlines of Pyrrhonism*, bk. 3.

49. The laws of logic are another area in which Hegel would accuse much of modern skepticism of timidity and dogmatism and would see the ancient skeptics as by contrast boldly extending their skeptical attack by means of the equipollence method. Schulze, the representative of modern skepticism in *The Relation of Skepticism to Philosophy*, was explicit about this dogmatic assumption of his skepticism. Enumerating a series of propositions which he regarded as valid beyond doubt in his *Aenesidemus*, he wrote: "General logic is the touchstone of all truth." Though Hegel is not directly concerned with this aspect of modern skepticism's dogmatism in *The Relation of Skepticism to Philosophy*, we can see that he considers it an unacceptable restriction on the scope of a genuine skepticism from his Jena review of Bouterwek's *Anfangsgruende der spekulativen Philosophie*, in *Jenaer Scriften*. He criticizes Bouterwek for being unfaithful to his own principles of only going as far in his philosophizing as the skeptic would allow "to the extent that he [i.e., Bouterwek] erects . . . on the basis that doubting is itself a thinking, the whole system of laws of thought, as logic. For on the contrary the consistent skeptic denies the concept of a law altogether" (p. 141).

Hegel was perhaps influenced in his belief that a genuine skepticism would not stop at the laws of formal logic by an interesting, if at points confused, criticism of Kant for dogmatism in this area by a largely forgotten contemporary, C. G. Bardili. Hegel's early interest in Bardili's work is evidenced by a letter from Schelling to Fichte of May 24, 1801, and by Bardili's appearance in Hegel's early essay *The Difference between the Fichtean and Schellingian Systems of Philosophy*. Kant had accorded the question, "How is synthetic a priori knowledge possible?" a central role in his *Critique of Pure Reason* and had sought to answer it by providing both an explanation of

such knowledge in terms of the structuring role of the mind and a justification of the more questionable (in particular, nonmathematical) parts of it by
means of transcendental arguments, such as those found in the Analogies of
Experience. But Kant had shown no comparable interest in raising or answering the question, "How is *analytic* a priori knowledge possible?" and
this was because he understood analytic propositions to be founded on the
law of noncontradiction and was satisfied that this law along with the other
laws of formal logic stood in no need of an epistemological investigation,
since they were "certain entirely a priori" (*Critique of Pure Reason,* B78,
A54) and constituted "a closed and completed body of doctrine" in all es-
sentials unchanged since Aristotle (B viii). Bardili—in his essay "On Bardili's
First, Kant's Transcendental and the hitherto General Logic," in K. L. Reinhold, *Beitraege zur leichteren Uebersicht des Zustandes der Philosophie
beim Anfange des 19. Jahrhunderts* (Hamburg, 1801–1802)—took Kant to
task for his uncritical acceptance of the laws of logic. He argued that Kant
had left these principles, which are presupposed by all others, "merely rhap-
sodically . . . gathered together" (p. 83), i.e., picked up uncritically from
tradition. He noted the oddity of Kant's juxtaposition of a demand for an
investigation of the grounds of possibility of other kinds of knowledge with
a completely uncritical acceptance of received logical principles: "The Kantian school has itself demanded an appropriate metaphysics for everything
which is supposed to be scientific in each kind of human knowledge, in
which the connection of this piece of knowledge with its a priori grounds
should be developed. Is only logic alone to do without such a metaphysics,
and yet be, and be called, a science, indeed quite pure science?" (p. 85). And
most interestingly for our purposes, Bardili pointed out that it seemed to be
an assumption underlying Kant's complacency about logical principles that
they had not been subjected to skeptical attack and he called into question
the historical accuracy of this assumption. Thus he wrote: "Kant thought he
had recognized that the dogmatists and skeptics had remained standing with
their quarrels only on the territory of metaphysics; and that on the territory
of logic on the contrary an eternal peace has always prevailed" (p. 88). And
he asked rhetorically in response to this view of Kant's "whether it is really
true that skepticism has only called into question the objective in human
cognition, or has not on the contrary also more than once dared to attack
the validity of the laws of our understanding themselves" (pp. 88–89).

In both Hegel and Bardili the perception that classical logical principles
were vulnerable to skepticism and lacked any secure epistemological basis
contributed to the inception of a theoretical project of providing a reformed,
epistemologically secure logic. Bardili sought to realize such a project in his
*Outline of the First Logic Purified of the Errors of Previous Logic in General
and of the Kantian in Particular* (*Grundriss der ersten Logik, gereinigt von
den Irrtuemern bisheriger Logik ueberhaupt, der Kantischen insbesondere;*
Stuttgart, 1800). Hegel sought to realize it in his—somewhat, and surely
not coincidentally, similar—"total reconstruction" of traditional logic in the
Science of Logic, tr. A. V. Miller (New York: Humanities Press, 1976),

which had its "justification" in the *Phenomenology* (*Science of Logic*, pp. 51, 48).

One may have grave doubts about the results of these attempts by Bardili and Hegel to revolutionize logic on an epistemologically secure basis. However, as a matter of history they were certainly both right to suggest that even the classical laws of logic had been subjected to skeptical attack. Perhaps the most interesting evidence of this is found in Cicero's *Academica*, tr. H. Rackham (London: Loeb Classical Library, 1979), II, 95–98, where among other things the Academic skeptic calls into question the law of excluded middle by means of a version of the Liar Paradox: "Clearly it is a fundamental principle of dialectic that every statement . . . is either true or false; what then? is this a true proposition or a false one—'If you say that you are lying and say it truly, you lie'?" The thought is that both the claim that this proposition is true and the claim that it is false lead to paradox, which constitutes grounds for classifying it as neither true nor false, contrary to the law of excluded middle.

It is a question worthy of serious consideration to what extent the equipollence method of the ancient skeptics might be successfully applied to classical logical laws. There have been numerous proposals in the past, of both a serious and a more hypothetical nature, to abandon one or another of these laws. And the equipollence skeptic might adduce these proposals or concoct similar arguments of his own in order to generate an equal balance of arguments for and against particular classical laws and thereby induce a suspension of belief concerning them. Among the more serious proposals which a skeptic might exploit, there have been various suggestions that the law of excluded middle should be given up in order to solve perceived difficulties in mathematics (the intuitionists), in quantum mechanics, and in logic itself. To give an example from logic, it has been proposed in connection with Russell's Paradox—in a manner reminiscent of the argument of the Academic skeptics mentioned above—that the paradoxical Russellian sentence which says that the class of all non-self-membered classes is a member of itself be coped with by instituting a three-valued logic in which the principle of excluded middle disappears and the Russellian sentence is assigned the middle truth-value. Again, H. Putnam has proposed in response to problems arising within quantum mechanics a logic which, though retaining the law of excluded middle, gives up the distributive law:

$$p \mathrel{\&} (q \lor r) \to (p \mathrel{\&} q) \lor (p \mathrel{\&} r).$$

Among the more hypothetical proposals which a skeptic might exploit are Wittgenstein's suggestion—at *Remarks on the Foundations of Mathematics*, tr. G. E. M. Anscombe (Oxford: Basil Blackwell, 1978), IV, 59—that one might respond to Russell's Paradox by dispensing with the principle of non-contradiction in the case of the Russellian sentence and his somewhat less dramatic suggestion—at *Philosophical Investigations*, tr. G. E. M. Anscombe (Oxford: Basil Blackwell, 1976), no. 554—that there might be a logic in which double negations were either meaningless or equivalent to single negations, so that, for example, the law of double negation elimination disappeared. Using such materials as these and others of his own devising, the equipollence skeptic might attempt to argue in relation to each classical law of logic that it is possible to think of an equally plausible alternative logic in which that law does not hold.

The Bardili-Hegel position sketched before implies that classical logic has been provided by Kant and his predecessors with no epistemological fortification capable of defending it against such skeptical attacks. This is again a persuasive claim. The question of the epistemological security of logical laws has in general received scandalously little attention from philosophers, who have compensated by showing indecent haste in attempting to reduce other kinds of principles to logical laws on the assumption that they were thereby extending the certainty and self-evidence of the latter to the former (e.g. Kant's explanation of analyticity in terms of the principle of noncontradiction and Frege's attempt to reduce arithmetic to logic). And while Kant was inaccurate in his suggestion that the formal logic of his day had made no advance beyond Aristotle—his own formal logic was in fact a blend of Aristotelian and Stoic elements—he would have been on firmer ground if he had said instead that the *epistemological securing* of logic had made no advance beyond Aristotle. In *Metaphysics*, bk. Gamma, Aristotle had given two major arguments in defense of classical logical principles against skeptical and other attacks. Taking the principle of noncontradiction as his example, he had argued to the conclusions (1) that it is impossible to believe a contradiction to be true (1005b22–35), and (2) that in order to mean or understand anything by words or be capable of thought, one must believe the truth of the principle of noncontradiction (1006a11–1006b34). When he claimed in the *Critique of Pure Reason* that formal logic "contains the absolutely necessary rules of thought without which there can be no employment whatever of the understanding" (B 76, A 52), Kant was just distantly echoing Aristotelian conclusions of one or both of these kinds.

Two things should be noted about this traditional Aristotelian defense of formal logic. First, it is by no means obvious—and the complexities of Aristotle's arguments show that *he* did not think it obvious—that conclusions of the two kinds in question are true. To use Aristotle's example, it is by no means obvious that we *cannot* believe particular contradictions or that we *cannot* think without believing the principle of noncontradiction. Many people have certainly seemed to be in one or both of these positions. But second, and perhaps more importantly, even if such conclusions *were* correct, they would constitute a much weaker epistemological defense of classical logic than Aristotle and those who follow him in his strategy of defense have supposed. Wittgenstein saw the Achilles' heel of this epistemological defense of classical logic. He was quite ready to acknowledge at least conclusions of type (1). For example, he wrote in the *Remarks on the Foundations of Mathematics* that the classical laws of logic "can be said to show: how human beings think, and also *what* human beings call 'thinking'" (I, 131). But he did not at all see this as a ground for holding the classical laws of logic to be indispensable or to enjoy exclusive correctness. For he recognized that there might always be something *similar* to what we call thought (or belief or meaning or understanding etc.), of which adherence to one or more of the classical laws was not an essential ingredient as it seems to be an essential ingredient of what we call that, and which was as good or useful an instrument as what we call that, if not a better or more useful instrument. Wittgenstein's most concise statement of this line of thought occurs not in relation to logical laws but in relation to the analogous case of mathematical laws: "I could imagine . . . that people had a different calculus, or a technique which we should not call 'calculating.' But would it be *wrong?*" *Philosophical Investigations,* pp. 226e–227e. Hence, when he considered Russell's Paradox in the *Remarks on the Foundations of Mathematics,* Wittgenstein in effect conceded to the Aristotelian that what we call propositions are *essentially* used in conformity with the principle of noncontradiction, but this did not at all prevent him from raising the possibility that it might be sensible in this case to violate that principle: "Why should Russell's contradiction not be conceived as something supra-propositional, something that towers above the propositions and looks in both directions like a Janus head? . . . Might one not even begin logic with this contradiction? And as it were descend from it to propositions" (IV, 59). Hegel, it seems to me, was as aware of this weakness in the traditional Aristotelian defense of classical logic as Wittgenstein. Hence, on the one hand, he conceded to Aristotle that classical logic is an essential ingredient of what men usually call thought or what Hegel himself refers to as the thought of the *Understanding* (at *Encyclopedia,* no. 82, he calls this logic "the logic of mere Understanding"). But on the other hand he recognized the possibility—and indeed claimed the actuality and the superiority—of a different kind of "thought" of which classical logic is *not* an essential ingredient and which he refers to as the thought of *Reason.*

50. *A Treatise of Human Nature,* bk. 1, pt. 4, sec. 7.

51. *Encyclopedia,* no. 39.

52. Descartes, *Meditations,* in *Descartes—Philosophical Writings,* p. 61.

53. Hence after attacking our beliefs by means of the Evil Genius Hypothesis in the *First Meditation,* Descartes concedes that they have only been shown to be "doubtful in a way . . . but are yet highly probable, and far more reasonably believed than denied." *Descartes—Philosophical Writings,* p. 65.

54. *Meditations,* Synopsis, in *The Philosophical Works of Descartes,* tr. E. S. Haldane and G. R. T. Ross (Cambridge: Cambridge University Press, 1978), vol. 1.

55. Note this is *not,* and is not consistent with, the presently fashionable and wholly implausible view that defeating skepticism was not a major concern of Descartes'.

56. Since this does indeed seem to be a necessary condition of successfully raising traditional skeptical equipollence problems, the present interpretation of Descartes has these two major advantages. First, it enables us to avoid supposing, as we would have to if we understood the *First Meditation* as an attempt to give a straightforward presentation of skepticism, that Descartes had such a poor grasp of the nature of skepticism as to have overlooked the fact that equipollence problems constituted its very core. Such a supposition

is implausible in view of the prominence of the equipollence method in Montaigne's characterization of skepticism in the *Apology for Raymond Sebond;* Descartes' allusion to equipollence problems in the *Discourse (Descartes— Philosophical Writings,* p. 12: "[Philosophy] has been cultivated by the most outstanding minds of several centuries, and . . . nevertheless up to now there is no point but is disputed and consequently doubtful"); and his early facility with the method of producing equipollent arguments, as witnessed by a public display at the home of Cardinal Bagni in about 1628 (see R. H. Popkin, *The History of Skepticism from Erasmus to Spinoza* [Berkeley: University of California Press, 1979], pp. 174–175). It is, furthermore, uncharitable. Second, the present interpretation attributes to Descartes a well-conceived strategy against equipollence skepticism.

57. There is a long tradition of interpretation of ancient skepticism which sees Academic skepticism, especially in its Carneadean form, as significantly more moderate than Pyrrhonist skepticism. Hume expresses allegiance to this tradition in *An Enquiry Concerning Human Understanding:* "There is, indeed, a more *mitigated* skepticism or *academical* philosophy, which may be both durable and useful, and which may, in part, be the result of this Pyrrhonism, or *excessive* skepticism, when its undistinguished doubts are, in some measure, corrected by common sense and reflection" (sec. 12, pt. 3). Contrary to this tradition of interpretation and in defense of the generality of his sharp contrast between a timid, dogmatic modern skepticism and a radical ancient skepticism based on the equipollence method, Hegel holds that the skepticism of the Academic skeptics Arcesilaus and Carneades is either more or less the same as, or has its logical completion in, the skepticism of the Pyrrhonists. He argues at one point, for example, that the Pyrrhonists had difficulty distinguishing their position from that of the Academics, that the distinction which they drew between the two positions was "very formal, and has but little signification," and that this distinction "often consists in the meanings of words only, and in quite external differences." *History of Philosophy,* vol. 2, p. 311. And at another point he says that "if this Academic standpoint is driven to its ultimate limit, it amounts to this, that everything is clearly for consciousness alone, and that the form of an existent, and of the knowledge of existence, also quite disappears as form; this, however, is skepticism [i.e., Pyrrhonism]." *History of Philosophy,* vol. 2, p. 328.

The tendency in much of the best modern scholarship on Academic skepticism is to bear out Hegel's general judgment (see for example work by Couissin, Burnyeat, Sedley and Frede). It may be useful to indicate one or two relevant features of the case. The first point to note is that both Arcesilaus and Carneades, as far as the existing evidence allows us to judge, shared with the Pyrrhonists the ideal of a general suspension of belief (*epochē*) and the view that the way to achieve this was to find opposing arguments of equal weight on each issue. This is well established for Arcesilaus, of whom Cicero reports that he spoke "against the opinions of all men" to persuade people that, "whereas equal weights of argument were always discovered on both sides of the same question, the more natural course was to withhold assent from both sides." *Academica*, I, 45. That it is also true of Carneades is highly probable in the light of such facts as that his aide and successor as head of the Academy, Clitomachus, praised him for championing *epochē* (Cicero, *Academica*, II, 108), and that Carneades used the method of balancing arguments for and against when arguing on successive days for and against justice during his ambassadorial visit to Rome.

The main source of the traditional misconception that the Academic skeptics were more moderate than the Pyrrhonists lies in a peculiarity of the Academic way of effecting a suspension of belief by means of the equipollence method. Sextus Empiricus remarks on this peculiarity, and it can be traced in many of the Academic arguments which have been preserved. For details, see especially P. Couissin, "The Stoicism of the New Academy," in *The Skeptical Tradition*, ed. Burnyeat; Burnyeat's unpublished paper "Carneades Was No Probabilist." The peculiarity was that the Academic skeptics, when confronted by a dogmatist's proposition about which they wished to produce a suspension of belief, did not draw their equally convincing counterargument from just any source, as the Pyrrhonists might, but looked instead for an equally convincing counterargument *based on premises drawn from the dogmatist himself*. This was in large measure a result of the continuing strong influence of Socratic elenchus in the Academy. Sextus Empiricus mentions this difference between Academic and Pyrrhonist practice in passing: "With regard to (the physical division of philosophy) we shall pursue again the same method of inquiry, and not delay long on particular points as Clitomachus has done and the rest of the Academic troupe (for by plunging into alien subject-matter and framing their arguments on the basis of dogmatic assumptions not their own they have unduly prolonged their counterstatement)." *Against the Physicists*, bk. 1. The Academic skeptics, in framing the argument against the proposition of a given dogmatist on the basis of premises drawn from that dogmatist himself were not evincing any conviction in the truth of those premises, any common ground with the dogmatist. On another occasion they might be expected to attack one or more of those same premises on the basis of some new set of premises drawn from the dogmatist. This was the point of Carneades' likening dialectic to an octopus which first grows its tentacles and then consumes them, on the ground that dialecticians eventually overturn their own arguments. See D. Sedley, "The Motivation of Greek Skepticism," in *The Skeptical Tradition*, ed. Burnyeat, p. 17. Still, it is easy to see how the Academic procedure—given the circumstances that (a) it was used mainly to attack the doctrines of a single philosophy, Stoicism, (b) only a fraction of its applications were preserved for later interpreters, and (c) the Academics had their Stoic dogmatists before them giving the positive arguments for their dogmas, so that they did not themselves need to formulate the positive arguments for these dogmas but only the negative arguments against them in order to attack them by means of the equipollence method—could give rise later to the false impression among interpreters that the Academics themselves shared a certain amount of common ground with their Stoic opponents and generated arguments which they actually believed on the basis of this common ground to certain conclusions hostile to other Stoic views. Hence, for example, the temptation to understand the Academic criticism of the Stoic doctrine that the cataleptic sense-presentation provides us with a criterion of truth as a criticism which proceeds against the background of a certain amount of theory of perception which the Academics share in common with the Stoics (such as that our perception of the world is mediated by sense-presentations which it impresses upon us) and as a criticism which is believed by the Academics actually to show that the cataleptic sense-presentation does not provide us with a criterion of truth. Modern veil of perception skepticism really is committed to some such theory of perception as the background for its problems and really does purport to demonstrate various negative conclusions on this basis. Academic skepticism, however, is in a quite different position: it merely borrows the background theory from the dogmatists for the sake of argument, and the argument to a negative conclusion which it produces on this basis is supposed to be equally balanced by arguments given by the dogmatists themselves to the opposed positive conclusion. Even Carneades' famous probabilistic theory is explicable in these terms. See Burnyeat, "Carneades Was No Probabilist." This, then, seems to be the explanation of the erroneous tradition of interpretation of Academic skepticism which perceives it to be more moderate than Pyrrhonism.

58. Thus at least one modern authority on ancient skepticism, M. Frede, would argue that the Hegelian picture of a radical Pyrrhonism painted so far fundamentally misrepresents the nature of Pyrrhonism. Ignoring Hegel's dubious suggestion, to be considered shortly, that the ten tropes of Aenesidemus do not attack the content of his own Philosophical Science, the tenor of his interpretation of the Pyrrhonists is to present them as intellectual revolutionaries seeking to eradicate all beliefs in order then to live an innovative life according to appearances, or the way things seem to them nonepistemically, that is, without belief. This interpretation conflicts sharply with the subtle and influential interpretation in M. Frede, "Des Skeptikers Meinungen," *Neue Hefte fuer Philosophie* 15/16 (1979). Frede's Pyrrhonists are fundamentally intellectual reactionaries, reacting against a wave of philosophers and scientists who have themselves launched a revolutionary assault on traditional beliefs, presuming to inform people on the strength of reason and argument how the world really is or is *by nature* beyond the in some degree illusory appearances which bind the traditional believer. The Pyrrhonists are not seeking to eradicate all beliefs, but only the beliefs distinctive of the philosophers and scientists (and those who imitate them in founding belief upon reason and argument). Far from the Pyrrhonists' life of appearances being an innovation to sustain them after an eradication of all beliefs, it is a life made up mainly of traditional beliefs held in the same way as before the rude intrusion of the philosophers and scientists.

Having indicated the nature of the conflict between Hegel and Frede, let me in a provisional way offer some arguments in Hegel's defense (in part borrowed from Burnyeat's "Can the Skeptic Live His Skepticism?" which gives an interpretation similar to Hegel's). First, consider some of the copious evidence which seems to support Hegel's reading against Frede's. (1) The ten tropes of Aenesidemus are aimed primarily at undermining the ordinary beliefs of the ordinary man, and the five tropes of Agrippa are quite indifferent as to the nature of the beliefs against which they are directed. (2) In the *Outlines of Pyrrhonism* Sextus Empiricus attacks not only philosophical or scientific subject matter but also such everyday concepts as causation, motion, time, and truth. (3) When Sextus Empiricus in the *Outlines of Pyrrhonism* illustrates the point that the skeptics avoid both positive and negative assertions, he chooses neither philosophical nor scientific assertions as examples but the quite mundane propositions "It is day" and "It is not day" (bk. 1, ch. 20). (4) Early critics of Pyrrhonism, such as Aristocles, who should have been in a position to know, assume that they are dealing with a philosophy intent on avoiding all beliefs; and the early stories relayed by Diogenes Laertius about the helplessness of Pyrrho himself suggest that this was the goal of the movement's figurehead (even if, as is possible, these stories were intended as caricature). (5) Sextus Empiricus characterizes the Pyrrhonist not merely as rejecting *dogmata*, a term which may connote philosophical or scientific principles—see J. Barnes, "The Beliefs of a Pyrrhonist," *Proceedings of the Cambridge Philological Society* 29 (1982), pp. 6–9—but also as living *adoxastōs*, or "without *doxai*," a term for beliefs which is surely either neutral or suggestive of the common man's beliefs. (6) Pyrrhonism stands in close relation to Academic skepticism but shows a persistent concern to distinguish itself by being more radical. Thus Aenesidemus, the founder of Pyrrhonism as a school, seems to have left the Academy because he found it too dogmatic in his time, and Sextus Empiricus is constantly at pains in his works to distinguish Pyrrhonism as a more radical position than Academic skepticism. Yet the founder of Academic skepticism Arcesilaus spoke "against the opinions of all men." Cicero, *Academica*, I, 45. And he constructed a theory of the possibility of action without assent with the clear purpose of thwarting the objection to his skepticism that a life completely without belief would make action impossible—an objection which he would surely not have gone to such pains to thwart if this had not indeed been the kind of life to which he aspired. See Frede, "Des Skeptikers Meinungen," pp. 107–109. (It makes little difference whether, as Frede reasonably says is unlikely, the theory was put forward as the truth, or as Frede reasonably says is more likely, it was put forward to counterbalance arguments that assent was necessary to action and so bring about a suspension of judgment on the issue. In either case the theory was almost certainly part of an effort to thwart the objection to the ideal of a life altogether without belief that such a life would make action impossible. And in either case his development of the theory therefore strongly suggests that Arcesilaus accepted the objector's assumption that he espoused the ideal of a life altogether without belief.) The question, then, is whether it is likely that the Pyrrhonists, who prided themselves on being at least as radical as the Academic skeptics, would have fallen short of Arcesilaus in his aspiration to undermine all belief. (7) According to Sextus Empiricus, the acceptance of appearances which is exempt from skeptical attack, makes up the content of the skeptic's philosophical position, and guides the course of the skeptic's life is an acceptance

by the skeptic that his mental impressions (the appearances) are thus and so
in him, not an acceptance that they correctly represent, or that there otherwise obtain, facts about the external world. Thus in the *Outlines of Pyrrhonism* Sextus writes that, "The criterion . . . of the skeptic school is, we
say, the appearance, giving this name to what is virtually the sense-
presentation (*dynamei tēn phantasian*); for since this lies in feeling and involuntary affection, it is not open to question" and that, "In his enunciation
of [the skeptical] formulae [the skeptic] states what appears to himself and
announces his own impression (*pathos*) . . . without making any positive
assertion regarding the external realities" (bk. 1, chs. 11, 10). For reasons
already discussed in our text this means that in Sextus Empiricus's eyes the
skeptic's acceptance of appearances is nonepistemic (without belief). Such
evidence as this constitutes a fairly strong prima facie case in favor of Hegel's
reading of Pyrrhonism as opposed to Frede's.

   We should now consider some of the evidence to which Frede appeals in
order nevertheless to support his reading. The strongest evidence in support
of this reading is threefold. (1) At *Outlines of Pyrrhonism,* bk. 1, ch. 7,
Sextus Empiricus distinguishes between a broad and a narrow sense of
dogma. In the broad sense this just means approval (*eudokein*) of something.
In the narrow sense it means assent to a nonevident object of scientific inquiry (*tini pragmati tōn kata tas epistēmas zētoumenōn adēlōn*). Sextus Empiricus, while renouncing *dogmata* in the narrow sense, is prepared to accept
them in the broad sense. See Frede, "Des Skeptikers Meinungen," pp. 111–
123. (2) Sextus Empiricus frequently uses qualifications such as "nonevident" (as we have just seen) or "so far as this is a matter of reason" to
characterize the subjects on wich he is suspending belief. See Frede, pp. 112–
113, 117–118. (3) When Sextus Empiricus discusses the "commemorative"
signs which he favors and the "indicative" signs which he opposes in *Against
the Logicians,* he writes: "We propose to devote all our investigation and
criticism not to the commemorative sign (*for this is generally believed by all
ordinary folk to be useful*) but to the indicative, *for this has been devised by
the dogmatic philosophers and by the logical physicians* . . . Hence *we are
not attacking the common preconceptions of mankind,* nor are we turning
life upside down by asserting that no sign exists, as some slanderously affirm
of us. For if we were abolishing every sign we might, perhaps, have been
attacking ordinary life (*tō biō*) and all mankind, but as it is, we ourselves
are of the same mind and infer fire from smoke, and a previous wound from
a scar" (bk. 2, 156–158, my emphasis). See Frede, p. 114.

   Faced with this conflict of evidence, one may perhaps be tempted to agree
with J. Barnes—"Ancient Skepticism and Causation," in *The Skeptical Tradition,* ed. Burnyeat, pp. 159–160—that there simply is no consistent account of the character or scope of the Pyrrhonists' attack on beliefs to be
found in Sextus Empiricus's texts. Barnes suggests indeed that we must resign
ourselves to finding not just two inconsistent versions of skepticism there but
a whole spectrum of mutually inconsistent degrees of skepticism, ranging
from the "sober" skepticism identified by Frede at one extreme to the
"drunken" skepticism identified by Hegel and Burnyeat at the other. And we

may be tempted to agree with Barnes further that the reason for this inconsistency is that Sextus Empiricus is primarily a compiler of earlier material rather than a systematic thinker. However, such a conclusion must surely, due to quite general principles of exegesis, represent a reading of last resort. Nor is Barnes's alternative way of coping with the conflict of evidence in "The Beliefs of a Pyrrhonist," pp. 18–19, satisfactory. There he argues that Sextus Empiricus's view implicitly was or at least should have been as follows. Since the suspension of belief, or *epochē*, is at root a kind of therapy designed to induce quietude in different patients, it is inevitably tailored to fit different patients' needs. Some patients are disquieted by any amount of belief, whereas in others a modicum of belief causes no disquietude. For the former patients the therapy required is a general suspension of belief, which explains the evidence supporting Hegel's reading of Sextus Empiricus's texts. For the latter patients the therapy required is only a limited suspension of belief, which explains the evidence supporting Frede's reading of Sextus Empiricus's texts. The problem with this reading as exegesis is that it goes well beyond and indeed conflicts with evidence in Sextus Empiricus's texts. First, while Sextus Empiricus certainly does think in terms of the therapy model and does hold that the ease of removing beliefs varies from one person to another, so that arguments of different strengths are required in applying the equipollence method to different patients (*Outlines of Pyrrhonism*, bk. 3, ch. 32), he nowhere suggests that the amount of belief compatible with quietude varies from one individual to another or that the skeptic's therapy should be tailored to match such variations. Second, in many of the apparently conflicting passages in Sextus Empiricus's texts Sextus is explicitly describing not mere alternative therapies but *the* therapy used by him and his school.

Let me, then, suggest in outline a way of defending Hegel's interpretation of Pyrrhonism against Frede's contrary evidence, as the correct interpretation of a Pyrrhonist position in all fundamentals consistent. Consider to begin with Frede evidence (1): Sextus Empiricus's distinction between two senses of *dogma*—the broad sense of an acceptance of something and the narrow sense of assent to a non-evident object of scientific inquiry—and his restriction of skeptical opposition to *dogmata* in the latter sense. First, it seems fairly clear from what Sextus Empiricus goes on to say in the relevant passage in explanation of the kind of "dogmatizing" or "accepting" which the skeptic allows that this is merely assent to the mental impressions which necessarily arise through sensation (*tois . . . kata phantasian katēnangkasmenois pathesi*), such as the feelings of being warmed or cooled (*thermainesthai ē psychesthai*). *Outlines of Pyrrhonism*, bk. 1, ch. 7. And this is precisely the kind of nonepistemic acceptance of an appearance that Hegel's reading would lead one to expect. In terms of Hegel evidence (7) cited previously, it is an acceptance by the skeptic that his mental impressions are thus and so in him, but without any implication that these represent the external realities correctly or that the external realities otherwise are a certain way. The reasons why such acceptance is nonepistemic or does not count as belief were given in our main text. Frede tries to argue against this natural reading of Sextus Empiricus's explanation—"Des Skeptikers Meinungen," pp. 124–

125—but his arguments strike me as forced. For some pertinent points in reply, see Burnyeat, "Can the Skeptic Live his Skepticism?" pp. 134–135. Second, Sextus Empiricus's limitation of his attack to nonevident (*adēla*) objects implies no more of a restriction than that he will only attack what lies beyond his own nonepistemic appearances. For the Stoics, from whom the Pyrrhonists borrow the terminology of nonevidence, not only mental impressions but also certain external realities were self-manifesting or evident (under certain conditions), so that only a subset of external realities were nonevident or in need of inference from something evident. For the Pyrrhonists, on the contrary, only their own mental impressions or appearances are self-manifesting or evident, and whatever is not a mental impression or appearance, whatever concerns external reality, stands in need of inference from something evident and is therefore nonevident. Thus at *Outlines of Pyrrhonism*, bk. 2, ch. 9, 88 Sextus Empiricus treats the appearances (*phainomena*) and the nonevident (*adēla*) as two jointly exhaustive classes of things, implying that anything which is not an appearance must be nonevident. Third, the reference to the sciences in the phrase *tini pragmati tōn kata tas epistēmas zētoumenōn adēlōn* does not, I think, function to *restrict* the class of nonevident things at issue but rather to *exemplify* them. Hence the objects of skeptical attack are not being said to be *just* scientific ones. See Barnes, "The Beliefs of a Pyrrhonist," p. 10. The fact that Sextus Empiricus makes special mention of the sciences is sufficiently accounted for by the situation I describe in response to Frede evidence (3) below.

Consider next Frede evidence (2): the frequent occurrence in Sextus Empiricus of tags such as "nonevident" of "so far as this is a matter of reason" to characterize the objects of his attack. The circumstance that for the Pyrrhonists only their own nonepistemic appearances or mental impressions are evident, so that everything going beyond them is nonevident or would require an application of inference or reasoning from evident appearances if it were to be grasped, explains how Sextus Empiricus can liberally use such tags to characterize the objects of his attack without this at all implying that he is restricting his attack to some *subset* of facts beyond nonepistemic appearances in the way Frede suggests.

Finally, consider Frede evidence (3): the passage from *Against the Logicians* in which Sextus Empiricus appears to emerge as the champion of the ordinary man's views (in particular accepting his "commemorative" signs) and the opponent only of the "dogmatic philosophers and . . . logical physicians" (in particular rejecting their "indicative" signs). The key to understanding passages such as this in which Sextus Empiricus allies himself with the ordinary man against the philosopher or scientist, and also to understanding the special hostility to the sciences implied in Sextus Empiricus's characterization of the objects of skeptical attack in Frede evidence (1), is as follows. The Pyrrhonists may reject any given belief in *one* or in *two* ways. They may reject the *form* of the belief only, reject it qua belief, while retaining allegiance to its propositional *content* in the new form of an appearance. Or they may reject not only its form, its existence as a belief, but also its propositional content, retaining no allegiance to this content qua appearance. In the case of their own skeptical formulae, for example, the Pyrrhonists' rejection has the former character. See *Outlines of Pyrrhonism*, bk. 1, ch. 7. But in the case of a scientific belief about, say, the underlying cause of certain medical symptoms or the nature of the universe their rejection has the latter character. The considered Pyrrhonist position is that one renounces the *form* of all beliefs, their existence as beliefs, and in this respect the Pyrrhonists are no less hostile to the ordinary man than to the philosophers and scientists. However, where the propositional *content* of beliefs is concerned, the Pyrrhonists are more discriminating: here they are decided allies of the ordinary man against the philosophers and scientists, accepting the propositional content of the beliefs of the former but rejecting the propositional content of the beliefs of the latter as appearances. One can readily see this from Sextus Empiricus's description of the four sources of appearances which the skeptics use to guide their lives at *Outlines of Pyrrhonism*, bk. 1, ch. 11, 23–24: the guidance of nature, the constraint of the passions, the tradition of laws and customs, and the instruction of the arts. Thus Barnes is guilty of a non sequitur, or at least a misleading oversimplification, when he argues in "The Beliefs of a Pyrrhonist": "Everyman has everyday beliefs; a rustic [i.e., Hegel/Burnyeat-style] Pyrrhonist has no beliefs; it is merely disingenuous for a rustic to pretend that he is on the side of Everyman" (p. 17). Sextus Empiricus suggests two reasons for favoring the content of the beliefs of the ordinary man over the content of philosophical and scientific beliefs in this way (while rejecting them all qua beliefs). First, he suggests that the content of the ordinary man's beliefs, once these have been discredited as beliefs, somehow *forces* itself upon us as an appearance, unlike the content of philosophical or scientific beliefs. Hence at *Outlines of Pyrrhonism*, bk. 1, ch. 20, 193 Sextus Empiricus writes: "We yield to those things that move us emotionally (*pathētikōs*) and drive us compulsorily (*anangkastikōs*) to assent." Second, he suggests that the content of the ordinary man's beliefs, unlike that of philosophical or scientific beliefs, is necessary for ordinary life (*bios*). Hence consider the passage quoted as Frede evidence (3) above. It is this allegiance to the ordinary man and hostility toward the philosophers and scientists with respect to the *content* of beliefs which is really at issue in the passage on the commemorative and indicative signs from *Against the Logicians* which served as Frede evidence (3). The Pyrrhonists accept as an appearance the content of the ordinary man's beliefs in commemorative signs (e.g. the inference on the basis of past experience that because there is smoke here therefore there must also be fire), but they do not accept as an appearance the content of the philosophers' or scientists' beliefs in indicative signs (e.g. the inference that because sweat is found on the skin, there must be unseen pores in the skin). This does *not* mean, however, that the Pyrrhonists accept the *form* of the ordinary man's beliefs in commemorative signs or the form of any other of the ordinary man's beliefs—it does not mean that they accept them *as beliefs*. Pace Frede, "Des Skeptikers Meinungen," p. 114. We can see that this is not Sextus Empiricus's position from the discussion of signs in the *Outlines of Pyrrhonism* corresponding to the discussion with which we have been concerned in *Against the Logicians*. For in the *Outlines of Pyrrhonism* Sextus, while he repeats his claim that the skeptics reject only the indicative sign and retain the commemorative sign required for ordinary life, makes explicit the qualification that this exemption of the ordinary man or ordinary life from attack takes the form of "lend[ing] it our support by assenting *nonbelievingly (adoxastōs)* to what it relies on." *Outlines of Pyrrhonism*, bk. 2, ch. 10, 102; my emphasis. (The question remains why Sextus Empiricus does not actually give any equipollence arguments against our beliefs in commemorative signs in order to induce us to give them up *as beliefs* and merely accept them as appearances. The answer is probably that he *has* given such arguments but in an indirect way by making equipollence attacks on beliefs in the premises and conclusions of commemorative inferences, which beliefs are essential components of any belief in commemorative inferences. For example, although he does not attack the belief in the commemorative inference 'In the past scars have always been preceded by wounds; this is a scar; therefore this was preceded by a wound' directly, he has attacked it indirectly by attacking the belief in its premises and conclusion in various ways.)

We might conclude this note by considering one remaining prima facie reason for thinking that the Pyrrhonist position is just incorrigibly inconsistent (a reason at work in Barnes's "Ancient Skepticism and Causation," pp. 159–160, for example). Sextus Empiricus generally characterizes appearances as mental impressions and the skeptic's acceptance of them as an acceptance that they are thus and so in him, but not that the external realities are any given way (see Hegel evidence (7) above). However, he sometimes implies that acceptance of an appearance involves at least an acceptance that there exists an external object which is doing the appearing (though not that that object is constituted any particular way). For example, at *Outlines of Pyrrhonism*, bk. 1, ch. 10, he says: "Honey appears to us to be sweet (and this we grant, for we perceive sweetness through the senses), but whether it is also sweet in its essence is for us a matter of doubt." The explanation for such apparent vacillations is not, I think, that Sextus is straightforwardly inconsistent. Rather, it is that the Pyrrhonists have a deliberate policy of not assigning precise technical definitions to their terms in the fashion of the dogmatists but rather of allowing their terms the same kind of vagueness and fluidity in sense that terms enjoy in ordinary use. Consider, for example, Sextus Empiricus's statement that the skeptics adopt their own formulae "in a loose and inexact sense." *Outlines of Pyrrhonism*, bk. 1, ch. 19, 191. One would expect the Pyrrhonists to extend this policy to their conception of their own appearances. And that they do so extend it we can infer from Sextus Empiricus's qualification of his equation of appearances with the sense-presentations, or *phantasiai*, of Stoic theory. He does not say simply that the appearance *is* the sense-presentation; rather he says that the appearance is "virtually *(dynamei)* the sense-presentation." *Outlines of Pyrrhonism*, bk. 1, ch. 11. We may conclude, then, that in their conception of their own appearances the skeptics are not guilty of any straightforward inconsistency but rather leave the line between appearances and external realities vague and fluid on principle. These observations are also important in helping to rectify the misleading impression which may have arisen, due to Hegel evidence (7) above, of an excessively dogmatic Pyrrhonist theory of appearances as mental impressions distinct from the external world. Frede reasonably objects to the attribution of such a theory to the Pyrrhonists in "Des Skeptikers Meinungen," pp. 118–119.

59. "Philosophical Science" is an expression sometimes used by Hegel to refer to the content of his own philosophical system, the system which finds mature articulation in his *Encyclopedia*. Hegel uses a plethora of names to denote this content, but I shall restrict myself to this one, characteristic of later rather than earlier texts, as far as possible. For the Hegel of *The Relation of Skepticism to Philosophy*, who did not yet have a theory of development and progress in the history of philosophy, this same content was expressed more or less adequately by all past philosophies worthy of the name (p. 216). By the time Hegel composed the passages on skepticism in the *History of Philosophy*, this content was instead envisaged, as in Hegel's mature thought, as the final result of a process of development in the history of philosophy proceeding through successive philosophical principles.

60. *History of Philosophy*, vol. 2, p. 346.

61. *The Relation of Skepticism to Philosophy*, pp. 237, 240. Hegel's crediting of the ten tropes of Aenesidemus with the in his eyes praiseworthy exemption of Philosophical Science from skeptical attack is fanciful. The last of these tropes in particular includes an attack on "dogmatic conceptions (*dogmatikas hypoleipseis*)" in general—a class which the Pyrrhonist would certainly understand to include such positions as Hegel's Philosophical Science. *Outlines of Pyrrhonism*, bk. 1, ch. 14, 145–147.

62. *The Relation of Skepticism to Philosophy*, pp. 237, 243. Hegel's view of the relative merits of the ten tropes of Aenesidemus and the five tropes of Agrippa underwent a shift between the composition of this essay and the composition of the relevant parts of the *History of Philosophy*. On the whole, *The Relation of Skepticism to Philosophy* is more favorable to the ten tropes of Aenesidemus for their usefulness in combating the dogmatism of the common Understanding and more critical of the five tropes of Agrippa for their tendency to be misused against genuine Philosophical Science, whereas the *History of Philosophy* is more critical of the ten tropes of Aenesidemus on the ground of their crudity and more favorable to the five tropes of Agrippa for their allegedly "profound knowledge of the categories." *History of Philosophy*, vol. 2, p. 359.

63. These two sides of Schulze's skepticism and their weaknesses are the most prominent themes in *The Relation of Skepticism to Philosophy*.

64. *The Relation of Skepticism to Philosophy*, pp. 219–220. Cf. p. 247 for the same charge against the five tropes of Agrippa when these are used to attack genuine Philosophical Science.

65. *The Relation of Skepticism to Philosophy*, p. 251.

66. *Critique of Pure Reason*, A601/B629.

67. *The Relation of Skepticism to Philosophy*, p. 251.

68. Someone might object to Hegel that Kant and Schulze require only the intensional distinguishability of an item and its concept, not extensional dis-

tinctness, for their skeptical case against God or the Absolute to go through. As we shall see in Part Three, Hegel denies them *both* where the concept of God or the Absolute is concerned.

2. The Limitations of Ancient Skepticism

1. *History of Philosophy,* vol. 2, p. 333. In note no. 42 to Chapter 1 I gave a partial explanation of this claim, but it was only partial.
2. *History of Philosophy,* vol. 2, p. 344.
3. Two possible occasions for qualifying this general judgment are (1) Aenesidemus's alleged Heracliteanism and (2) the Academic strategy of constructing equipollence arguments from materials drawn from a single dogmatic opponent (see note no. 57 to Chapter 1), which might be understood as an attempt to demonstrate an implicit contradiction in his position.
4. *History of Philosophy,* vol. 2, pp. 365, 359.
5. *The Relation of Skepticism to Philosophy,* p. 228.
6. *History of Philosophy,* vol. 2, p. 331.
7. *History of Philosophy,* vol. 2, p. 356.
8. *History of Philosophy,* vol. 2, p. 365.
9. *History of Philosophy,* vol. 2, p. 344.
10. On Aristotle, see H. F.. Cherniss, *Aristotle's Criticism of Presocratic Philosophy* (Baltimore, 1935). For Hegel's position see *History of Philosophy,* Intro., esp. "Results Obtained with Respect to the Notion of the History of Philosophy."
11. *Phenomenology,* nos. 205–206: "[Skepticism] lets the unessential content in its thinking vanish; but just in doing so it is the consciousness of something unessential. It pronounces an absolute vanishing, but the pronouncement *is,* and this consciousness is the vanishing that is pronounced. It affirms the nullity of seeing, hearing, etc., yet it is itself seeing, hearing etc. It affirms the nullity of ethical principles, and lets its conduct be governed by these very principles. Its deeds and its words always belie one another and equally it has itself the doubly contradictory consciousness of unchangeableness and sameness, and of utter contingency and non-identity with itself. But it keeps the poles of this its self-contradiction apart, and adopts the same attitude to it as it does in its purely negative activity in general. Point out likeness or identity to it, and it will point out unlikeness or non-identity; and when it is now confronted with what it has just asserted, it turns round and points out likeness or identity . . . In skepticism consciousness truly experiences itself as contradictory."
12. Though naive in the sense that it does not apply to the *considered* position of the Pyrrhonist, Hegel's criticism does, I would concede, apply to positions found at certain points in Sextus Empiricus's texts—as for example at *Against the Logicians,* bk. 2, 479–481, where Sextus likens the skeptic's equipollence arguments to fire which "after consuming the fuel destroys also itself" or to purgatives which "after driving the fluids out of the bodies expel themselves as well."
13. *The Relation of Skepticism to Philosophy,* p. 249: In its unrestricted attack

on objective claims "skepticism had to become inconsistent, for the extreme cannot maintain itself without its opposite. Therefore pure negativity or subjectivity is either nothing at all, in that it destroys itself in its extreme, or it would have to become quite objective at the same time; the recognition of this point suggests itself readily and is what the opponents urged."

14. *The Relation of Skepticism to Philosophy*, p. 249, notes Sextus Empiricus's crucial qualification "that one must always think in addition to whatever the skeptic says: 'according to us,' 'as far as I am concerned,' or 'as it seems to me.'"

15. *History of Philosophy*, vol. 2, pp. 371, 374–375.

16. *History of Philosophy*, vol. 2, p. 372.

17. For Hegel's view of skepticism as a kind of *liberation* in the sense indicated in the first half of this sentence see Verneaux, "L'essence du scepticisme selon Hegel," pp. 128–129.

18. *History of Philosophy*, vol. 2, pp. 371–372.

19. *Phenomenology*, no. 88.

20. *An Enquiry Concerning Human Understanding*, sec. 12, pt. 2.

21. *History of Philosophy*, vol. 2, p. 330.

22. *The Relation of Skepticism to Philosophy*, p. 249.

3. The Theory of a Historical Ur-teilung

1. *History of Philosophy*, vol. 2, p. 366.

2. I do not mean to suggest that Hegel was unaware of or unprepared to defend the fact that he did history in this way. Consider his own pronouncement on the structure of history depicted in the *Philosophy of History*: "All this is the a priori structure of history to which empirical reality must correspond." G. W. F. Hegel, *Vorlesungen ueber die Philosophie der Weltgeschichte* (Hamburg: Felix Meiner Verlag, 1976), vol. 1, p. 157. Some of my translations from the first volume of this work are borrowed from G. W. F. Hegel, *Lectures on the Philosophy of World History—Introduction*, tr. H. B. Nisbet (Cambridge: Cambridge University Press, 1980).

3. F. Hoelderlin, *Urteil und Sein*, in *Hoelderlin Werke und Briefe* (Frankfurt am Main: Insel Verlag, 1969): "Judgment (*Urteil*) is in the highest and strictest sense the original separation of the object and subject which are most intimately united in intellectual intuition, that separation through which object and subject first become possible, the original division (*Ur-teilung*) . . . Being (*Sein*) expresses the connection of subject and object. Where subject and object are not only partly united but so united that no separation at all can be undertaken without violating the essence of that which is to be separated, there and nowhere else can one speak of *Being simpliciter*, as is the case with intellectual intuition."

4. Preface to the penultimate version of *Hyperion*, in *Hoelderlin Werke und Briefe*.

5. Cf. the reference in the *Fragment von Hyperion*, in *Hoelderlin Werke und Briefe*, to the course which people as individuals *and as a species* follow

"from one point [of more or less pure simplicity] to the other [of more or less complete culture]."

6. Letter to Hegel, 26 January 1795, in *Hoelderlin Werke und Briefe; Urteil und Sein.*

7. F. W. J. Schelling, *System of Transcendental Idealism (1800),* tr. P. Heath (Charlottesville: University Press of Virginia, 1981), p. 232, speaks of the need to return from the dividing cognition of science to the unifying cognition of poetry: "In mythology . . . [the medium for this return of science to poetry] existed, before the occurrence of a breech now seemingly beyond repair."

8. For Schelling, the state of unity coincides with the prevalence of mythical thought, and the event of Ur-teilung presumably with the disappearance of mythical thought, but this is very vague.

9. Hegel considers the Schellingian version of the theory at one point and expresses considerable skepticism about it, partly for reasons of the kind just given. See *Encyclopedia,* no. 246, Zusatz.

10. *Science of Logic,* p. 625: "The judgment is the self-diremption of the concept; this unity is, therefore, the ground from which the consideration of the judgement . . . begins. It is thus the original division (*Ur-teilung*) of what is originally one; thus the word judgement (*Urteil*) refers to what judgement is in and for itself."

11. *Phenomenology,* nos. 446, 476.

12. Thus the shapes of consciousness which, as we shall see shortly, correspond to Greek Ethical Life—those in the chapter entitled "Consciousness"—already contain the distinction between a subject and an object.

13. *Phenomenology,* no. 442.

14. *Phenomenology,* no. 442.

15. G. Lukács, *The Young Hegel* (Cambridge: MIT Press, 1976), pp. 470–471.

16. *Phenomenology,* no. 528.

17. See *Phenomenology,* nos. 750–754, 768.

18. *Phenomenology,* nos. 444–445.

19. *Phenomenology,* no. 464. Cf. 465, 701.

20. *Phenomenology,* no. 479. Cf. 199.

21. *Phenomenology,* no. 480.

22. Someone familiar with Hegel's philosophy of history might confront my emphasis on the naturalistic rather than merely metaphysical character of the explanation Hegel gives with the following objection. For Hegel, all historical processes are ultimately to be explained as part of a unitary teleological development aimed at the genesis of that self-knowledge of Absolute Spirit in the modern world which his own philosophy embodies. Each historical process is therefore to be explained in terms of its contribution to the emergence of the philosophical principle which is borne by the nation holding the torch of world history at the time when it occurs. Must not the explanation of the demise of Greek Ethical Life therefore be for Hegel a metaphysical rather than naturalistic one, an explanation in terms of the contribution of this demise to the unitary teleological process just mentioned? The answer to this objection is that though for Hegel the most fundamental level

of historical explanation does indeed have the teleological, metaphysical character indicated, so that all historical processes must receive such an explanation, this neither in Hegel's eyes nor in fact excludes nonteleological, naturalistic explanations of the same processes. It is in Hegel's nonteleological, naturalistic explanations that we shall be interested in what follows.

4. The Collapse of Greek Ethical Life

1. See Gen. 3:7–11.
2. *History of Philosophy*, vol. 2, p. 320.
3. *History of Philosophy*, vol. 2, p. 321.
4. G. W. F. Hegel, *The Positivity of the Christian Religion,* in *Early Theological Writings,* tr. T. M. Knox (Philadelphia: University of Pennsylvania Press, 1981), pp. 152–153.
5. *Phenomenology*, nos. 446–476.
6. This is not to say that it is just *obvious* that for Hegel an interest in the decline of Greek ethics and an interest in the decline of Greek religion must go hand in hand. For he accords to Greek ethics a much greater degree of autonomy from religion than to the ethics associated with the revealed religions, where God is regarded as both the source of the authority of all moral law and the model of right behavior. See e.g. *The Positivity of the Christian Religion,* p. 155: "[The Greeks'] will was free, obeyed its own laws, they knew no divine commandments."
7. *Phenomenology*, no. 750: "The religion of art [i.e. Greek religion] belongs to the ethical Spirit." For the simultaneous and identical explanation, see *Phenomenology*, no. 746.
8. See *Philosophy of History*, vol. 2, p. 640: "The concrete vivacity of the Greeks is Ethical Life, living for religion and state . . . Law is present, and Spirit is in it . . . The principle of thought is destructive for the condition on which the existence of the whole Greek world rests." See *Philosophy of History (Vorlesungen ueber die Philosophie der Geschichte;* Stuttgart: Reclam, 1961), pp. 378–379: "Through the rise of the inner world of subjectivity the breach with reality occurred . . . Now the question was raised whether gods are and what they are."
9. The reasons why Hegel subsumes a model of cognition in general under the title "Ethical Life" and gives examples of that model which are primarily ethical in the usual sense are complex. First, Hegel believes that for the Greeks social and natural objects were in general imbued with ethical meaningfulness in a way that they no longer are for us (we shall illustrate this by reference to two such objects, the community or state and the natural process of death, in Chapter 5). Second, Hegel sees in the sphere of ethics in the usual sense a paradigm of each of the three characteristics about to be described in my text as constituting the general form of cognition in which he is interested—hence the prevalence of examples drawn from ethics. Third, it is, as we are about to see, an essential aspect of this form of cognition in general that within it judgment is at its foundations determined by social

norms rather than individual insight or justifications and in this sense has an ethical character.

10. Thus in the *Phenomenology* Hegel says of the "matter in hand," which he identifies with the "ethical substance" (no. 420), that its nature is "such that its being is the action of the single individual and of all individuals" and that it exists "only as the action of each and everyone" (no. 418). And he says that the law of such a community is "the absolute pure will of all" (no. 436). The distinction between fundamental and nonfundamental principles drawn in my text is not explicit in Hegel but is rather inferred from his choice of examples and the general tendency of his account.

11. *Phenomenology*, no. 437.

12. *Phenomenology*, no. 421.

13. *Phenomenology*, no. 437.

14. *History of Philosophy*, vol. 2, p. 366.

15. As shown earlier, Greek Ethical Life corresponds to the whole "Consciousness" chapter of the *Phenomenology*, including the shapes of consciousness Sense-Certainty, Perception, and Understanding. The latter two of these shapes incorporate a conception of error, as the full title of the section dealing with Perception, "Perception; or the Thing and Deception," indicates. Hence the immediacy characteristic of the forms of consciousness within Ethical Life clearly cannot consist in an ignorance of the possibility of error. Moreover, since Understanding is characterized by a recognition of the distinction between appearance and reality (i.e., between those constitutions and forces which seem to the untutored observer to make up the world and those underlying constitutions and forces which in fact do so), the immediacy in question also cannot consist in an ignorance of the possibility that subjects are systematically misled in their judgment of the world through only paying attention to its outward appearance to the neglect of its underlying reality.

16. *Phenomenology*, no. 466. My emphasis.

17. *History of Philosophy*, vol. 2, p. 355. My emphasis.

18. *Euthyphro*, 6d: "What I wanted you to tell me was not one or two of the numerous actions that are pious, but the actual form that we spoke of, which makes them all pious." Cf. *Theaetetus* 146e; *Laches*, 191c–192b; *Meno*, 72a–c; *Hippias Major*, 287d–e.

19. *History of Philosophy*, vol. 2, p. 366.

20. *The Positivity of the Christian Religion*, pp. 155–156: "Fortunate campaigns, increase of wealth, and acquaintance with luxury and more and more of life's comforts created in Athens and Rome an aristocracy of wealth and military glory. The aristocrats then acquired a dominion and an influence over the masses and corrupted them by their deeds and still more by the use they made of their riches. The masses then readily and willingly ceded power and preponderance in the state to the aristocrats, conscious as they were that they had given them their power and could take it away again at the first fit of bad temper. But gradually the masses ceased to deserve a reproof so often brought against them on the score of their ingratitude to their leaders; when they could choose between [subjection] and this wrong

[of ingratitude], they ceased to prefer the latter and [were now ready] to curse in an individual those virtues which had saved their country from ruin. Soon the preponderance freely granted to the rulers was upheld by force." With this loss of freedom by the majority of men in the communities of Athens and Rome the collapse of polytheistic religion became inevitable, since it was essentially a religion of free peoples: "Greek and Roman religion was a religion of free peoples only, and, with the loss of freedom, its significance and strength, its fitness to men's needs, were also bound to perish" (p. 154).

21. Though the *Phenomenology* regards the economic aspect of the development as a secondary feature capable of an ulterior psychological explanation, the bondsman performing labor on objects at the behest of the lord *in order to avoid the risk of death;* whereas *The Positivity of the Christian Religion* regards the economic aspect as the primary cause of the whole development, the accumulation of wealth by an aristocratic class enabling it to acquire power and coerce.

22. Since, as we have seen, the subsequent two stages Stoicism and Skepticism are firmly located in the history of the Roman Empire and the preceding chapter "Consciousness" corresponds to Greek Ethical Life, it seems that Lordship and Bondage must be assigned to Roman and later Greek history.

23. *Phenomenology,* no. 197. Hegel's theory of an intimate connection between Stoicism and slavery is no doubt heavily influenced by the historical facts that the early Stoic Cleanthes was extremely poor and supported himself in Athens by menial labor, while the later Stoic Epictetus actually was a slave. On Cleanthes see Diogenes Laertius, *Lives of Eminent Philosophers,* tr. R. D. Hicks (London: Loeb Classical Library, 1979), bk. 7, ch. 5.

24. *Phenomenology,* nos. 197, 202.

25. According to Hegel, the Stoics, having posited this sharp division, seek to restrict their claims to those which can be validated from the thought side of the divide. Thus the Stoic consciousness withdraws "from existence only into the self," since "its aim is to be free, and to maintain that lifeless indifference which steadfastly withdraws from the bustle of existence . . . into the simple essentiality of thought." The problem with this position, which the skeptics exploit against the Stoics, is that the claims which the Stoics seek to validate purely by considering the thought side of the divide are supposed to be about the reality side, and since the possibility of independent variations of the two sides has been built into their model of the divide, the Stoics cannot reasonably claim that such validation is possible. This is Hegel's diagnosis of the purpose and inevitable failure of the Stoics' "cataleptic sense-presentation" as a criterion of truth: "Stoicism was perplexed when it was asked for what was called a 'criterion of truth as such,' i.e. strictly speaking for a *content* of thought itself. To the question, *What* is . . . true, it again gave for answer the contentless thought." *Phenomenology,* nos. 201, 199, 200.

26. Hegel indeed suggests the more alarming interpretation that skepticism represents a destruction of the reality side of the division altogether. *Phenomenology,* nos. 202, 204. This interpretation was considered in Part One.

27. *History of Philosophy*, vol. 2, pp. 315–318. On Hegel's account of the transition from Stoicism to Skepticism, see Verneaux, "L'essence du scepticisme selon Hegel," pp. 113–117.

28. For the reference back see *Phenomenology*, nos. 464–465.

29. *Phenomenology*, no. 466.

30. *Phenomenology*, no. 472.

31. *Phenomenology*, no. 740.

32. *Philosophy of History* (Reclam), p. 375.

33. *Philosophy of History* (Reclam), pp. 375–376.

34. *Philosophy of History* (Reclam), pp. 378–379.

35. *History of Philosophy*, vol. 1, pp. 368–369.

36. See W. K. C. Guthrie, *The Sophists* (Cambridge: Cambridge University Press, 1979), pp. 181–182.

37. Thus, when Plato in the *Theaetetus* gives his account of the Heraclitean "secret doctrine" on which he assumes Protagoras's relativist theory to be based, he cites the fact of opposite appearances as something which the secret doctrine is supposed to explain: "If you speak of something as big, it will also appear small; if you speak of it as heavy, it will also appear light; and similarly with everything, since nothing is one—either one thing or qualified in one way" (152d). While there is good reason to doubt that Protagoras's relativism was based on a Heraclitean secret doctrine, it probably was intended to respond to the problem of opposite appearances, as Plato's account implies. Later in the dialogue, when Socrates undertakes to defend Protagorean relativism against the objection that at least the views of such people as dreamers and madmen cannot be true (for them) by arguing that one cannot tell whether one is dreaming rather than awake since all features of the two states correspond exactly, he comments revealingly on this example of how one would defend the Protagorean theory: "Well then, you see that it isn't hard to get a dispute going, since there are disputes even about whether we are awake or asleep" (158c–d).

38. See Guthrie, *The Sophists*, p. 234.

39. *History of Philosophy*, vol. 1, pp. 383–384.

40. Gorgias's case for the sharp general distinction rests largely on the observation that there are particular objects of thought—such as a man flying, a chariot running over the sea, Scylla or the Chimera—which do not exist. For this case and the two skeptical theses quoted see Sextus Empiricus, *Against the Logicians*, bk. 1, 65–87. The reader is invited to see in this paragraph of my text the beginnings of a case against V. Brochard's profoundly mistaken judgment that ancient skepticism owes nothing to Sophism. *Les Sceptiques grecs* (Paris, 1923), pp. 45–47.

41. *History of Philosophy*, vol. 2, p. 355.

42. *Phenomenology*, no. 466.

43. *Against the Physicists*, bk. 1, 1–2.

44. The age-old example of jaundice causing yellow perceptions is in fact a myth but I shall use it for illustrative purposes anyway. See J. Annas and J. Barnes, *The Modes of Skepticism* (Cambridge: Cambridge University Press, 1985), p. 42.

45. C. Kahn, *The Verb "Be" in Ancient Greek*, Foundations of Language, Supplementary Series, vol. 16.

46. The conception of the medium of conceptual thought in general as distinct from and capable of misrepresenting reality seems to require the full existential use of "be," because it appears that in order to have this conception, one must recognize such circumstances as that, though we have a concept of God, there may *be* no God, and this recognition is essentially articulated by means of the full existential use of "be." Conversely, the full existential use of "be" seems to require a conception of the medium of conceptual thought in general as distinct from and capable of misrepresenting reality, to the extent that it is plausible to analyze "exists" as a second-order concept, expressing the satisfaction of other concepts. For if this analysis is correct, then it is necessary for a person to have the notion of a concept as such (i.e., as something distinct from reality, which may or may not satisfy it) in all cases where that person has the notion of existence.

47. *Philosophy of History* (Felix Meiner Verlag), vol. 1, p. 178.

48. *Philosophy of History* (Felix Meiner Verlag), vol. 1, p. 178.

49. *Philosophy of History* (Felix Meiner Verlag), vol. 1, p. 178.

50. *Phenomenology*, no. 472; cf. no. 740.

51. *The Positivity of the Christian Religion*, p. 155: "[The Greeks'] will was free, obeyed its own laws, they knew no divine commandments."

52. *The Positivity of the Christian Religion* (*Die Positivitaet der christlichen Religion*), in *Fruehe Schriften* (Frankfurt am Main: Suhrkamp, 1979), p. 190.

53. *The Positivity of the Christian Religion*, in *Early Theological Writings* (University of Pennsylvania Press), pp. 152–153.

54. *Phenomenology*, no. 746.

55. *Philosophy of History* (Felix Meiner Verlag), vol. 1, p. 178.

56. *The Relation of Skepticism to Philosophy*, pp. 241–242.

57. Hegel neglects Montaigne in his discussions of modern skepticism, which is a pity since Montaigne perhaps comes closest among modern philosophers of note to representing the kind of skepticism which Hegel considers genuine.

58. Diogenes Laertius, *Lives of Eminent Philosophers*, bk. 9, ch. 11.

59. See Guthrie, *The Sophists*, pp. 262–263.

60. Thus Democritus enjoyed a great reputation as a traveler in antiquity. See e.g. Diogenes Laertius's report that according to others "he traveled into Egypt to learn geometry from the priests, and he also went into Persia to visit the Chaldeans as well as to the Red Sea," and "he associated with the Gymnosophists in India and went to Ethiopia." *Lives of Eminent Philosophers*, bk. 9, ch. 7. Consider also Xenophanes' observation, "The Ethiopians say that their gods are snub-nosed and black, the Thracians that theirs have light blue eyes and red-hair." G. S. Kirk, J. E. Raven, and M. Schofield, *The Presocratic Philosophers* (Cambridge: Cambridge University Press, 1983), pp. 168–169.

61. *History of Philosophy*, vol. 2, p. 355.

62. From at least the time of Thales, of course, rival fundamental principles concerning various subjects were offered *within* communities by Presocratic

philosophers and provided grist for skeptical mills. But that an awareness of the unfamiliar fundamental principles of alien communities was nevertheless a precondition for the generation of skeptical problems is probable because, as Kirk points out, the scientific or philosophical innovations of the Presocratics were probably *themselves* stimulated by "the comparison of Mesopotamian, Egyptian and Greek versions [of myths], which first became possible and probable at just about this time." G. S. Kirk, *The Nature of Greek Myths* (Harmondsworth: Penguin, 1974), p. 295. As for the precondition of raising the concept-instantiation problem in its full force and generality, that one recognize a sharp division between the conceptual medium of thought in its entirety and the world which it is supposed to depict, Hegel nowhere explicitly connects this with an acquaintance with the thought of alien communities. However, such an acquaintance was probably a crucial factor in the establishment not only of the previous two preconditions but of this one as well. For it was presumably the experience that members of an alien community had basic, unanalyzable concepts (of mythical creatures, for example) for which their own myths and experience of the world provided no instances and for which they were loathe to posit a new set of entities that initially induced people to develop a conception of the possibility that even basic, unanalyzable concepts could exist without instances in the world and must therefore be distinct from them, which is the core of the precondition in question. The same experience would also have been originally responsible for the genesis of the full existential use of "be" characterized by Kahn, if my earlier suggestion that this use is interdependent with the precondition of skepticism here in question is correct. A good text in which to observe the pressures which arise from a reflective acquaintance with the entities posited in the thought of alien communities toward establishing this precondition of skepticism and the full existential use of "be" is the *Histories* of Herodotus.

5. The Alienated Realms of Culture and Faith

1. *Phenomenology*, no. 442.
2. *Phenomenology*, no. 208.
3. *Phenomenology*, no. 213.
4. *The Positivity of the Christian Religion*, p. 163.
5. G. W. F. Hegel, *The Spirit of Christianity*, in *Early Theological Writings*, tr. T. M. Knox, p. 205.
6. Recalling the account Hegel gave of the decline of Greek polytheism in *The Positivity of the Christian Religion*—that this was a form of religion essentially belonging to free men, so that their loss of freedom robbed men of its foundation—we should not be surprised to find that his account in the same work of the emergence of the alienated religion of Christianity turns largely on his view that this form of religion is appropriate to and arises because of man's social and political subjugation. According to Hegel, the flight from this world to the remote beyond of Christian faith was initially an impotent reaction to the misery of life under the despotism of the Roman emperors,

and man's sense within Christianity of the insignificance of his own power, knowledge, and moral worth in comparison with God's and his willingness to abase himself before God and humbly accept God's commands are reflections of the mentality of the slave. Thus Hegel writes of the rise of Christianity within the Roman Empire: "The despotism of the Roman emperors had chased the human spirit from the earth and spread a misery which compelled men to seek and expect happiness in heaven; robbed of freedom, their spirit, their eternal and absolute element, was forced to take flight to the deity. [The doctrine of] God's objectivity is a counterpart to the corruption and slavery of man, and it is strictly only a revelation, only a manifestation of the spirit of the age . . . The spirit of the age was revealed in its objective conception of God when he was no longer regarded as like ourselves, though infinitely greater, but was put into another world in whose confines we had no part, to which we contributed nothing by our activity, but into which, at best, we could beg or conjure our way" (pp. 162–163). Likewise, the account of Judaism in *The Spirit of Christianity* ascribes the alienated attitude of the Jews toward God and the realm of Nature, as well as other nations, to their historical enslavement by virtue of which they could only act "either [as] mastered or masters" (p. 196). Hence their retention of Abraham's attitude that "nothing in Nature was supposed to have any part in God; everything was simply under God's mastery . . . Abraham . . . likewise was supported by God" (p. 187). Hence also their retention of the trait that "mastery was the only possible relationship in which Abraham could stand to the infinite world opposed to him" (p. 187), i.e., to "the Nature which he regarded as infinite and hostile (for the only relationship possible between hostile entities is mastery of one by the other)" (p. 186). In this connection it is also significant that the sections on the divided realms of Culture and Faith in the *Phenomenology* arise immediately out of the section Legal Status which culminates in a description of the despotic power of the Roman emperor. And Hegel's association of forms of religion characterized by faith in a remote, infinite, inscrutable, and commanding deity with social and political institutions which deprive men of freedom survives even in later works, where Catholicism is the paradigm. This explanation of the emergence of the consciousness divided between a harshly objective world and a remote, infinite, despotic deity in terms of social and political subjugation was very important for Hegel, and on its religious side it had an enormous impact on subsequent thinkers, such as Feuerbach, Marx, and Nietzsche.

7. *History of Philosophy*, vol. 2, pp. 371, 374–375.
8. *Phenomenology*, no. 206.
9. *Phenomenology*, no. 442. Note that for Hegel the two sides of this alienation somehow belong together or complement each other: "The present actual world has its antithesis directly in its beyond . . . just as the beyond has in the present world its actuality, but an actuality alienated from it" (no. 485).
10. Culture (*Bildung*) only fully disappears for Hegel with the establishment of his own philosophy. See esp. *Phenomenology*, no. 33; G. W. F. Hegel, *The Difference between the Fichtean and Schellingian Systems of Philosophy*

(*Differenz des Fichteschen und Schellingschen Systems der Philosophie*), in *Jenaer Schriften*, the section entitled "The Need for Philosophy."

11. *The Spirit of Christianity*, p. 193: "From the pictures, feelings, inspiration and devotion of Eleusis, from these revelations of god, no one was excluded."

12. *Phenomenology*, no. 477.

13. *The Positivity of the Christian Religion*, p. 154.

14. *The Positivity of the Christian Religion*, pp. 154–155.

15. *Phenomenology*, no. 452: "The dead individual, by having liberated his *being* from his *action* . . . is an empty singular, merely a passive being-for-another, at the mercy of every lower irrational individuality and the forces of abstract material elements, all of which are now more powerful than himself . . . The family keeps away from the dead this dishonoring of him by unconscious appetites and abstract entities, and puts its action in their place, and weds the blood-relation to . . . the elemental imperishable individuality. The family thereby makes him a member of a community which prevails over and holds under control the forces of particular material elements and the lower forms of life, which sought to unloose themselves against him and to destroy him."

16. *The Positivity of the Christian Religion*, p. 157.

17. Unfortunately, its treatment there involves a confusion with the quite separate question of a distinction between mind and body.

18. *The Spirit of Christianity*, p. 300. Much in this passage turns on Hegel's highly ambiguous use of the word Spirit (*Geist*) which enables him to express several quite different theses simultaneously.

19. Another thing he means in addition to those discussed in my text is that we conceive of God (Spirit) as an infinite being infinitely removed from man and his world, in the manner described in the Faith section of the *Phenomenology*, rather than as something present and manifested in man's life and world, in the manner of, for example, Greek polytheism.

20. *The Positivity of the Christian Religion*, p. 164.

21. *Phenomenology*, no. 466.

22. *Phenomenology*, no. 468.

23. *Phenomenology*, no. 436.

24. B. Snell, *The Discovery of the Mind* (New York: Dover, 1982), p. 24. Snell emphasizes belief in the religious sphere, but his point transfers to other subject matters.

25. *Phenomenology*, no. 468.

26. *Phenomenology*, no. 468.

27. G. W. F. Hegel, *Philosophy of Right*, tr. T. M. Knox (Oxford: Oxford University Press, 1980), no. 14: The finite will is "tied to this content as to the specific determinations of its nature and its external reality."

28. *Philosophy of Right*, no. 14: "The ego . . . is the possibility of determining myself to this or to something else, of *choosing* between these specific determinations." At this level "freedom of the will is arbitrariness" (no. 15).

29. *Phenomenology*, no. 472; *Philosophy of History* (Felix Meiner Verlag), vol. I, p. 178.

30. One might accept Hegel's implication that the spring of *intellectual* explanation (i.e., explanation by reference to rational grounds) runs dry at this point while not despairing of an explanation altogether. According to Hegel's most plausible account of the emergence of the preconditions for raising the skeptical difficulties, the context in which historical individuals find themselves in the position of having to decide what kind of conscious commitment to fundamental principles in exclusion of contrary principles they are going to engage in is one in which an acquaintance with the thought of alien peoples has enabled them to see beyond the homogeneity of their own community's fundamental principles and has brought them to the realization that there are contrary fundamental principles which one might adopt. This means, in effect, that the competition between contrary fundamental principles with which individuals are confronted runs parallel to the competition between living communities in which the same individuals are participants. Individuals with their inherited stock of fundamental principles are faced with a situation where their intellectual rivals (the representatives of contrary fundamental principles) are at the same time the economic and military rivals of themselves and their community, whereas their intellectual comrades (the representatives of their own fundamental principles) are at the same time their comrades in arms and in economic activity, other members of their own community. Although Hegel does not make the point, this situation suggests that we might explain the emergence of the kind of conscious exclusive commitment identified by Hegel as belonging to Culture (a simple commitment going beyond the expression of the force of available reasons), rather than the alternative kind of commitment which we considered (a commitment wholly expressive of subjective or egocentric reasons of one kind or another), in terms of the greater functional usefulness of the former practice to communities existing in a state of economic and military competition with one another. By instituting a simple, irreducible commitment to people's own principles in exclusion of contraries, the former practice helps to shore up intellectual cohesion within the community and the exclusion of alien ways of thinking—which, especially in areas of thought closely bound up with social conduct, such as ethics and religion, translates into a strengthening of social bonds within the community and a reinforcement of hostile and exclusive attitudes toward other communities. The alternative practice of making exclusive commitment to a principle wholly dependent on a certain kind of egocentric reason would, by contrast, be detrimental to the competing community: if the reasons were diverse in character, this would encourage the development of heresies and the importation of foreign ideas, with consequent harm to the intellectual cohesion and exclusiveness of the community and hence to its cohesion and exclusiveness in general; if the reasons concerned only the maintenance of the received tradition of one's community, this would still weaken the intellectual (and hence also practical) ardor of individuals, a fact which the ancient skeptics recognized and praised as a personal benefit, but without considering the consequences for the community. See *Outlines of Pyrrhonism*, bk. 1, ch. 12.

31. *Phenomenology*, no. 442.
32. *Phenomenology*, no. 207.
33. *Phenomenology*, no. 217.
34. *Philosophy of History* (Felix Meiner Verlag), vol. 1, p. 178.
35. *History of Philosophy*, vol. 2, pp. 374, 384–385. Contrast with this the usual attitude of the Greek philosophers and poets toward divine knowledge. As Snell points out, they do not usually regard the acceptance of divine inspiration as *exclusive* of human means of evaluation. For example, the goddess says to Parmenides: "Do not trust sense experience . . . but judge by means of the *logos* the much-contesting proof which is expounded by me." *The Discovery of the Mind*, p. 149.
36. *The Positivity of the Christian Religion*, in *Fruehe Schriften* (Suhrkamp), p. 190.
37. *The Spirit of Christianity*, p. 196.
38. *Phenomenology*, no. 220.
39. *Phenomenology*, no. 228: "This mediator, having a direct relationship with the unchangeable Being, ministers by giving advice on what is right. The action, since it follows upon the decision of someone else, ceases, as regards the doing or *willing* of it, to be [consciousness's] own."
40. *Philosophy of History* (Felix Meiner Verlag), vol. 1, p. 178.
41. *Phenomenology*, no. 486.
42. *Phenomenology*, no. 485.
43. *History of Philosophy*, vol. 2, p. 385.
44. Preface to the penultimate version of *Hyperion*, in *Hoelderlin Werke und Briefe*.
45. *Phenomenology*, no. 442.
46. *Encyclopedia*, no. 24, Zusatz 3.

6. Hegel's Epistemology?

1. *Science of Logic*, p. 50.
2. R. Scruton, *From Descartes to Wittgenstein* (New York: Harper and Row, 1982), p. 178.
3. J. B. Baillie, *The Origin and Significance of Hegel's Logic* (London, 1901), p. 42.
4. *The Origin and Significance of Hegel's Logic*, p. 42.
5. *The Origin and Significance of Hegel's Logic*, p. 42.
6. *The Origin and Significance of Hegel's Logic*, p. 43.
7. *Hegel in Berichten seiner Zeitgenossen*, ed. G. Nicolin (Hamburg: Felix Meiner Verlag, 1970), p. 306.
8. These claims also apply to thinkers closely associated with the idealists, in particular Hoelderlin and von Sinclair. These figures are discussed below. See also D. Henrich, "Hoelderlin ueber Urteil und Sein," *Hoelderlin Jahrbuch*, 14.
9. J. G. Fichte, "Review of Aenesidemus," in *Between Kant and Hegel*, tr. di Giovanni and Harris, p. 137.
10. Kant, *Prolegomena to Any Future Metaphysics*, tr. P. Carus (Indianapolis:

Hackett, 1982), p. 5. Kant's considerable debt to ancient skepticism is less widely known. See G. Tonelli, "Kant und die antiken Skeptiker."

11. Fichte's *Aenesidemus* review is the crucial text for tracing this route taken to his own philosophical system. See D. Breazeale, "Fichte's *Aenesidemus* Review and the Transformation of German Idealism," *Review of Metaphysics* 34 (1981); Breazeale, "Between Kant and Fichte: Karl Leonhard Reinhold's 'Elementary Philosophy,'" *Review of Metaphysics* 35 (1982).

12. F. W. J. Schelling, *System of Transcendental Idealism (1800)*, pp. 7–8: Transcendental philosophy "necessarily begins with a general doubt as to the reality of the objective," i.e., with an "absolute skepticism . . . which is directed not against individual prejudices, but against the basic preconception, whose rejection leads automatically to the collapse of everything else."

13. See esp. G. W. F. Hegel, *On the Nature of Philosophical Critique* (*Einleitung. Ueber das Wesen der philosophischen Kritik ueberhaupt und ihr Verhaeltnis zum gegenwaertigen Zustand der Philosophie insbesondere*), in *Jenaer Scriften*, for the *theory* of the method of Critique, and G. W. F. Hegel, *Faith and Knowledge* (*Glauben und Wissen*), in *Jenaer Schriften*, for a paradigm of its application.

14. See R. Haym, *Hegel und seine Zeit* (Hildesheim: Georg Olms Verlagsbuchhandlung, 1962), pp. 183–184.

15. *The Relation of Skepticism to Philosophy*, p. 255.

16. *Encyclopedia*, no. 10.

17. See F. W. J. Schelling, *Further Presentations from the System of Philosophy* (*Fernere Darstellungen aus dem System der Philosophie*), in *F. W. J. Schelling Ausgewaehlte Schriften* (Frankfurt am Main: Suhrkamp, 1985), vol. 2, pp. 105–106.

18. *Phenomenology*, no. 27.

19. *Phenomenology*, no. 76.

20. *Phenomenology*, no. 76.

21. *Phenomenology*, no. 76.

22. *Science of Logic*, p. 48; *Encyclopedia*, no. 25.

23. *Encyclopedia*, nos. 61–78. Hegel sees appeals, of a kind which he associates with Descartes, to the self-evidence of certain propositions as akin to, and no more acceptable than, Jacobi's appeals to immediate knowledge. *Encyclopedia*, no. 64.

24. See *Phenomenology*, nos. 6–10.

25. See *Encyclopedia*, no. 63. See also W. C. Zimmerli, "Inwiefern wirkt Kritik systemkonstituierend?" *Hegel-Studien*, supplementary vol. 20.

26. *Encyclopedia*, no. 71: "Since the criterion of truth is found, not in the nature of the content, but in the mere fact of consciousness, every alleged truth has no other basis than subjective certitude and the assertion that we discover a certain fact in our consciousness . . . But there can be nothing shorter and more convenient than to have the bare assertion to make, that we have a certain fact in our consciousness, and are certain that it is true."

27. *Encyclopedia*, no. 72: "A . . . corollary which results from holding immediacy of consciousness to be the criterion of truth is that all superstition or idolatry is allowed to be truth, and that an apology is prepared for any

contents of the will, however wrong and immoral. It is because he believes in them . . . that the Hindu finds God in the cow, the monkey, the Brahmin, or the Lama." Cf. *Encyclopedia*, no. 74: "The form of immediacy is altogether abstract: it has no preference for one set of contents more than another, but is equally susceptible to all: it may as well sanction what is idolatrous and immoral as the reverse."

28. *Encyclopedia*, no. 77: "It abandons itself to wild vagaries of imagination and assertion, to a moral priggishness and sentimental arrogance, or to a reckless dogmatizing and lust of argument."

29. The former point is witnessed by some sixty pages on modern and ancient skepticism in *The Relation of Skepticism to Philosophy* written during the early Jena period, as many pages on the skepticism of the New Academy and the Pyrrhonists in the *History of Philosophy* probably dating mostly from the Jena period, a number of pages on Cartesian and ancient skepticism in the *Phenomenology*, and several remarks on skepticism in the *Encyclopedia*.

30. *History of Philosophy*, vol. 2, p. 367.

31. In Part Two we found that Hegel's account of the emergence and impact of a skeptical culture displayed a similar emphasis on the development of equipollence problems with respect to *fundamental* principles. I suggested there in partial explanation and justification of such emphasis that and why the emergence of equipollence problems in these cases was arguably a necessary condition of such problems coming to have force against *any* kind of principle. This same suggestion may in part explain and justify Hegel's emphasis on the equipollence problem which arises for fundamental assumptions made without ulterior grounds in his own attempts to *combat* skepticism.

32. *The Relation of Skepticism to Philosophy*, p. 244. For Sextus Empiricus's own statement of this trope, see *Outlines of Pyrrhonism*, bk. 1, ch. 15. As we saw earlier, Hegel would have no patience with appeals to immediate knowledge or to the self-evidence of certain propositions as an answer to this kind of skeptical problem.

33. *Encyclopedia*, no. 1.

34. An example of a recent interpretation of Hegel based on this assumption is T. Rockmore, *Hegel's Circular Epistemology* (Bloomington: Indiana University Press, 1986).

35. *Encyclopedia*, no. 86.

36. *Encyclopedia*, no. 10.

37. *Phenomenology*, no. 84.

38. *On the Nature of Philosophical Critique*, pp. 173–174.

39. *On the Nature of Philosophical Critique*, p. 174.

40. *The Relation of Skepticism to Philosophy*, p. 253.

41. For the singularity of the claim which articulates Hegel's philosophical system, see *Zwei Anmerkungen zum System*, in *Jenaer Systementwuerfe II* (Hamburg: Felix Meiner Verlag, 1982), p. 366: "Philosophy has no proposition except this single one which constitutes her whole content, so that she never steps outside it or proceeds to another. Her organization as a whole system is itself nothing but the expression of this her Idea."

42. *The Relation of Skepticism to Philosophy*, p. 247.
43. For the singularity of the concept which articulates Hegel's philosophical system, see *Science of Logic*, p. 39: "A concept is . . . implicitly *the* Concept, and the latter is only one and is the substantial foundation."
44. *The Relation of Skepticism to Philosophy*, p. 257.
45. *The Relation of Skepticism to Philosophy*, pp. 227–228: "A true philosophy necessarily itself has a negative side at the same time, which is turned against everything limited and thus against the heap of facts of consciousness . . . and against limited concepts, . . . against this whole realm of finitude."
46. For the rejection see also *Phenomenology*, no. 27.
47. L. Wittgenstein, *On Certainty*, tr. D. Paul and G. E. M. Anscombe (Oxford: Basil Blackwell, 1977), no. 192.
48. *The Difference between the Fichtean and Schellingian Systems of Philosophy*, p. 25. On the self-contradictoriness of presuppositions cf. *Encyclopedia*, no. 78, where Hegel makes it clear that the dialectic (i.e., demonstration of self-contradictions) within Philosophical Science will dispose of all presuppositions.
49. Though I confess that Hegel often *seems* to have this naive criticism in mind. See not only *Encyclopedia*, no. 10, but also e.g. no. 41, Zusatz; *Encyclopedia* (Heidelberg, 1817), no. 36.
50. *Encyclopedia*, no. 10: "A main line of argument in the critical philosophy bids us pause before proceeding to inquire into God or into the true being of things, and tells us first of all to examine the faculty of cognition and see whether it is equal to such an effort."
51. For Hegel's criticisms of Kant's epistemology in general, see further M. J. Inwood, *Hegel* (London: Routledge and Kegan Paul, 1983), ch. 5.
52. *Phenomenology*, no. 74: "To be specific, it presupposes certain ideas about cognition as an instrument and as a medium, and assumes that there is a difference between ourselves and this cognition. Above all it presupposes that the Absolute stands on one side and cognition on the other, independent and separated from it, and yet is something real; or in other words, it presupposes that cognition which, since it is excluded from the Absolute, is surely outside of the truth as well, is nevertheless true."
53. *Encyclopedia* (Heidelberg), no. 36: Hegel says more specifically that "the assumption of a faculty of knowledge prior to real knowing is already a presupposition both of the unjustified category or determination of faculty or power and of a subjective cognition."
54. *Encyclopedia*, no. 40. This fundamental Hegelian objection to Kantian epistemology that it rests on presuppositions has been rightly emphasized by J. Habermas, *Knowledge and Human Interests* (Boston: Beacon Press, 1971), pp. 17–19. However, Habermas does not see the ancient skeptical background which explains what Hegel means by "presuppositions." Hegel was by no means the first thinker of his generation to draw attention to and criticize the skeptically vulnerable presuppositions of Kant's critical philosophy. The self-styled skeptics Schulze and Maimon preceded him. So too did Reinhold for whom such criticisms were a major force impelling him to attempt to restructure the Kantian philosophy on the firm foundation of a

self-evident principle (the "proposition of consciousness") in his "Elementarphilosophie." Hence in K. L. Reinhold, *The Foundation of Philosophical Knowledge,* in *Between Kant and Hegel,* tr. di Giovanni and Harris, we read: "The foundation of the *Critique of Pure Reason* is . . . not firm enough: for however true all that the *Critique* presupposes as established regarding its own groundwork may be . . . it is equally true that none of it *has been established* as true. The concepts of the possibility of experience, and of the nature and actuality of synthetic a priori judgements, which are laid down in the *Critique* as the foundation of the edifice of Kantian doctrines, are assumed . . . without proof . . . The *reality* of the concepts at issue . . . is *presupposed*" (pp. 92–93; cf. p. 95). For this aspect of Reinhold's reaction to Kant, see Breazeale, "Between Kant and Fichte: Karl Leonhard Reinhold's 'Elementary Philosophy,'" pp. 796–798.

55. Cf. Hegel's observation at *Encyclopedia,* no. 78, that the presupposition made in Jacobi's epistemology of an opposition between immediate and mediate knowledge is, like other presuppositions, to be cleared away by the dialectic of Philosophical Science (which exhibits self-contradiction).

56. Thus when repeating his argument against Kantian epistemology in his *Lectures on the Philosophy of Religion,* in *G. W. F. Hegel: On Art, Religion, Philosophy,* ed. J. G. Gray (New York: Harper and Row, 1970), Hegel writes: "Reason is to be examined, but how? It is . . . to be known; this is, however, only possible by means of rational thought . . . It is impossible to make any preliminary examination of rational activity without being rational" (p. 176).

57. *Science of Logic,* p. 72.

58. *Phenomenology,* nos. 13, 26.

59. *Further Presentations from the System of Philosophy,* p. 106.

60. *Phenomenology,* no. 84. My emphasis.

61. *On the Nature of Philosophical Critique,* p. 174. My emphasis.

62. *The Difference between the Fichtean and Schellingian Systems of Philosophy,* p. 25.

63. *Phenomenology,* no. 26.

64. *Encyclopedia,* no. 25.

7. Two Defenses against Skepticism

1. For Hegel, to say that they are absolutely identical is not the same as to say that they are identical. The latter claim is only a distorted version of the former, "expressed for Reflection." In an absolute identity both sides are *aufgehoben* (abolished, elevated, and preserved): "Both are posited and both are destroyed, neither and both together are." *The Difference Between the Fichtean and Schellingian Systems of Philosophy,* pp. 114–115; cf. *Phenomenology,* no. 39.

2. These skeptical opponents include at least the following: (1) Schulze's skepticism regarding the noumenal subject matter of metaphysics, which takes its cue from the Kantian critique of the ontological argument, being founded on the idea that "all rational knowledge aims at . . . *plucking out . . . a being*

from thinking, existence from concepts" (*The Relation of Skepticism to Philosophy*, p. 253); (2) any version of a general veil of perception skepticism based on the thought that "the human faculty of knowledge is a thing which has concepts, and because it has nothing more than concepts it cannot go out to the things which are outside it. It cannot find out about them or explore them—for the two things are . . . different in kind. No rational person in possession of the representation of something will imagine himself at the same time to possess this something itself" (*The Relation of Skepticism to Philosophy*, pp. 253–254); (3) any version of ancient skepticism which exploits a general assumption of a sharp distinction between concepts and their instances—thus the *Relation of Skepticism to Philosophy* notes that Kant only succeeded in impressing the existence of such a rift upon the "culture of *more recent* times" (p. 251; my emphasis), and the *History of Philosophy* includes the ancient skeptics, particularly the Academic skeptic Arcesilaus, among those who propagated it in earlier times.

3. F. W. J. Schelling, *Bruno*, tr. M. G. Vater (Albany, N.Y.: State University of New York Press, 1984), p. 141.

4. *The Difference between the Fichtean and Schellingian Systems of Philosophy*, pp. 20–25; cf. Hegel's introduction to his *Encyclopedia* lectures of 1818, in G. W. F. Hegel, *Theorie Werkausgabc* (Frankfurt am Main: Suhrkamp, 1981), vol. 10, pp. 406–408.

5. Hegel from an early stage in the development of the philosophy of identity took the lead in emphasizing that the two aspects of the identity were of unequal importance—that the Self and its social organization enjoyed priority over Nature as an aspect of the Absolute. See e.g. G. W. F. Hegel, *On the Scientific Ways of Treating Natural Law*, in *Natural Law*, tr. T. M. Knox (Philadelphia: University of Pennsylvania Press, 1975), p. 111: "If both, as attributes, are real, Spirit is higher than Nature." This emphasis on the spiritual side of the identity did not, however, fundamentally affect the bearing of the philosophy of identity on skepticism in Hegel's eyes. Nor did the fact that within the later Logic, which expounds the nature of the Absolute in its purest form, an analogue of the rift between object and subject or reality and concept reappears in the form of the distinction between the categories of the Objective Logic and those of the Subjective Logic.

6. Letter to Schiller, 4 September, 1795, in *Hoelderlin Werke und Briefe*.

7. I. von Sinclair, *Philosophische Raisonnements*, in H. Hegel, *Isaak von Sinclair zwischen Hoelderlin und Hegel* (Frankfurt am Main: Vittorio Klostermann, 1971), p. 277: "The skeptic accords equal being to each and sets them in absolute opposition to one another."

8. *Philosophische Raisonnements*, pp. 263–264: The goal of philosophy is "to communicate certainty about everything, even if it showed that there was no certainty still it would have to show that at least with certainty."

9. *Philosophische Raisonnements*, pp. 265–266: "Only . . . when one could no longer oppose the manifold to itself and thus no longer to the self either, when one had the feeling of the whole and thus no longer any feeling, can one think of unity as being present. Then also the certainty of the object could no longer be opposed to that of the subject. If we found nothing more

which contradicted the demand for unity then we should no longer ask after certainty ... The demand for certainty would be fulfilled. Consciousness and the object of consciousness would be one. So what could still be uncertain?"

10. *Philosophische Raisonnements*, p. 275: "One would ... be wanting to posit for a self that something was not posited for a self."

11. *Philosophische Raisonnements*, p. 275.

12. That is, in Hoelderlin's terms, a knowledge in which "the unification of subject and object" is accomplished (Hoelderlin's letter to Schiller, 4 September, 1795), a knowledge of what Hoelderlin in *Judgment and Being* calls Being.

13. See e.g. *Philosophische Raisonnements*, p. 268: "Others despaired about the dissolution of the contradictions, the skeptics."

14. Thus Parmenides writes of the path on which "mortals wander knowing nothing, two headed, ... they are carried along, deaf and blind at once, dazed, undiscriminating hordes, who believe that to be and not to be are the same and not the same." And in the second part of Parmenides' poem the mortals' opposition between being and not being receives articulation as the opposition between light and night and is used to construct a mortal cosmology in fulfillment of the goddess's statement that Parmenides would learn not only the truth but also "the opinions of mortals in which there is no true reliance." Kirk et al., *The Presocratic Philosophers*, pp. 247, 255–257, 243.

15. Another point in favor of the general plausibility of this suggestion: At an early date—in his *On the Scientific Ways of Treating Natural Law* and *Logic, Metaphysics, and Nature Philosophy* (*Logik, Metaphysik, und Naturphilosophie*), in *Jenaer Systementwuerfe II* (Hamburg: Felix Meiner Verlag, 1982)—Hegel understood Plato's *Parmenides* as a negative proof of a Platonic principle of absolute unity and approved of both the principle and the proof. In the *History of Philosophy* Hegel remarks that Plato's dialogue was "written in the spirit of the Eleatic school" (vol. 1, p. 250). Thus presumably at the time of *On the Scientific Ways of Treating Natural Law* and the *Logic, Metaphysics, and Nature Philosophy* he identified the Platonic principle of absolute unity which he understood to be proved in the *Parmenides* with Parmenides' principle of Being. If so, then at that time he approved of both Parmendes' principle of Being and what he understood to be Plato's proof of it. It is therefore hardly surprising if Hegel's own philosophical principle owes essential traits to Parmenides'.

16. *History of Philosophy*, vol. 1, p. 252; cf. Parmenides, fragment 6, in *The Presocratic Philosophers*, p. 247.

17. We can still detect this debt to Parmenides' argument in Hegel's treatment of the category Nothing in the *Science of Logic:* "So far as intuition or thinking can be spoken of here, it counts as a difference whether something or *nothing* is intuited or thought. Thus intuiting or thinking nothing signifies something; both are distinguished, thus there *is* (exists) nothing in our intuiting or thinking" (p. 82). The debt is even clearer in the corresponding treatment in the Nuremberg *Logic* of 1808/1809, in *Nuernberger und Hei-*

delberger Schriften (Frankfurt am Main: Suhrkamp, 1979), p. 9: "[Being] is
. . . the same thing as Nothing, which in thought is likewise and thus has the
same being as Being itself."

18. *The Relation of Skepticism to Philosophy*, p. 247.
19. *Phenomenology*, no. 39.
20. *Phenomenology*, no. 39.
21. This doctrine is part of what Hegel means by his well-known dictum "The
true is the whole." *Phenomenology*, no. 20.
22. *Science of Logic*, pp. 39, 49.
23. *Science of Logic*, pp. 44, 60, 49. Cf. pp. 62–63: True thought "should no
longer be called consciousness; consciousness embraces within itself the opposition of the ego and its object which is not present."
24. *Encyclopedia*, no. 24, Zusatz.
25. G. W. F. Hegel, *Lectures on the Proofs of God's Existence* (*Vorlesungen
ueber die Beweise vom Dasein Gottes;* Hamburg: Felix Meiner Verlag,
1973), pp. 172–177.
26. *Science of Logic*, p. 58; *Encyclopedia*, no. 24. Hegel thus sees himself in the
tradition of Anaxagoras, who "first declared that *nous*, thought, is the principle of the world, that the essence of the world is to be defined as thought."
Science of Logic, p. 50.
27. *Science of Logic*, p. 50.
28. After expounding the series of lesser categories in the Logic, Hegel writes
that the Absolute Idea's "true content is only the whole system of which we
have hitherto been studying the development." *Encyclopedia*, no. 237. On
the Absolute Idea's recognition of itself in the series, see *Science of Logic*, p.
843: "The Idea is itself the pure Concept that has itself for subject matter
and which, in running itself as subject matter through the totality of its
determinations develops itself into the whole of its reality, into the system of
the science, and concludes by apprehending this process of comprehending
itself." Cf. *Encyclopedia*, no. 237: "The Absolute Idea . . . contemplates its
contents as its own self . . . What we have now is the knowledge that the
content is the living development of the Idea."
29. *Science of Logic*, p. 39: "A concept is determinate . . . but the determinateness of the concept is a specific form of this substantial oneness, a moment
of the form as totality, of the same Concept which is the foundation of the
specific concepts." Cf. *Encyclopedia*, no. 243: "The Idea is presented as a
systematic totality which is only one Idea, of which the several elements are
each implicitly the Idea." Cf. *Science of Logic*, p. 61: "What is to be considered is the whole Concept, firstly as the Concept in the form of Being, sec-
ondly as the Concept."
30. Thus at its end the Logic, "in the Absolute Idea, has withdrawn into the
same simple unity which its beginning is [i.e., Being]." *Science of Logic*, p.
842. Note that this return to the beginning of the Logic from its culmination
in the Absolute Idea is not a dialectical development *beyond* the Absolute
Idea such as occurs in the transition from one self-contradictory category to
the next earlier in the Logic. Hegel firmly dispels the interpretation that there
is "an infinite retrogression in proof and deduction," saying: "It has been

shown a number of times that the infinite progression as such belongs to reflection that is without the Concept; the absolute method . . . cannot lead into that." *Science of Logic,* p. 839.

31. For Aristotle's own inchoate version of the theory, see *De Interpretatione,* 16a3–8; *De Anima,* 432a3–8; *Posterior Analytics,* 100a15–100b6.

32. *Meditations,* pp. 62–63: "Well, suppose I am dreaming, and these particulars, that I open my eyes, shake my head, put out my hand, are incorrect, suppose even that I have no such hand, no such body; at any rate it has to be admitted that the things that appear in sleep are like painted representations, which cannot have been formed except in the likeness of real objects. So at least these general kinds of things, eyes, heads, hands, body, must be not imaginary but real objects . . . Even if these general kinds of things, eyes, head, hands, and so on, could be imaginary, at least it must be admitted that some simple and more universal kinds of things are real, and are as it were the real colors out of which there are formed in our consciousness all our pictures of real and unreal things. To this class there seem to belong: corporeal nature in general, and its extension; the shape of extended objects; quantity, or the size and number of these objects; place for them to exist in, and time for them to endure through; and so on."

33. The objection in question might equally be raised against using Hegel's doctrine that the Rational has no negation for antiskeptical purposes.

34. Thus Descartes' skeptic draws attention to the possibility that an omnipotent God or evil genius could be giving me even my most fundamental thoughts and concepts without their corresponding to anything in existence and that the Aristotelian doctrine might therefore be false: "But there has been implanted in my mind the old opinion that there is a God who can do everything . . . How do I know he has not brought it about that, while in fact there is no earth, no sky, no extended objects, no shape, no size, no place, yet all these things should appear to exist as they do now?" *Meditations,* pp. 63–64.

35. *Lectures on the Proofs of God's Existence,* pp. 174–175.

36. Spinoza holds that one cannot have a clear idea or concept of a triangle without making particular affirmations about a triangle's nature, such as that the sum of its internal angles is equal to the sum of two right angles. Similarly, he holds that one cannot have a clear idea of God without making particular affirmations about God's nature, especially that God is necessarily existent. Thus in a footnote to the *Tractatus,* in *Benedict de Spinoza—A Theologico-Political Treatise/A Political Treatise,* tr. R. H. M. Elwes (New York: Dover, 1951), he writes: "We doubt of the existence of God . . . so long as we have no clear and distinct idea of God, but only a confused one. For as he who knows not rightly the nature of a triangle, knows not that its three angles are equal to two right angles, so he who conceives the Divine nature confusedly, does not see that it pertains to the nature of God to exist" (p. 270). Indeed Spinoza thinks that the affirmations essential to the possession of clear ideas must go beyond tentative belief to include knowledge that one knows what one affirms and certainty about it: "He who has a true idea, simultaneously knows that he has a true idea, and cannot doubt of the

truth of the thing perceived." *Ethics*, in *The Chief Works of Spinoza*, tr. R. H. M. Elwes (New York: Dover, 1955), proposition 63. Because of this doctrine of the essential role of certain affirmation in the possession of clear ideas, Spinoza can say that the skeptics, who fail to make any certain affirmations, do not doubt anything either and that if they "deny, grant or gainsay, they know not that they deny, grant or gainsay, so that they ought to be regarded as automata, utterly devoid of intelligence." *On the Improvement of the Understanding*, in *The Chief Works of Spinoza*, vol. 2, p. 17.

37. *Lectures on the Proofs of God's Existence*, p. 175.
38. *Science of Logic*, p. 61.
39. Hegel would probably argue similarly, in defense of the antiskeptical doctrine that the Rational has no negation, that one cannot even understand the concept of Philosophical Science—the Absolute Idea or Concept—without recognizing that it has no negation and that negation only occurs within its dialectical self-exposition. He would do so on the grounds that, as the Logic shows, the articulation of the Absolute Idea essentially includes a dialetical demonstration of the self-contradictoriness of the category of Nothing, or Not-being, when taken by itself, and a demonstration that this category is embraced within or is implicitly one with the Absolute Idea. Note that Hegel would be unimpressed by the suggestion that the skeptic could still raise problems concerning the concept or claim of Philosophical Science even without understanding it by referring to it indirectly as, say, "Hegel's concept/claim, whatever it may be." For as we shall see in the next chapter, he does not believe that there is a coherent viewpoint from which such an indirect reference could be made.
40. There is evidence that Aristotle holds the general view that the acceptance of certain true principles is a necessary condition of having clear thoughts or meanings. The discussion of the principle of noncontradiction in the *Metaphysics* provides a good example of this: Aristotle attempts to prove that this principle is the firmest of all principles because it is "what is necessarily part of the equipment of one who apprehends any of the things that are" or "what one necessarily understands who understands anything" (1005b15–18), i.e., a principle which must be affirmed by anyone who is to mean or think anything at all. There are also indications that for Aristotle the internality of the affirmation of particular principles to thought or meaningful expression operates at the more parochial level of specific subject matters.
41. The Aristotelians might make just this response to the Cartesian skeptic who attacked their thesis by suspending judgment about it on the ground that an omnipotent God or evil genius might be furnishing him with even his most fundamental concepts and thoughts without these corresponding to anything in reality. That is, the Aristotelians might respond that the skeptic's apparent suspension of judgment about the Aristotelian thesis just shows that the skeptic lacks a clear concept of such things as concepts and thoughts, that he is confused and unable even properly to understand the Aristotelian thesis. They might add that even before the skeptic's apparent suspension of judgment on that thesis, his claim that the evil genius hypoth-

esis described a *possible* state of affairs showed that he was in such a state of confusion and incomprehension, for in order to have had a clear concept of concepts or thoughts, he would have had to recognize that one's most fundamental concepts and thoughts *necessarily* correspond to real features of the world and that therefore the hypothesis of an evil genius supplying us with our most fundamental concepts without these having any instantiation in reality is not a hypothesis of a possible state of affairs.

42. Note that the general thesis put forward here as a means of defending the antiskeptical doctrines of Hegel and the Aristotelians against the skeptics' counterattack—the thesis tht the possession of concepts essentially involves the affirmation of certain principles—is independently hostile to skepticism. For if it is true of a given subject matter, then the skeptics will not be able genuinely to discuss or think about that subject matter without affirming the principles pertaining to it, thus abandoning suspension of judgment, and if it is true of all subject matters, then they will not be able genuinely to discuss or think about *anything* without affirming some principles.

43. See, e.g., Hegel's remark in relation to his absolute identity thesis that to talk merely of a "unity of subject and object, of finite and infinite, of being and thought, etc. is inept, since subject and object, etc. signify what they are *outside* of their unity." *Phenomenology*, no. 39. Cf. Hegel's distinction in the *Encyclopedia* between the ordinary and the properly philosophical concepts of truth: "In common life truth means the agreement of an object with our conception of it . . . In the philosophical sense of the word, on the other hand, truth may be described in general abstract terms, as the agreement of a thought-content with itself. This meaning is quite different" (no. 24).

44. Thus in the *Encyclopedia* (Heidelberg) Hegel points out that the traditional epistemological problematic deriving from Kant, which demands a critical investigation of our faculty of knowledge, involves "a presupposition both of the unjustified category or determination of faculty or power and of a subjective cognition" (no. 36). That these categories are presuppositions ultimately signifies for Hegel that they prove to be self-contradictory. How convincing we find this suggestion will depend largely on how persuaded we are by Hegel's project discussed in the next chapter of showing all nonscientific categories to be self-contradictory.

45. On Hegel's concepts being the only self-consistent ones see the next chapter. What would be Hegel's response if a variety of ancient skepticism were to exploit Hegel's acknowledged change of meanings and, so to speak, seal itself off from a confrontation with his two doctrines (that there is an absolute identity of concept and object in the Rational and that the Rational lacks a negation) by strictly confining its skeptical objections to claims about knowledge and how things really are articulated in the *old* set of concepts (those with which the epistemological discussion begins and which Hegel rejects as incoherent)? Hegel would, I think, respond that a skepticism which avoided falling foul of his two doctrines in this way was possible and indeed desirable, since he only has an interest in thwarting skeptical attacks directed against the claims of Philosophical Science, which are articulated using the new concepts. At the same time he would deny that all forms of ancient

skepticism actually achieve such immunity to his two doctrines, since they do not all refrain from attacking the claims which Philosophical Science makes using the new concepts. These two sides of Hegel's response are apparent from the different attitudes he takes in *The Relation of Skepticism to Philosophy* toward the ten tropes of Aenesidemus and the five tropes of Agrippa. The ten tropes of Aenesidemus he endorses for the reason that they strictly confine their skeptical attacks to those claims about reality and our knowledge of it which the ordinary Understanding makes (using the old set of concepts). The five tropes of Agrippa he criticizes on the ground that, unlike the ten tropes of Aenesidemus, they do not strictly confine their skeptical attacks to such claims of the Understanding but in addition attack the corresponding claims which Philosophical Science makes (using the new set of concepts).

46. One might encourage this suspicion further by pointing out, for example, the extent to which, although the Absolute Idea and the categories which articulate it within the Logic are supposed to be absolutely identical with their objects or reality, Hegel nevertheless continues to speak of them very much in terms derived from and appropriate to our descriptions of categories in the usual sense.

8. Further Defenses against Skepticism

1. In this text Hegel points out the difficulty that Spinoza and Descartes merely *presuppose* the principle which he sees himself as sharing with them that God's concept is absolutely identical with his being: "That this is a presupposition is what is unsatisfactory." *Lectures on the Proofs of God's Existence*, p. 175. As we have seen, Hegel uses the term "presupposition" not in an everyday sense (as it might be used of any proposition which is accepted without ulterior justification) but in the precise sense acquired from the fourth trope of Agrippa of a proposition which is posited without ulterior grounds or justification *and therefore succumbs to the difficulty that its negation or a contrary principle may with equal justification be posited in the same way.* The difficulty Hegel is confronting in the *Lectures on the Proofs of God's Existence* is thus the special version of the equipollence difficulty with which we are familiar from *On the Nature of Philosophical Critique* and the *Phenomenology*. The solution to the difficulty which Hegel proposes in the *Lectures on the Proofs of God's Existence* follows a strategy equally familiar from these earlier texts: "The finite and subjective is . . . not only a finite measured by the standard of that presupposition: it is finite in itself and therefore the opposite of itself; it is the unresolved contradiction" (p. 175). Once again Hegel is proposing to defend the principle of his own philosophy against equipollence difficulties by showing that all the other (all "finite") viewpoints are self-contradictory.

2. Though original, Hegel's strategy is not *entirely* unprecedented. First, it shares certain characteristics with the, in other respects very different, strategy of such fideists as Montaigne and Charron. Like Hegel, the fideists are interested in defending a lofty religious world-view; like him, they use as

their main method of defense an attack upon all *competing* forms and sources of belief, an attack against which they suppose their own world-view to be immune; and like him, they choose as their weapon for this attack a discipline which they consider a form of skepticism. A second precedent is the idea which occasionally surfaces in Plato's dialogues that the true view on a given subject is distinguishable from all false views by virtue of the fact that the true view alone is self-consistent, the false views all being self-contradictory, and that the justification of a view accordingly consists in exhibiting these features of it and its competitors. See esp. *Gorgias,* 509a, 527a–b. This precedent, like the previous one, shares with Hegel the thought that the justification of an account is to be effected by showing all alternative accounts to be flawed in some way in which it is not. This precedent is not as close to Hegel as the fideist precedent in one respect: it does not in the manner of Hegel and the fideists understand the flaw in question to be demonstrated by a version of skepticism. But in another respect it is closer, namely in focusing on the same flaw as Hegel focuses on: self-contradictoriness. The third precedent almost certainly had a direct influence on Hegel. We considered earlier a letter written by Hoelderlin in which he expressed the desire to show "to what extent the skeptics are right and to what extent not." Presumably, both sides of this bear, for Hoelderlin, on the justification of the principle of his own philosophy (described in his letter as "the unification of subject and object in an absolute"). Thus Hoelderlin appears, like Hegel, to envisage a justification of his principle which consists in showing, on the one hand, the vulnerability of all other accounts to a form of skepticism (i.e., those accounts which Hoelderlin calls "theoretical" and which are distinguished by being posited within an assumed opposition of subject and object) and, on the other hand, the invulnerability of his principle to this skepticism (a principle grasped in what Hoelderlin calls an "aesthetic" or "intellectual intuition," distinguished by the absence of any opposition of subject to object). Moreover, on the reasonable assumption that Hoelderlin like von Sinclair understands the skepticism in question as a matter of pointing out *contradictions,* his position is still closer to that of Hegel, who also understands it in this way.

3. *On the Scientific Ways of Treating Natural Law,* p. 61.
4. K. Rosenkranz, *Hegels Leben* (Darmstadt: Wissenschaftliche Buchgesellschaft, 1977), p. 191; *The Relation of Skepticism to Philosophy,* p. 228.
5. *History of Philosophy,* vol. 2, p. 365; *The Relation of Skepticism to Philosophy,* p. 228.
6. *The Relation of Skepticism to Philosophy,* p. 228.
7. For example, Hegel says in the *Lectures on the Proofs of God's Existence:* "The finite and subjective is . . . finite in itself and therefore the opposite of itself; it is the unresolved contradiction" (p. 175).
8. *Prolegomena to Any Future Metaphysics,* no. 39.
9. For Reinhold, the scientific status of philosophy required that it be presented as a system derived from a single, self-evident principle. In his "Elementarphilosophie" he attempted to present Kantian philosophy as just such a system, with not Kant's logical forms of judgment but his own "proposition of

consciousness" playing the role of the single, self-evident foundation of the system. Fichte took over this Reinholdian ideal as a central aspect of his own philosophy. But for Fichte the single, self-evident foundation of the system of philosophy was neither Kant's logical forms of judgment nor Reinhold's proposition of consciousness but his own principle of the deed or *Tathandlung* of the self's self-positing. See Breazeale, "Fichte's *Aenesidemus* Review and the Transformation of German Idealism"; Breazeale, "Between Kant and Fichte: Karl Leonhard Reinhold's 'Elementary Philosophy.'"

10. *On the Concept of the Science of Knowledge* (*Ueber den Begriff der Wissenschaftslehre*), in *J. G. Fichte—Gesamtausgabe* (Stuttgart-Bad Cannstatt: Friedrich Frommann Verlag, 1965), ser. 1, vol. 2, p. 129.

11. *On the Concept of the Science of Knowledge*, p. 130.

12. *Science of Knowledge*, p. 22.

13. *The Difference between the Fichtean and Schellingian Systems of Philosophy*, p. 9.

14. The first evidence of a quasi-Fichtean dialectical method in Hegel occurs surprisingly early, in *The Difference between the Fichtean and Schellingian Systems of Philosophy*, pp. 26, 46–47. The method plays a leading role in all of Hegel's disciplines which are most important for the destructive project being explained in the present chapter: the early Logic of the *Logic, Metaphysics, and Nature Philosophy*, the *Phenomenology*, and the later Logic. It is the means employed in all these disciplines to demonstrate both the complete systematicity and hence the exhaustiveness of the collection of categories or similar items destroyed and also their self-contradictoriness. That Hegel in large part owes his dialectical method to Fichte can easily be put beyond dispute by comparing his method to Fichte's.

15. *On the Concept of the Science of Knowledge*, pp. 130–131.

16. Thus the early Logic of the *Logic, Metaphysics, and Nature Philosophy* begins with abstract Unity ("The Logic began with Unity itself"—p. 136), the *Phenomenology* begins with Sense Certainty, and the later Logic begins with Being. In the case of the latter two disciplines at least, the initial category or similar item is not only self-contradictory but also the most abstract or inadequate of all the self-contradictory categories or similar items dealt with.

17. *On the Concept of the Science of Knowledge*, pp. 130–131.

18. Thus circularity is striven for in each of the three texts which are most important as attempts to realize Hegel's destructive project: the early Logic of the *Logic, Metaphysics, and Nature Philosophy*, the *Phenomenology*, and the later Logic of the *Science of Logic*. In the *Logic, Metaphysics, and Nature Philosophy* the Logic begins with a merely abstract Unity, and this category is eventually reached again at the end of the Logic in the shape of the absolute Unity with which the Metaphysics begins: Thus at the start of the Metaphysics Hegel writes: "The Logic began with Unity itself . . . It provided no justification for this, something which first happens here, in that the in-itself posits itself here . . . That initial Unity is a result, but that it is a result was not at all evident from it . . . Here in the absolute return to itself it exists as this result" (p. 136). In the *Phenomenology* we are told that once the dialectical development of the work has reached Philosophical Science

proper, that Science "contains within itself [the] necessity of externalizing itself from the form of the pure Concept, and it contains the passage of the Concept into consciousness. For the self-knowing Spirit . . . is the immediate identity with itself which, in its difference, is the certainty of immediacy, or Sense Consciousness—the beginning from which we started" (no. 806). Thus there is eventually a return to the Sense Certainty from which the *Phenomenology* set out. Hegel goes on to explain that this circular return to Sense Certainty occurs through the fact that Spirit sacrifices or externalizes itself into Nature, and Nature then "reinstates the *Subject*" (no. 807), i.e., it occurs via that free self-release of the Absolute Idea into Nature which occurs at the end of the Logic and forms the transition to the Philosophy of Nature and the subsequent transition from the Philosophy of Nature to the Philosophy of Spirit which returns us to the human and the spiritual subject. For in the Philosophy of Spirit, as presented in the *Encyclopedia,* the subject matter of the *Phenomenology* beginning with Sense Consciousness receives a scientific retreatment in a section bearing the same name as the *Phenomenology.* The *Science of Logic* again displays a circular structure. Thus Hegel writes: "The essential requirement for the science of Logic is . . . that the whole of the science be within itself a circle in which the first is also the last and the last is also the first" (p. 71). The dialectic in this text starts out from the category of Being and returns to it at the end of the work. The process of beginning with this category was, we are told, something "merely formal," since the category was left in need of mediation and deduction (p. 839). When returned to at the end of the work the category has received this mediation and deduction through the dialectical development which has proceeded from it and now returned to it, so that it is "no longer something merely picked up, but something deduced and proved" (p. 838). The initial beginning from Being, though not made on purely arbitrary grounds, was therefore provisional and hypothetical, in need of the confirmation of its correctness which comes from the circular return of the dialectical derivation to it: "Each step of the *advance* in the process of further determination, while getting further away from the indeterminate beginning, is also *getting back nearer* to it, and . . . therefore, what at first sight may appear to be different, the retrogressive grounding of the beginning, and the *progressive further determining* of it, coincide and are the same. The method, which thus winds itself into a circle, cannot anticipate in a development in time that the beginning is . . . already something derived; it is sufficient for the beginning in its immediacy that it is simple universality . . . and there is no need to deprecate the fact that it may only be accepted *provisionally* and *hypothetically*" (p. 841). Note finally that in none of these three texts does the circular return find the initial category or similar item under exactly the same aspect or with exactly the same meaning as it had at its first appearance.

19. In connection with the circularity of the dialectic in Hegel's destructive disciplines, it should be noted that Hegel also characterizes his mature philosophical system as a whole (comprising the later Logic, the Philosophy of Nature, and the Philosophy of Spirit) as a circle, or a "circle of circles." *Science of Logic,* p. 842; *Encyclopedia,* no. 15. This circular structure of the

whole system is expressed by the literal Greek meaning of the title of the work in which the system is presented: *Encyclopedia,* or *en* (in) *kyklō* (a circle) *paideia* (education). And it is realized by virtue of the fact that the system's dialectic, after starting from the Logic and proceeding through the Philosophies of Nature and Spirit, comes at the end of the Philosophy of Spirit, in the culmination of the section on Absolute Spirit, to an account of philosophy which returns us to the Logic. *Encyclopedia,* no. 574.

Hegel has three main reasons for wishing his system as a whole to have this circular structure. First, there is the more or less mystical assumption that the circle is the best spatial representation of God or the Absolute. This is an assumption which Hegel shares with Schelling, who writes in his *Bruno:* "The circle is the figure that is the most perfect expression of Reason, which is the identity of the universal and the particular" (p. 170). Thus in the *Science of Logic* Hegel writes: "The image of genuine infinity, bent back into itself, becomes the circle, the line which has reached itself, which is closed and entirely present, without beginning and end" (p. 149). Second, Hegel shares with Reinhold and Fichte the view that, in order to be scientific, a presentation of philosophy must constitute a complete system. And he sees as the criterion of complete systematicity in his philosophy as a whole the circularity of its dialectical course, in agreement with Fichte before him and in keeping with his own strategy for showing complete systematicity in his destructive disciplines. *Encyclopedia,* nos. 14–15. But third, Hegel has an epistemological motive for the circularity of his whole system, a motive which has recently been emphasized in T. Rockmore, *Hegel's Circular Epistemology.* Since this motive bears on the topic of the present part of my book, I would like to make a few comments on it and on Rockmore's account of it.

The main lines of Rockmore's interpretation of the role of circularity in Hegel's mature system are as follows. Hegel is concerned not to begin his Philosophical Science with a *presupposition* in the sense of a principle asserted without further grounds, an "undemonstrated initial principle" (pp. 89–90). In order to avoid this, or presumably the equally unacceptable alternative of an infinite regress of grounds, he constructs his system in a circle so that every claim within it, including the claim with which it begins, is grounded by other claims: "Since philosophy cannot justify itself through its deduction from its initial principle, its beginning, which itself is not justified, it must be the case that the result of the theory justifies its beginning ... It is the result which justifies the entire reasoning process, including its onset. In a word, philosophy, which must justify itself in part and in whole, can carry out this process only through itself in the form of a circle" (p. 90). However, this epistemological strategy is ultimately unsuccessful, because even if philosophy can be shown to constitute a system of mutually supporting propositions, this still leaves undecided the question of whether or not this system is true of the world: "Although in virtue of the fact that it can presuppose nothing philosophy is necessarily circular, it at best can justify the certainty of certainty, but not the transition to truth. But since circular philosophy is inadequate to demonstrate the unity of thought and being, it is inadequate to provide the solution of the problem which is its central task" (p. 158).

Let me first indicate a few weaknesses in this reading of Hegel's epistemological strategy before going on to indicate the qualified sense in which I think it is correct. One general weakness should be obvious from my text: this reading gives a greatly oversimplified picture of Hegel's complex epistemological strategy. A more specific weakness is that it overlooks the fact demonstrated in my text that the problem of presupposition which Hegel is concerned to avoid is not the problem of beginning Philosophical Science with an ungrounded claim per se but rather the problem of doing so *in a context where an opposite claim can then be set up against it in the same way and so with equal right.* In short, it is the fourth trope of Agrippa problem of presupposition. Furthermore, if Hegel *had* seen beginning Philosophical Science with an ungrounded claim as a problem per se, then the circularity of his system would have been a much weaker solution to this problem than Rockmore realizes. For even if circularity had prevented any individual claim within the system from being ungrounded, it would have done nothing to prevent a reiteration of the putative problem at the level of the system as a whole: What are we to do about the fact that the *system as a whole* is ungrounded? Hegel makes no attempt to preclude or answer such a question and this reinforces the impression that he did not really perceive the putative problem as a problem in the first place.

A similar weakness would afflict any attempt to use the circularity of the whole system as a solution to the fourth trope of Agrippa problem of presupposition with which Hegel really *is* concerned. As Inwood has in effect noted, such circularity would by itself give no satisfactory answer to the problem, since it would allow a reiteration of the problem at the level of ungrounded and opposing circular systems: "If the circle is interpreted as an epistemic one, then it is on the face of it vicious, or at least ineffectual. The fact that a series of elements . . . is self-sustaining in this sense does not in itself guarantee that it is the only possible self-sustaining system and does not, therefore, establish that it is to be accepted in preference to some alternative . . . Hegel would still need to establish the uniqueness of his system, and for this other arguments are required." *Hegel,* p. 154. Indeed, if the circularity of the system consisted in a circle of implications, it would automatically be possible to find an opposing circular system to cause a reiteration of the problem, for if there exists a circular system

$$p \rightarrow q \rightarrow r \rightarrow s \rightarrow p$$

then necessarily by modus tollendo tollens there exists an opposing circular system

$$-p \rightarrow -s \rightarrow -r \rightarrow -q \rightarrow -p.$$

Of course, Hegel has a more promising strategy overlooked by Rockmore for solving the fourth trope of Agrippa problem of presupposition—a strategy which, if it could be properly executed, would not succumb to a reiteration of the problem in the form of ungrounded, opposed systems. This strategy is to avoid the problem not by preventing the claim of Philosophical Science from being put forward without further ground but rather by preventing it from being put forward *in the face of opposing claims.* As we have seen, Hegel's means for achieving this are his doctrine that the claim of Philosophical Science has no negation and his demonstration that all claims other than that of Philosophical Science turn out to be self-contradictory. It is here that Hegel's main response to the problem of presupposition in which he is interested lies. And although circularity plays a role in this response, it is the circularity of Hegel's destructive disciplines, whose contribution toward the demonstration of the self-contradictoriness of all nonscientific claims we have considered in this chapter, not the circularity of Hegel's whole system, on which Rockmore focuses.

Nevertheless, Rockmore is right in the following qualified sense: the circularity of Hegel's whole system does play a minor supporting role in his attempts to answer the fourth trope of Agrippa problem of presupposition threatening Philosophical Science. Hegel wishes to avoid having Philosophical Science be a presupposition in the sense of both (a) making ungrounded claims and (b) having these ungrounded claims confronted by similarly ungrounded opposites. His main solution to this challenge, as indicated, is to show that (b) cannot occur, but he does also in some degree try to prevent or minimize (a) by giving the whole system a circular structure, even though by itself this response is inadequate, and when accompanied by Hegel's main solution—the exclusion of (b)—it is, strictly speaking, superfluous. That Hegel in this way uses the circularity of the whole system as at least an auxiliary answer to the problem of presupposition is clear from the *Encyclopedia*: "Philosophy seems in general to begin with a subjective presupposition like the other sciences as the start which it must make, that is, it seems to have to make a particular object into the subject of its thought . . . But . . . the standpoint which in this way appears immediate must make itself within Science into a result, and indeed Science's last result, in which Science reaches its beginning again and returns into itself. In this way philosophy proves itself to be a circle returning back into itself, which has no beginning in the manner of other sciences, so that the beginning is only in relation to the subject, who resolves to philosophize, but not to Science as such" (no. 17).

As for Rockmore's claim that the circularity of Hegel's system fails to prove the "unity of thought and being," my text should make clear that, whatever exactly Rockmore means by this vague phrase, Hegel's attempt to prove it does not lie primarily, let alone exclusively, in the strategy of giving his system as a whole a circular structure. Hence a failure of such circularity to prove the "unity of thought and being" has little bearing on the question of whether or not Hegel succeeds in proving this or on the general question of the success of his epistemology.

20. *The Relation of Skepticism to Philosophy,* p. 228.

21. *Encyclopedia,* no. 78; *Encyclopedia* (Heidelberg), no. 36. That Hegel's phrase refers to his own early Logic is made fairly certain by the fact that Schelling in 1803 refers to a dialectical Logic of the kind then being developed by his friend and collaborator Hegel as a "scientific skepticism." *Vorlesungen ueber die Methode des akademischen Studiums* (Hamburg: Felix

Meiner Verlag, 1974), p. 63. On the identity of Schelling's "scientific skepticism" with Hegel's early Logic, see also K. Duesing, "Idealistische Substanzmetaphysik," *Hegel-Studien,* supplementary vol. 20, pp. 32–33; Duesing, "Das Problem der Subjektivitaet in Hegels Logik," *Hegel-Studien,* supplementary vol. 15, pp. 101–102.

22. *Phenomenology,* no. 78.

23. *Encyclopedia,* no. 81.

24. *On the Scientific Ways of Treating Natural Law* articulates the dependence of the equipollence of a claim and its negation on the deeper fact of their self-contradictoriness as follows: "Since . . . a specific detail, maintained by positive scientific opinion, is the very opposite of itself, it is equally possible for either of the two parties, holding one of the opposite details, to refute the other" (pp. 120–121). That equipollence problems are ultimately due to the self-contradictoriness of the *concepts* used to articulate claims is implied in this complaint in the *History of Philosophy* about the way the ten tropes of Aenesidemus exhibit equipollence problems: "From content and form we see in these tropes their early origin; for the content . . . shows its change only, takes up only the variability of its manifestation, without showing its contradiction in itself, i.e. in its concept" (vol. 2, p. 356).

This position of Hegel's helps to explain why he considers the second half of Plato's *Parmenides* such a perfect model of skepticism (*The Relation of Skepticism to Philosophy,* p. 228) and why he emulates it in several versions of his first destructive discipline, the early Logic (in particular in *On the Scientific Ways of Treating Natural Law* and the *Logic, Metaphysics, and Nature Philosophy*). For the second half of Plato's dialogue can with some plausibility be seen as an elaborate presentation of all the elements contained in Hegel's own explanation of the skeptic's equipollence problems, as follows. The contradictory hypotheses "The one is" and "The one is not" are shown in the dialogue to be equally justified or equipollent, the former being justified by the refutation of the latter in the second part of Parmenides' performance, and the latter being justified by the refutation of the former in the first part of that performance. These refutations are achieved by reducing each of the hypotheses to absurdity, showing each to be self-contradictory. The hypotheses are self-contradictory because the concept which articulates them both, unity, is self-contradictory (*On the Scientific Ways of Treating Natural Law* and the *Logic, Metaphysics, and Nature Philosophy* under stand the dialogue as a demonstration of the self-contradictoriness of the concept of unity when this is taken in abstraction from the many, and that this reading of the dialogue has textual support can be seen from such passages as *Parmenides,* 129b–130a, where Socrates challenges his Eleatic opponents to show him that there is self-contradictoriness in "forms apart just by themselves," such as the form of unity, and not only in the world of appearances).

In tracing the skeptics' equal balance of arguments for and against each claim to the self-contradictoriness of each claim and its negation, and beyond that, to the self-contradictoriness of the concepts through which each claim and its negation are articulated, Hegel is adopting and giving a wider application to the model of Kant's Mathematical Antinomies. Hegel hints at this program in the Nuremberg *Logic* of 1810/1811: "Kant has especially drawn our attention to the Antinomies, however he has not exhausted the antinomical aspect of reason, in that he has only expounded a few forms of it." *Nuernberger und Heidelberger Schriften*, p. 184. Kant had claimed that a genuine proof could be given for each side of his Antinomies, e.g. for both the claim "The world has, as to time and space, a beginning" and the claim "The world is, as to time and space, infinite." And he had argued that in the case of the Mathematical Antinomies, of which this example is one, this was to be explained by the fact that both claims were false because self-contradictory, this being possible because the subject concept common to both claims (here, "the world") was self-contradictory. The debt which Hegel's explanation of skeptical equipollence owes to this Kantian model should be evident.

25. Inwood, *Hegel*, esp. pp. 125–134, discerns a similar epistemological strategy in Hegel to the destructive strategy for answering the problem of equipollence on behalf of Philosophical Science outlined in this chapter. While generally helpful, his account has two weaknesses: (1) it does not recognize the crucial role played by the circularity of the dialectic in Hegel's attempts to demonstrate the complete systematicity and hence exhaustiveness of the collection of nonscientific viewpoints destroyed (although Inwood *does* see various other roles which Hegel assigns to circularity), and (2) it gives an inadequate and insufficiently charitable interpretation of the dialectical method itself (a deficiency which I hope to make up in Chapter Ten).

26. Thus the *Lectures on the Proofs of God's Existence* were written explicitly in connection with the later Logic: "These lectures can be regarded as a rounding out of the Logic" (p. 1). And Hegel's description of his destructive strategy there clearly refers to categories and developments from the later Logic: "Being in its immediacy is something contingent; we have seen that its truth is necessity. The Concept necessarily contains Being in addition" (p. 175).

27. Rosenkranz, *Hegels Leben*, p. 191.

28. G. W. F. Hegel, *The Idea of the Absolute Being (Die Idee des absoluten Wesens)*, unpub.; passage quoted in *Jenaer Systementwuerfe II*, p. ix.

29. *The Relation of Skepticism to Philosophy*, p. 228.

30. *Logic, Metaphysics, and Nature Philosophy*, p. 134. H. S. Harris, *Hegel's Development—Night Thoughts (Jena 1801–1806)* (Oxford: Clarendon Press, 1983), p. 385, notes that the stages of the early Logic are mirrored in those of the Metaphysics. In the sketch of the early Logic transmitted by Rosenkranz Hegel says: "Finally the destruction (*Aufheben*) of . . . finite cognition through Reason must be shown." Rosenkranz, *Hegels Leben*, p. 191. And in the unpublished original manuscript from which this sketch is drawn Hegel indicates what the destruction would involve: "Finite cognition or Reflection only abstracts from the absolute identity of what in rational knowledge is connected together or made equal, and through this abstraction alone it becomes a finite cognition. In rational knowing or philosophy the material is indeed this finite cognition, its forms are indeed also

posited as finite forms, but at the same time their finitude is destroyed through the fact that in Speculation they are connected together. For they are what they are merely through opposition, so that when this opposition is destroyed, when they are identical, their finitude is destroyed at the same time. Mere Reflection, however, knows them only in their opposition."

31. Thus Hegel says: "The object of a true Logic will . . . be this: to set up the forms of finitude, and, to be sure, not empirically gathered together but as they step forth out of Reason, though, robbed of Reason by the Understanding, appearing only in their finitude." Rosenkranz, *Hegels Leben*, p. 190.

32. For the dialectical method of the Logic described in *The Difference between the Fichtean and Schellingian Systems of Philosophy*, see pp. 26, 46–47 of the work. My claim that the Logic of the *Logic, Metaphysics, and Nature Philosophy* does not essentially presuppose information from the Metaphysics represents a minority reading of this text (on which see Chapter Nine).

33. See the fundamental principle of Reinhold's "Elementarphilosophie," his "proposition of consciousness": "In consciousness the representation is distinguished by the subject from the subject and the object and is related to both." Fichte accepts this proposition of consciousness, but for him it is a derived not a fundamental principle. Only two of its three elements have any claim to be fundamental in his system: the self's self-positing, which is the first principle of the *Science of Knowledge,* and the self's positing of a not-self, which is the second principle of the *Science of Knowledge.* Concerning these two elements Fichte writes: "Self-consciousness and consciousness of something that is to be—not ourselves—are necessarily connected." *Science of Knowledge,* p. 33.

34. Hegel accepts the two elements of Reinhold's proposition of consciousness which are fundamental for Fichte: "Consciousness is, on the one hand, consciousness of the object, and on the other, consciousness of itself" (*Phenomenology,* no. 85); "Consciousness embraces within itself the opposition of the ego and its object" (*Science of Logic,* p. 63). He also accepts the third element which is fundamental in Reinhold but derived in Fichte, namely consciousness of one's representation of something other than oneself as such: "Consciousness is . . . consciousness of what for it is the true, and consciousness of its cognition of the truth" (*Phenomenology,* no. 85); "The distinction between the in-itself and cognition is already present in the very fact that consciousness has cognition of an object at all. Something is for it the in-itself; and cognition, or the being of the object for consciousness, is, for it, another moment" (*Phenomenology,* no. 85).

35. It is plausible to suppose that a demonstration of the self-contradictoriness of all the concepts articulating a claim guarantees the self-contradictoriness of the claim itself. This becomes less clear where shapes of consciousness are in question instead of concepts. Might not a claim made within a particular self-contradictory shape of consciousness be rearticulated in a self-consistent manner within a different, self-consistent shape or, if no shapes turn out to be self-consistent, within the medium which Hegel envisages superseding all shapes? Hegel must intend a negative answer to this question: the demonstration that a given shape of consciousness is self-contradictory is supposed

to show at the same time that all concepts and claims articulated within it are self-contradictory. Perhaps the thought is that since there turns out to be an internal contradiction among the interdependent concepts of self, cognition, and reality definitive of each shape, each shape has an implicitly self-contradictory concept of reality, so that the very assertion that things *really are* a certain way made within any given shape is implicitly self-contradictory, and all concepts articulated within the shape, being essentially understood as articulations of aspects of *reality*, are implicitly self-contradictory too.

36. The self-contradiction arises when one of the interdependent elements belonging to the subject in a given shape, its consciousness of its cognition, proves to contradict another, its consciousness of the object (referred to by Hegel as the "criterion" which "consciousness provides . . . from within itself"). *Phenomenology*, nos. 84–85. The development to a new shape occurs when the conscious subject changes its cognition in response to this conflict with the object or criterion, attempting thereby to bring them into agreement. Because the two elements of the shape are interdependent, this necessarily alters the subject's consciousness of the object as well, so that a new object is posited: "In the alteration of the cognition, the object itself alters for it too, . . . as the cognition changes, so too does the object, for it essentially belonged to this cognition." *Phenomenology*, no. 85. In this way a new shape is reached. Concerning the exhibition of the shapes of consciousness as a necessarily connected series or system by this means, Hegel writes: "The necessary progression and interconnection of the forms of the unreal consciousness will itself bring to pass the completion of the series." *Phenomenology*, no. 79. And he writes that the series thus generated constitutes "the entire system of consciousness." *Phenomenology*, no. 89. On the circular structure of the dialectic, see *Phenomenology*, nos. 806–807.

37. This is demonstrated in Chapter Nine.

38. Hence for example Hegel's statement in regard to the dialectical path of the *Phenomenology* that "the individual has the right to demand that Science should at least provide him with the ladder to this standpoint [i.e., Science's]." *Phenomenology*, no. 26. Cf. Hegel's description of the *Phenomenology* as the "deduction" of the "Concept of pure Science." *Science of Logic*, p. 49. Cf. *Encyclopedia*, no. 25.

39. Fichte in effect raised this difficulty in *On the Concept of the Science of Knowledge*, p. 131, but offered no satisfactory solution to it.

40. *Encyclopedia*, no. 78. Cf. *Encyclopedia* (Heidelberg), nos. 35–36. Cf. Hegel's observation at *Encyclopedia*, no. 24, Zusatz 3, that the proof of Philosophical Science's claim "has first of all the significance that it is shown that the other forms of cognition are finite forms. The superior ancient skepticism accomplished this by showing that all these forms contained a contradiction in themselves . . . All the forms of finite thought will appear in the course of the logical development and indeed in a necessary fashion. In the logical treatment itself . . . the negative side of these forms is shown."

41. See *Logic, Metaphysics, and Nature Philosophy*, p. 134: "Knowing [*Das Erkennen*, i.e., the final viewpoint treated within the Logic], in that it passes

over into Metaphysics, is the overcoming (*Aufheben*) of the Logic itself, *as of dialectic.*" My emphasis.

42. *Encyclopedia*, nos. 79–82: "In point of form logical doctrine has three sides: (a) the abstract side or that of the Understanding, (b) the dialectical or that of negative Reason, (c) the speculative or that of positive Reason . . . (a) Thought, as Understanding, sticks to fixed determinacy and its contrast with other things; such a limited abstract thing it treats as having a subsistence and being of its own . . . (b) In the dialectical stage such finite determinations abolish themselves, and pass into their opposites . . . (c) The speculative stage, or the stage of positive Reason, apprehends the unity of determinations in their opposition." At *Encyclopedia*, no. 25 Hegel explains more fully from what perspective the categories of the Logic are seen merely in manner (a): "First, they are only subjective, and the antithesis of an objective permanently clings to them. Second, they are always of restricted content, and so persist in antithesis to one another and still more to the Absolute."

43. *Encyclopedia*, no. 78; *Encyclopedia* (Heidelberg), no. 36; *Lectures on the Proofs of God's Existence*, p. 175.

44. For Hegel's mature judgment on the early Logic, see *Encyclopedia*, no. 78; *Encyclopedia* (Heidelberg), no. 36. The general question of Hegel's later attitude to the *Phenomenology* is vexed. Three points which indicate that he did not simply abandon the discipline are the following. First, in none of his later discussions of the *Phenomenology*—particularly at *Encyclopedia*, nos. 25, 78; *Encyclopedia* (Heidelberg), no. 36—does Hegel state or imply its abandonment. Second, when Hegel discusses the proof of God at *Encyclopedia*, nos. 12, 50, the proof he has in mind is identical or very similar to that found in the *Phenomenology*. For example, he says that the starting point of the ascent to a knowledge of God is the immediate, sense-oriented consciousness (*Bewusstsein*), that the ascent involves experience (*Erfahrung*), and that it concerns the appearance (*Erscheinung*) of God—all of which ideas are distinctive components of his conception of the *Phenomenology* and have an exact sense in relation to that work but would be inappropriate as descriptions of any other discipline of Hegel's (in particular, of the later Logic). Third, Hegel began revising the *Phenomenology* for a new edition shortly before his death, which he would hardly have done if he had simply abandoned it.

45. *Phenomenology*, nos. 76, 38.

46. In the *Science of Logic* Hegel explains the category of Appearance (*Erscheinung*) as one which mediates between the realm of Law or Essence and the realm of mere Existence: "The realm of Laws is the *stable* content of Appearance; Appearance is the same content but presenting itself in restless flux . . . It is Law as the negative, simply alterable Existence" (p. 504). Thus when he calls the *Phenomenology* an appearance of Philosophical Science, he means that it considers the essential subject matter of Philosophical Science in a manner distorted by an admixture of mere existence. See e.g. *Phenomenology*, no. 35: "The element of immediate existence is what distinguishes this part of Science [i.e., the *Phenomenology*] from the others."

47. Thus at *Phenomenology,* no. 805 Hegel, looking forward to the Logic which begins Philosophical Science, writes: "In [Science] the moments of [Spirit's] movement no longer exhibit themselves as specific *shapes of consciousness,* but . . . as *specific concepts* and as their organic self-grounded movement." And he observes that there is a one-to-one correspondence between these shapes of consciousness and pure categories: "To each abstract moment of Science corresponds a shape of manifest Spirit as such." Reflecting his conception of Appearance as mediating between Essence and mere Existence, he adds: "To know the pure concepts of Science in this form of shapes of consciousness constitutes the side of their reality, in accordance with which their essence . . . breaks asunder the moments of this mediation [i.e., in the transition to the Logic]."

48. *Science of Logic,* p. 69. Cf. *Encyclopedia,* no. 12, where Hegel indicates that the knowledge of God "devours" its own proof or mediation (i.e., the *Phenomenology*), and *Encyclopedia,* no. 50, where he says of the proof of or ascent to God that "by being a transition and mediation this ascent [to God] is just as much *Aufheben* of the transition and mediation" and that "in this mediation even the mediation gets *aufgehoben.*" That the *Phenomenology* suffers *Aufhebung* will not surprise anyone who has recognized its descent from the early Logic, since the *Aufhebung* of the early Logic, upon transition to the Metaphysics or Philosophical Science proper, was a constant feature of Hegel's early system. See esp. *The Difference between the Fichtean and Schellingian Systems of Philosophy; Logic, Metaphysics, and Nature Philosophy.* For the gesture in the *Phenomenology* toward the scientific retreatment of its own content, see *Phenomenology,* nos. 806–807.

49. This doctrine is presupposed in *The Difference between the Fichtean and Schellingian Systems of Philosophy,* pp. 37–40, where Hegel explains that the antinomical "proposition of cause" (*Satz des Grundes*) is "the highest possible expression of Reason through the Understanding." It is also presupposed in the early Logic's general strategy of affording the self-contradictory nonscientific viewpoint a provisional acquaintance with Philosophical Science by making it concentrate on the *highest* forms of self-contradictory untruth of which it is capable. This strategy is indicated in the sketch of the early Logic transmitted by Rosenkranz when Hegel says that in order to serve as an introduction to philosophy, the Logic "holds forth the image of the Absolute so to speak in a reflection, and in this way makes it familiar." Thus the Logic "must present the striving of the Understanding as it imitates Reason in a production of identity, but is only able to produce a formal identity"; it must show "what meaning and what content" the finite forms which it destroys "have for Reason"; and it must show that the Understanding's syllogisms "are merely an imitation of Reason by the Understanding." *Hegels Leben,* pp. 190–191.

50. Thus at *Phenomenology,* no. 27 the *Phenomenology* is referred to as the "process of coming-to-be [of Science]." This is clarified a little at *Phenomenology,* no. 26, where we are told that "Science on its part requires that self-consciousness should have raised itself [to Science] in order to be able to live—and actually to live—with Science and in Science"—for the raising of

the ordinary consciousness to Science said here to be essential to the existence of Science is something which it is the job of the *Phenomenology* to effect. For the more precise significance of these passages, see my description of the "metaphysical" goal of the *Phenomenology* in Chapter Nine.

51. Note Hegel's statement at *Encyclopedia*, no. 64 concerning the maxim that "the being of God is immediately and inseparably bound up with the thought of God": "It is the endeavor of philosophy to *prove* such a unity, to show that it lies in the very nature of thought and subjectivity to be inseparable from being and objectivity."

52. For the earliest version of this strategy, see the sketch of a Logic in *The Difference between the Fichtean and Schellingian Systems of Philosophy*, esp. pp. 26, 28, 115, which proposes to reduce to absurdity the assumption that there are two distinct totalities of Self and Nature by means of a derivation of these two distinct totalities which is irremediably dialectical in a (here Schelling-inspired) Logic.

53. *Logic, Metaphysics, and Nature Philosophy*, p. 136.

54. *Logic, Metaphysics, and Nature Philosophy*, p. 3.

55. *Logic, Metaphysics, and Nature Philosophy*, p. 3.

56. *Logic, Metaphysics, and Nature Philosophy*, p. 3.

57. *Logic, Metaphysics, and Nature Philosophy*, p. 3.

58. *Logic, Metaphysics, and Nature Philosophy*, p. 134.

59. *On the Scientific Ways of Treating Natural Law*, pp. 71, 82.

60. *Logic, Metaphysics, and Nature Philosophy*, p. 125.

61. *Logic, Metaphysics, and Nature Philosophy*, p. 3.

62. *Logic, Metaphysics, and Nature Philosophy*, p. 125.

63. *Logic, Metaphysics, and Nature Philosophy*, p. 136. It may be asked how Hegel can simultaneously lay the blame for all the self-contradictions exhibited in the course of the Logic at the doorstep of the abstract unity from which it starts, as we see him doing here, and impute it to all the various concepts of the Understanding considered along that course, as we saw him doing earlier in this chapter. The answer must, I think, be that he regards the concept of abstract unity as part of the essence or nature of each specific concept of the Understanding, so that the source of a given self-contradiction may lie both in the essence of the specific concept of the Understanding in connection with which it arises and in the concept of abstract unity which is part of that essence.

64. *The Difference between the Fichtean and Schellingian Systems of Philosophy*, pp. 43–44.

65. *Lectures on the Proofs of God's Existence*, p. 1.

66. *Lectures on the Proofs of God's Existence*, p. 175.

67. See the passages quoted in note no. 42 to this chapter from *Encyclopedia*, nos. 25, 79–82 (the parts referring to (a) and (b)).

68. *Lectures on the Proofs of God's Existence*, p. 175.

69. The phrase is from *Phenomenology*, no. 39. I distinguish this demonstration from the process described in Chapter Seven in which the Absolute Idea or Concept expounds itself as Being. For this demonstration concerns the dialectical development of categories considered in *abstraction* from one an-

other and from the Absolute Idea. How clearly Hegel marks this distinction is another question.

70. *Encyclopedia*, nos. 49–50: "These are the two elements, abstract identity, on the one hand, which is spoken of in this place as the Concept, and Being, on the other—which Reason seeks to unify . . . To carry out this unification two ways or two forms are admissible. Either we may begin with Being and proceed to the abstraction of thought; or the movement may begin with the abstraction and end in Being."

9. The Proof for Nonbelievers

1. This goal lies behind the remarks from *Phenomenology*, nos. 26, 27 quoted in note no. 50 to Chapter 8.

2. Baillie, *The Origin and Significance of Hegel's Logic*; O. Poeggeler, "Hegels Jenaer Systemkonzeption," *Philosophisches Jahrbuch der Goerres-Gesellschaft*, no. 71 (1974).

3. Haym, *Hegel und seine Zeit*; J. H. Trede, "Hegels fruehe Logik," *Hegel-Studien* (1972); Poeggeler, "Hegels Jenaer Systemkonzeption."

4. Thus Baillie holds the Logic of the *Logic, Metaphysics, and Nature Philosophy* to be "merely Logic of the Understanding and . . . illuminated by no analysis of Understanding and its relation to Reason." *The Origin and Significance of Hegel's Logic*, pp. 95–96. Note that the designation of this Logic as "Logic of the Understanding" is Hegel's own. *Logic, Metaphysics, and Nature Philosophy*, p. 3.

5. H. F. Fulda, *Das Problem einer Einleitung in Hegels Wissenschaft der Logik* (Frankfurt am Main: Vittorio Klostermann, 1975), pp. 163–164.

6. *Phenomenology*, nos. 87, 88.

7. The Logic described in *The Difference between the Fichtean and Schellingian Systems of Philosophy* differs from the Logic of the sketch transmitted by Rosenkranz and of *The Idea of the Absolute Being* and anticipates the Logic of the *Logic, Metaphysics, and Nature Philosophy* and also the *Phenomenology* in the following respects: it does not essentially presuppose information from the Metaphysics or Philosophical Science proper, and it uses a quasi-Fichtean dialectical method supposed compelling for nonscientific viewpoints in order to give both the destructive and the constructive sides of its proof of Philosophical Science. Because of these two properties, it furnishes a proof of Philosophical Science which can hope to be compelling for nonscientific viewpoints on the basis of their own views and criteria.

8. Rosenkranz, *Hegels Leben*, p. 191.

9. Rosenkranz, *Hegels Leben*, p. 191.

10. *On the Nature of Philosophical Critique*, p. 174.

11. *On the Nature of Philosophical Critique*, p. 174.

12. See e.g. Hegel's observation that the skepticism of the *Parmenides*, on which his own Logic is modeled, "is itself the negative side of the knowledge of the Absolute *and immediately presupposes Reason as the positive side.*" *The Relation of Skepticism to Philosophy*, p. 228; my emphasis. See also his

remark that such a skepticism "is itself most intimately one with each true philosophy." *The Relation of Skepticism to Philosophy*, p. 227.

13. *The Relation of Skepticism to Philosophy*, p. 237.
14. *The Relation of Skepticism to Philosophy*, p. 241.
15. *The Relation of Skepticism to Philosophy*, p. 240.
16. See Hegel's complaint that ancient equipollence skepticism "exercises its dialectic contingently, for just as the material comes up before it, it shows in the same that implicitly it is negative." *History of Philosophy*, vol. 2, p. 331.
17. *On the Scientific Ways of Treating Natural Law*, p. 88: the argument we are about to consider is an example of the work of "dialectic" which proves that "relation is nothing whatever in itself" (this is one of Hegel's earliest uses of the term "dialectic").
18. *On the Scientific Ways of Treating Natural Law*, p. 86: "If the power and, with it, the possible compulsion by either side is given unequal strength, then the result is that—in proportion as the one part has more power than the other, or as each has an excess over the other—only one part, and not its opposite, is under compulsion, which ought not to happen."
19. *On the Scientific Ways of Treating Natural Law*, p. 86: "But if . . . action and reaction, position and opposition, are equally strong, the power on both sides is reduced to equilibrium and all activity, action, and expression of the will is thereby canceled." Hegel says that it is no solution to this problem to propose that "no member reacts directly on that by which it is moved (producing equilibrium), but always on some other member, so that the first moves the last and the last the first," because "such a *perpetuum mobile* whose parts are all supposed to follow one another round the circle, will, instead of moving, settle at once into complete equilibrium and become a complete *perpetuum quietum;* for pressure and counterpressure, coercing and being coerced, are entirely equal, and they stand directly against each other and effect the same reduction of forces as in the first conception." *On the Scientific Ways of Treating Natural Law*, pp. 86–87.
20. *On the Scientific Ways of Treating Natural Law*, pp. 119, 121.
21. *On the Scientific Ways of Treating Natural Law*, pp. 118–119. My emphasis.
22. In addition to the ancient skeptics' publicly persuasive demonstrations of equipollence problems, several precedents of publicly persuasive demonstrations of self-contradictoriness probably influenced Hegel in taking this step—in particular, the arguments of Kant's Antinomies, especially those of the Mathematical Antinomies which Kant understood to reveal self-contradictions in concepts, and Socratic elenchus.
23. Two bits of evidence speak for this. First, whereas *On the Scientific Ways of Treating Natural Law* contains clear allusions to the publicly graspable destruction of various categories in the Logic, it contains no clear allusion to any publicly accessible necessary development from one destroyed category to the next. Second, Hegel in *On the Scientific Ways of Treating Natural Law* refers to a stage in the Philosophy of Spirit called "Intelligence" (*die Intelligenz*) which appears to correspond to a final stage of the Logic in which there occurs a simultaneous destruction of all the Understanding's previously set-up categories and a transition to the Metaphysics. *On the*

Scientific Ways of Treating Natural Law, pp. 110–111. The stage "Intelligence" seems to have the same function as or even to be identical with the stage called "The Negative or Freedom or Crime" in the roughly contemporary *System of Ethical Life* which, as Trede has convincingly argued, corresponds to the final portion of the Logic in the sketch transmitted by Rosenkranz, where all the Understanding's categories, having been previously set up, are destroyed together and the transition is made to Metaphysics. Trede, "Hegel's fruehe Logik." Thus the Logic alluded to in *On the Scientific Ways of Treating Natural Law* seems not to have set up its system of categories by means of a publicly compelling dialectical development from one category to the next (such as is found later in the Logic of the *Logic, Metaphysics, and Nature Philosophy,* for example), for this would have involved a demonstration of the self-contradictoriness of each individual category as soon as it was set up, rather than in a single destructive phase encompassing all categories together and following their setting-up. The Logic of *On the Scientific Ways of Treating Natural Law* seems instead to have set up the system of the categories to be destroyed in some other way before going on to exhibit their self-contradictoriness all at once, as in the Logic of the sketch transmitted by Rosenkranz—the initial setting up of the system presumably being effected in a way presupposing esoteric knowledge from the Metaphysics, as in that sketch.

24. This may already have been so at phase three without any publicly compelling dialectical development playing a role, but one cannot tell from *On the Scientific Ways of Treating Natural Law.*

25. *Logic, Metaphysics, and Nature Philosophy,* p. 4. The transition from Logic to Metaphysics is the transition to the category of Knowing (*Erkennen*) which is "no longer a subject of Logic . . . but of Metaphysics." *Logic, Metaphysics, and Nature Philosophy,* p. 131. Hence it is also significant that Hegel describes Knowing as first posited in the transition from Definition to Division (the two preceding categories) and says that this transition cannot be effected by a dialectical development. *Logic, Metaphysics, and Nature Philosophy,* pp. 123–124. See further the transition from Divison to Knowing in the text (p. 116), where one notices the absence of that emphasis on contradiction as the means of transition and on the necessary character of the transition which always appears in Hegel's descriptions of dialectical transitions within the Logic, and where Hegel instead simply urges that Knowing must be posited if we are to overcome the division into independent, particular kinds.

26. Nevertheless, Hegel's marginal note at the point of transition beyond the Logic—"Dialectic of Division" (*Logic, Metaphysics, and Nature Philosophy,* p. 116)—suggests that he attempted such a remedy before eventually abandoning the discipline altogether.

27. *Encyclopedia* (Heidelberg), no. 36; cf. *Encyclopedia,* no. 78.

28. *History of Philosophy,* vol. 2, p. 331.

29. *Phenomenology,* no. 26; *Encyclopedia,* no. 25.

30. *Phenomenology,* no. 89. My emphasis.

31. *Phenomenology,* no. 806.

32. *Phenomenology,* no. 807.

33. For a slightly fuller description of this circularity in the *Phenomenology,* see note 18 to Chapter 8. Hegel also seems to envisage a more direct return to Sense Certainty once Philosophical Science is reached at the end of the *Phenomenology.* For before discussing the return described in my text, he writes that "the self-knowing Spirit, just because it grasps its Concept, is the immediate identity with itself which, in its difference, is the certainty of immediacy, or Sense Consciousness—the beginning from which we started" (no. 806). The return described in my text is said to be necessary in addition because "this externalization is still incomplete" (no. 807).

34. It enables the *Phenomenology* to offer such a demonstration both for all nonscientific viewpoints (the concern of the present chapter) and simpliciter (the concern of the preceding chapter). The flaw in the *Logic, Metaphysics, and Nature Philosophy* prevented it from accomplishing either kind of demonstration.

35. *Phenomenology,* no. 28: "The single individual must also pass through the formative stages of universal Spirit so far as their content is concerned, but as shapes which Spirit has already left behind."

36. This is true whether the proof of exhaustiveness is being effected for all nonscientific viewpoints (our concern in this chapter) or simpliciter (our concern in the preceding chapter).

37. *The Difference between the Fichtean and Schellingian Systems of Philosophy,* p. 25.

38. Thus the Logic of *The Difference between the Fichtean and Schellingian Systems of Philosophy* dialectically expounds the two totalities of Self and Nature (pp. 26, 115) which express the organization of the Absolute (p. 30), and it does so in a manner which is supposed to be compelling for nonscientific viewpoints. But this expression of the Absolute has an untrue, oppositional form in the Logic and only becomes synthesized into its true form once the Logic has done its work and the synthesizing operation of intuition can be introduced as a postulate (pp. 43–44). The situation in the Logic of the *Logic, Metaphysics, and Nature Philosophy* is rather similar.

39. *Encyclopedia,* no. 25 implies this.

40. The quoted phrase is from *Phenomenology,* no. 38.

41. The quoted phrase is from *Phenomenology,* no. 26.

42. *Encyclopedia,* no. 25.

10. *The Dialectical Method in Hegel's Epistemology*

1. The demonstration in this case runs: "*Being, pure being,* without any further determination . . . It is pure indeterminateness and emptiness. There is *nothing* to be intuited in it . . . Just as little is anything to be thought in it . . . Being, the indeterminate immediate, is in fact *nothing,* and neither more nor less than nothing." *Science of Logic,* p. 82.

2. On the positive outcome of the negative result Hegel writes "The negative is just as much the positive, or . . . what is self-contradictory does not resolve itself into a nullity." *Science of Logic,* p. 54. On the necessity of the positive

outcome, see e.g. *Phenomenology,* no. 34: "[The] movement of pure essences constitutes the nature of scientific method in general ... It is the necessary expansion of [the] content into an organic whole." On "the negative of the negative," see e.g. *Science of Logic,* p. 835. On the positive outcome uniting the two mutually implying contrary categories, see e.g. *Science of Logic,* p. 56: It is "the grasping of the opposites in their unity."

3. See Hegel's treatment of Plato in the *History of Philosophy.*

4. Hegel in effect reads his own dialectical metaphysics into works which either generate contradictions merely as aporiai to be resolved later (the *Parmenides*) or are concerned with the development of a contradiction-free metaphysics (the *Sophist* and the *Philebus*). On Hegel's misinterpretation of the later Plato, see K. Duesing, "Ontologie und Dialektik bei Plato und Hegel," *Hegel-Studien* (1980).

5. H. G. Gadamer, *Hegel's Dialectic* (New Haven: Yale University Press, 1976), p. 22. See also Duesing, "Ontologie und Dialektik bei Plato und Hegel."

6. *History of Philosophy,* vol. 2, p. 64.

7. *Apology,* 21a–22e. I agree with R. Robinson—*Plato's Earlier Dialectic* (Oxford: Oxford University Press, 1984), ch. 3—contrary to what is becoming the prevailing wisdom, that Plato/Socrates understands elenchus as a demonstration of a self-contradiction in the interlocutor's hypothesis. In addition to the evidence cited by Robinson, consider the description of the behavior of the interlocutor's hypotheses as turning into their negations by themselves at *Euthyphro,* 11b–e.

8. See *Laches,* 197d. But see especially Socrates' subtle parody of the abuse of Prodicean distinctions of sense to avoid acknowledging a contradiction at *Protagoras,* 338e–341e, where Socrates in effect puts himself in the shoes of the victim of elenctic refutation for a while by undertaking to defend the consistency of Simonides' poem in the face of the demonstration of its self-contradictoriness which Protagoras gives. Socrates' sensitivity to the bearing of ambiguity on elenctic refutation and his lively awareness of the temptation to appeal to it illegitimately in order to avoid acknowledging refutation have not received the attention they deserve in the secondary literature.

9. Hence at *Protagoras* 347e Socrates ridicules the whole business of conducting an exegesis of texts on the ground that there is no way of determining the correct interpretation when the author is not present to be questioned on his meaning, in the manner of Socratic cross-examination.

10. This allows us to save Robinson's conception of elenctic arguments as attempted demonstrations of the self-contradictoriness of an interlocutor's initial hypotheses without accepting his implausible view that Plato/Socrates simply overlooked the role in these arguments of other premises conceded by the interlocutor. See *Plato's Earlier Dialectic,* pp. 27–28.

11. *On the Scientific Ways of Treating Natural Law,* p. 119.

12. In Hegel's eyes, the moral to be drawn from this is that the Antinomies represent "the rising of Reason above the limitations of the Understanding and the resolving them." *Science of Logic,* p. 46.

13. *Science of Logic,* p. 46: Kant's reaction was to have cognition flee "to sen-

suous existence, imagining that in this it possesses what is solid and self-consistent," though "since this knowledge is self-confessedly knowledge only of appearances, the unsatisfactoriness of the latter is admitted . . . as much as to say that admittedly, we have no proper knowledge of things in themselves, but we do have a proper knowledge of them within the sphere of appearances, as if, so to speak, only the *kind of objects* were different, and one kind, namely things in themselves, did not fall within the scope of our knowledge but the other kind, phenomena, did."

14. *Science of Logic,* p. 46.
15. Like the rest of the general structure of Hegel's dialectical method, this aspect of it was borrowed from the method of Fichte's *Science of Knowledge.* Hence Baillie is wrong to suggest that Hegel constructed his Logic "without . . . help as to content or method from Fichte." *The Origin and Significance of Hegel's Logic,* p. 45.
16. *Hegel,* p. 130.
17. *Science of Logic,* p. 56.

Index